I CALLED IT

I CALLED IT
MAGIC

GARETH KNIGHT

SKYLIGHT PRESS

First published in Great Britain in 2011 by Skylight Press,
210 Brooklyn Road, Cheltenham, Glos GL51 8EA

Designed and typeset by Rebsie Fairholm
Printed and bound in Great Britain by Lightning Source, Milton Keynes

www.skylightpress.co.uk

ISBN 978-1-908011-15-2

To Katie Belle

for persuading me this tale was worth the telling

"See how eagerly the lobsters and the turtles all advance!
They are waiting on the shingle – will you come and join the dance?"

Contents

Sir Gareth as a young knight.

The Rocky Road of the Seeker
1930-53

I called it magic – Kathleen Raine called it poetry – J. R. R. Tolkien called it enchantment – others have called it a variety of things – from mysticism to mumbo jumbo. All I know is, that it works – and that for better or worse I have lived most of my life by it. Now seems the time to take stock of it – not so much in self justification – but in order to dust it off, look it up and down, and make some kind of appraisal of what it was all about. Was it all worth it? What did it serve? Was it a public service for the greater good or a fanciful diversion – a flight from the real in pursuit of the ideal?

I originally thought to call this story "A Magical Life" because magic seems to have been what it was all about. But then comes the question "what do I mean by *magic*?" I suppose it has taken most of a lifetime to find out.

I only know I did what I felt I had to do. And a large part of that was to rescue the word magic – and all that it could and should stand for – from the misunderstandings of those who fear it, condemn it, ridicule it, or abuse it – each according to their prejudice or lack of information.

The child is father of the man, wrote William Wordsworth, who was also something of a magician in his way.

> My heart leaps up when I behold
>   A rainbow in the sky:
> So was it when my life began;
> So is it now I am a man;
> So be it when I shall grow old,
>   Or let me die!
> The Child is father of the Man;
>   I could wish my days to be
> Bound each to each in natural piety.

If the poet's words are worth anything, what portents did my childhood show of my concerns as a man? For magic was my natural piety – even if I could not give it a name.

At a very tender age, making mud pies in the garden, I chose to call them "witches' pies". Was that a predisposition to the esoteric?

And when hardly out of infant school, and something of a natural leader among my peers, my ambition in life was to be leader of a group of people "who went around doing good". Easier said than done of course, but was this the foreshadowing of the ideals of an esoteric group?

I must have been of an age to read when I recall being much affected by a children's book about three pixies, or similar creatures, who went on a long and arduous journey in search of their "goodnesses". I cannot think who can have written that tale. In retrospect it seems like Enid Blyton, but the names of the three heroes that come to mind are Wynken, Blynken and Nod, which is the name of a sentimental children's poem by an American journalist, Eugene Field – a bed-time story of three fishermen sailing and fishing in the stars. Anyhow, the book that I pored over inspired within me thoughts of a spiritual Quest.

Tending towards a secret and intimate communion with beings of another kind, another treasured volume of childhood was *The Bee's Song*. Who wrote it I do not know and I have never been able to trace the book. I could identify with its hero because he too was a lonely child whose given name began with the letter B – which enabled him to commune with a bee who came to visit and befriend him, dancing up and down his bedroom window with a coded song.

A rather more awesome connection with windows was, however, the odd feeling I used to get, when playing in the garden, of being watched from the window of my bedroom by a strange woman. Who it was I did not know, and did not care to mention it or enquire. Within the house however, a source of irrational childish fear was my parent's bedroom, which had a vague air of menace – perhaps because it was the room in which I was born.

Also in those early years I recall returning from a holiday in Devon with the enamel badge of a Cornish Pixie, which I treasured as a special talisman for a year or more before, having lost it, I felt I had lost a friend. And in rare visits to my uncle's flat over a garage in Holland Park Mews, at a time when such were occupied by the chauffeurs of the great houses of Holland Park near by, I recall being intrigued by a framed picture that hung in the hall – of pillars and globes and what I now realise must have been some kind of freemasonic illustration.

Moving on to grammar school my thoughts turned to a more scientific bent and with intense anticipation I looked forward to learning chemistry. It held for me all the fascination that must have dominated the alchemists of old. Had I perhaps been one? I have to say that in this life I was doomed to disappointment. I did reasonably well at the subject, and on leaving school my first job was as a laboratory assistant, but found that life in a plastics factory was no great route to finding gold or the elixir of life.

In the school science society, clandestine experiments with an ouija board were a temporary frisson that led to nowhere, likewise scanning the spiritualism and psychical research shelves of the local public library. As with chemistry I also looked forward to experiments in physics with coloured light but was soon put off when it turned out to be more a mathematical concern with angles. And Euclid's geometry seemed utterly pointless. Why go through all that mind boggling rigmarole to prove the angles at the base of an isosceles triangle were equal when it was perfectly obvious that they were? Intuition scored over intellect with me, every time.

As it turned out, the dominant interest in my life became music, at any rate until I realised I was not as good at it as I thought. Not that I showed any early promise. My mother sent me for piano lessons with the village organist but only got me to go there with threats and a stick. She had been denied the chance to learn the piano as a child and was determined I should not be similarly deprived. But as far as I was concerned the half hour of purgatory was hardly worth the shilling she paid.

I bore this affliction with some ill grace until I chanced one day to be listening on the radio to the American Forces Network from Munich, and heard some sounds that electrified me – it turned out to be Count Basie. From then on my ambitions turned to jazz, not that I knew how to pursue such a career. I used to spend quite a lot of time playing the piano loudly in our front room in the hope and fond expectation that some talent spotter might come along and hear me. But alas none ever came my way, or if they did were not impressed.

Then one night I took a more positive approach and turned up early at a dance at the Moot Hall in Colchester before any but the band had arrived, sat down at the grand piano and started to play. I was soon asked to shut up by the bass player, who said he had a headache already, but to my great delight the trumpet player, a soldier in the Army Fire Service, asked me if I would like to join the band at his station.

It was a six piece group, of trumpet, alto saxophone, accordion, guitar and drums and in desperate need of a pianist. The gigs were a monthly sergeant's mess Saturday night dance with an occasional visit to similar events at other barracks in the military town of Colchester. For this I was paid a pound a time. Somewhat below the union rate but at least I could call myself a "semi-pro".

Approaching the age of eighteen I felt the time had come to spread my wings and try to hit the big time, but would need some money if I wanted to start a band of my own. As it happened the RAF were seeking to recruit air crew in the immediate post war period and were offering a bounty to anyone who would sign up for five years. To my callow teenage mind this seemed a golden chance of freedom from the endless vista of factory work with evening classes tacked on for three nights a week which had been my lot up until then. And so I went off to a selection panel at North Weald, only to fall at the first hurdle. In common with most who applied, I was not found to have sufficient aptitude to hurl aircraft about the sky. But as I was due to be called up for a couple of years' National Service anyway, why not sign on as ground crew instead? "Learn a trade and see the world!" as the silver tongued recruiting officer said. Which is what I did – for eight years. "Act in haste, repent at leisure" is an old saying, the truth of which I learnt the hard way.

Nonetheless my undistinguished service career had its advantages. I met a few other jazz musicians, including a budding clarinet player whose sister Roma I later married after a long and desultory courtship. And when stationed in Malta, managed to get a traditionalist jazz band together which played on the local Forces Broadcasting Service under the name of Bazz Wilby's USAWOM Jazz Band – the acronym standing for Unrehearsed, Spontaneous and Without Music. No doubt it sounded like it, and fortunately none of the acetate discs from the recordings have survived!

Bazz Wilby (with trumpet, third from right) and the USAWOM Jazz Band in Malta, early 1950s.

One of the more inspiring things to come from this period was acquaintance with an American saxophonist, Juice Wilson, a former Duke Ellington and Benny Carter sidesman, who had apparently been washed up in Europe just before the war. Whenever we could we would visit him in one of the clip joints in which he played on the Sliema waterfront, and organised the occasional Sunday afternoon jam at a slightly more salubrious location.

But my musical ambitions came to an end on return to England when I met a real professional pianist who was doing his National Service. A shaft of reality then struck. The gap in natural talent, dedication and formal training was painfully obvious. I was never going to be anything more than a moderately talented amateur.

I did have other interests however, including politics, which I picked up largely from meeting another National Serviceman Illtyd Harrington. A charismatic character of decidedly left wing views who later became a prominent member of the Greater London Council. He did not hide his political light under a bushel and found me a ready listener, my radicalism helped by a popular Penguin book of the time, *I Choose Peace* by Konni Zilliacus, exacerbated with the sight of the appalling wounds of soldiers coming back via Malta from Korea at the time. As a consequence of my loudly proclaimed left wing views I was henceforth kept clear of active service stations, as a possible security risk, and spent the rest of my RAF career as an instructor at No. 2 Radio School, Yatesbury.

I was at this time in a confused state of mind which I think epitomises the problems of the Seeker. I found great stimulus in the heady rhetoric of Marx and Engels yet at the same time fascinated but repelled by their philosophy of dialectical materialism. The dialectic seemed irrefutable but I could not accept the uncompromising materialism. Indeed what they had done, as they openly boasted, was turn the dialectical idealistic philosophy of Hegel on its head. And that was what I was really searching for without knowing quite where to look.

So at the same time I began to look to the fringes of the esoteric movement such as the Theosophical Society and similar bodies but without feeling the call to join any one of them. And my political ardour cooled to more realistic levels after I enrolled with Wolsey Hall correspondence college to study for an Intermediate B.Sc. with a view to eventual entry to the London School of Economics. This never came to pass but this first brush with higher education taught me that there was another side to the issues involved than revolutionary rhetoric.

While impaled on the horns of this dilemma however, I was about to find the way ahead.

·2·

ᚱhe Lesser Mysteries
1953-59

David, one of my fellow instructors at No. 2 Radio School, was thought a bit weird, though in my naïvety I found him quite impressive.

His bunk was always a fug of Balkan Sobranie mixture, smoked in a curved meerschaum pipe, and he was given to secretive remarks about vaguely symbolic objects in his possession. One was a set of circular copper plates. I never did find out the purpose of them, possibly there was none.

He had a disconcerting trick on occasion of staring you fixedly in the eye to read your thoughts – which he kept to himself with a significant look. I guessed his method was to visualise a link between his brow centre and my own, along with the hypnotic glare. So one day I imagined a set of whirling lawn mower blades in front of my own. Easier to conjure than a magic sword and apparently as effective, for he shook his head in bafflement and never tried it again. My first self taught lesson in practical occultism, if at a low level.

He had a few books, fleetingly revealed, as fit only for the eyes of the elect. A favourite was *Le Comte de Gabalis,* the reprint of a seventeenth century novella on Elemental beings, all the more impressive for having been translated and privately published by an outfit called The Brothers. But one day he lent me a less impressive looking publication (it was in "duplicated" format – an early form of office printing), that had an electrifying effect upon me.

It was written by someone called Dion Fortune and called *The Esoteric Orders and their Work.* Who Dion Fortune was I did not know, but I felt I had found a kindred spirit, even if at first I thought the author was a man.

What was the attraction of this book, the reading of which set the course for the rest of my life? I suppose it was summed up in the first few words of the introduction:

"In all ages and among all races there has existed a tradition concerning certain esoteric schools or fraternities, wherein a secret wisdom unknown to the generality of mankind might be learnt, and to which admission was obtained by means of an initiation in which tests and ritual played their part."

The chapter headings also jumped out at me with compelling force: the Origin of the Mysteries; the Paths of the Western Tradition; the Training and Work of an Initiate; Orders, Fraternities and Groups; the Path of Initiation…

Wow! This was heady stuff! If there were such things as initiates I wanted to be one. If there were such things as esoteric orders then I wanted to join. What is more, there was a notice inviting enquiries. I needed no second bidding.

I could hardly contain my impatience awaiting the arrival of the first course material from the Society of the Inner Light. Indeed I still recall the pang of disappointment at being too late to get to the mail room on Saturday, and having to wait the rest of the weekend, consumed with curiosity, until able to claim and open the precious package on Monday. It contained an introduction to the Tree of Life as expounded in Dion Fortune's book *The Mystical Qabalah*, along with instructions for practical work. This was a commitment to ten or twenty minutes meditation each day upon a selected topic; a mental "salutation to the masters" at noon; and an evening review – running through the events of the day in reverse order on retiring to bed.

Meditation was by no means the commonplace practice it is today. I must say I found it something of a trial, and about as inspiring as practising scales on the piano (which I had always skimped!) But circling the mind round a metaphysical topic has the effect of boring a hole in the solid walls of the workaday mind. One day, thick as you had seemed to be, light should start to shine through.

The Course was in three parts, which could take up to a year, the later exercises moving on to the practice of visualisation – of a room once familiar, or going for a remembered walk. This was quite fun although not particularly esoteric. That came with the final "Threshold" part which was based on visualisation of key symbols – such things as temple pillars, a dawning sun, a serpent-twined staff and the like. But before being allowed to take this, one had to attend the Interview.

This was a meeting with two senior members of the Society at their headquarters in Bayswater. It was my first personal contact with anyone claiming to be a real initiate, and I wondered if I was going to have my aura clairvoyantly examined. My conceptions of an esoteric fraternity were highly influenced by Dennis Wheatley's occult blood and thunder, *The Devil Rides Out*. However, the event was unremarkable enough. Conducted by the bluff and breezy General Secretary Richard Mallock, and Miss G. P. Lathbury, an elderly little lady with great black luminous eyes, it was much like attending an ordinary job interview.

Having been deemed worthy of acceptance, after the short Threshold Course I was invited to submit my measurements for a ritual robe to be made – and to present myself for initiation on the afternoon of October 23rd 1954.

Ritual initiation, for all its reputed glamour, is no sudden blinding transformation. As the word implies, it simply marks a stage already gained and the opportunity to begin something new. Certainly, high spiritual dynamics may apply, but as often as not are beyond the conscious awareness of the average candidate. Nonetheless, it was in rather nervous expectation of something spectacular that I turned up on the day.

However a slightly ludicrous mundane concern was the first thing to strike me. When left in a room to change out of my street clothes into my ceremonial robe, the middle aged lady deputed to introduce me to the lodge said, somewhat primly, on departing, "You may take your trousers off if you wish."

Having the demeanour of a tightly buttoned down headmistress there were obviously no erotic overtones in this well meant instruction. Nonetheless it did cross my mind to wonder how she would know when it was all right for her to come back to the room without finding me in my shirt tails. Or was she covertly watching on the astral plane to see when I was respectably robed? In which case what was the point of her withdrawing anyway? Such were the lofty thoughts of an aspiring young initiate in the repressed cultural climate of the early 1950s.

My naïvety may be gauged from a sense of disappointment at finding the initiating magus to be wearing spectacles. To my mind, an occult adept ought be a perfect being – far beyond such mortal weaknesses!

Nonetheless the effect of a well conducted initiation ceremony is quite impressive. To stand at the door of the lodge upon which three knocks are given on one's behalf, to meet with the challenge as the door swings slightly ajar, bringing with it a waft of incense, *"Stranger from the outer world, why seek ye to enter our secret places and hidden mysteries?"* and being prompted to answer (as from your own Higher Self) *"I desire to know in order to serve"*. To be admitted blindfold (to represent your own stumbling forward in spiritual darkness) to where the hooded brethren are assembled. Then, in due course, the hoodwink removed, to observe the symbolic furniture of the temple as you are ceremoniously processed around for instruction, admonishment and contact by the various officers of the lodge.

It was the tradition to choose a "mystery name" for yourself – a motto to represent your current aspiration. I chose *"I Cast Me"* – lifted from Sir Thomas Malory's *Le Morte D'Arthur*, which was required background reading for all students, together with an introduction to Jungian psychology by Jolande Jacobi. With this somewhat archaic phrase, signifying my dedication to the task or quest or whatever might befall, so commenced the progress of Frater I.C.M. through the three grades of the Lesser Mysteries.

Becoming an initiate of the 1st Degree was not much different from being a student in "the Outer Court", but supplemented by the opportunity, or indeed the duty, to attend a ritual meeting every month.

This had a somewhat hazardous aspect as I had to work until midday on a Saturday – which meant a rapid ride by motorbike from Yatesbury up the Great West Road (no motorway in those days), through Marlborough, Hungerford, Newbury, Reading, Maidenhead, Slough, Chiswick to the west end of London. The meeting began at three but the door was closed at half past two and remained closed – ring at the bell as you might.

Mr Mallock did urge me to ride with caution on these forays but I secretly deplored his lack of faith, convinced that while engaged upon such mighty business no ill could possibly befall me. Hopefully there are angels deputed to watch over aspiring young neophytes – especially ones on motorbikes.

Ritual meetings could take one of three forms – a rehearsal of the catechism of the degree; a directed visualisation; or a trance address.

Rehearsal of the catechism I privately considered rather boring, but it did not do to admit the fact. Indeed the exercise had its importance, in going formally in question and answer form over the tenets of the symbolism of the degree in a ritual environment rather than in individual meditation.

Directed visualisation was much looked forward to, in the form of a "path working" based upon one of the Paths of the Tree of Life. For the 1st Degree the relevant ones being the 32nd, 31st and 29th that ray forth from Malkuth, the Kingdom (the lowest sphere on the Tree of Life) that represents mundane consciousness. They were conducted by the Magus of the Degree, unscripted, although broadly based upon the published attributions of the Golden Dawn tradition.

Once every quarter, in the meeting closest to the Spring and Autumnal Equinoxes and the Summer and Winter Solstices, there was a trance address. These were given by a remarkably gifted psychic, Margaret Lumley Brown, known in more esoteric terms as the Pythoness, in contact with an Inner Plane Adept who was known as the Chancellor.

This was a tradition begun by Dion Fortune from back in the early days, when she used to be stretched out on a couch (or "pastos") in the middle of the lodge in full trance. Margaret Lumley Brown was a lot more matter of fact and just used to sit on a chair in the middle, before the altar, and give forth, almost in a conversational tone. She was pretty good too, so much so that I later published (in *Pythoness*) some of her work received in this manner.

In those days before tape recorders, a scribe would discreetly take down the text in shorthand for later typing, duplicating and dissemination to the membership.

My membership of the Fraternity gave me the opportunity to visit Chalice Orchard, Dion Fortune's old headquarters at the foot of Glastonbury Tor, where so much had started, including the writing of *The Mystical Qabalah*. It was a plot of land occupied by a large officers' army hut, supplemented by a number of small chalets. Time was when Chalice Orchard had been a kind of guest house and out of town base for the Fraternity's work, but the war and post-war years had brought an end to all that. It was now occupied by two old stalwarts of the Society who acted as live-in caretakers in their declining years.

Mary Gilchrist was a former spiritualist medium, and perhaps from lack of a new ear to talk to, extremely loquacious. She gave me chapter and verse of all that "he said to her" and "she said to him" in recalling past disputes and grievances with both esoteric and exoteric antagonists, including the local coal merchant, who apparently jibbed at heaving coal part way up the Tor – and who can blame him?

Her companion, Robbie, a retired dental surgeon, was much quieter, indeed there was not much chance to be anything else when Mary was in full flow, but you had to watch your thoughts with him. He had a way of anticipating what you were about to say, or were thinking but did not quite like to say. His remark *"I expect you think I am rather a poor old chap?"* struck a little too close for comfort!

Nonetheless there were anecdotes well worth remembering, such as their presence when Dion Fortune was diagnosed with leukaemia shortly before her death in 1946. In fact it had been Robbie who had been the first to realise her condition, when asked to take a look at the cavity of an extracted tooth that was troubling her. Their account served for my eventual biography of Dion Fortune.

There was also an atmosphere about the main chalet that brought home the presence of Dion Fortune in some indefinable way. Whether it was the great long refectory table by the window that took up almost the whole of the room, or the brass accoutrements in the grate of the open fire – somehow it seemed a place where the spirit of Dion Fortune remained imprinted. I don't know how it has appeared to subsequent owners of the place, which include the Arthurian scholar Geoffrey Ashe. One of

Margaret Lumley Brown by the sea with the Society's Warden Arthur Chichester.

the chalets had a particularly potent atmosphere about it, despite having become a repository for old furniture, and had once been the vaunted Shrine opened there in 1932 and last used by Dion Fortune in 1945.

All this to me was the epitome of Glastonbury, along with the sight of Glastonbury Tor, seen from a distance, overlooking the Somerset plain from the Shepton Mallet road. Once seen, never forgotten. My first memory of it stays with me – in the company of mystagogue Dave – two young romantics sitting astride our motorbikes, feeling like latter day knights on our chargers, on which I also embarked on an Arthurian pilgrimage to Winchester and Tintagel.

It was in the 2nd Degree that I had my first vivid psychic experience, in the less than romantic aura of RAF sergeants' quarters. In the midst of a quite routine meditation I was startled by the imaginative impression, very powerful, of the bearded head and shoulders of an ancient looking man. Some time later I recognised its likeness to a statue of Melchizedek at Chartres cathedral – an early Biblical figure, strangely described as "without father or mother, without descent" who appeared to the patriarch Abraham, bearing bread and wine, in an ancient priestly function. What was particularly striking was the sense of power and benevolence that came with this vision. It was an isolated incident, but it gave me the feeling that I was beginning to get somewhere – and would not have to rely for ever on the spiritual or psychic impressions of others.

Being a member of the 2nd Degree also entailed being on the rosta of "diary supervisors" – checking the meditation records of students on the

Study Course. Performing this chore brought home the good sense of the somewhat austere discipline of the Outer Court, in which diary entries had to be no more than ten lines long, and supervisory remarks kept to an absolute minimum. Apart from corrections to errors of fact, they were limited to an assessment of "Adequate", "Adequate plus", "Adequate minus", or the dreaded "Inadequate" as a result of each month's work.

There were good reasons for this less than sociable regime. It weeded out the emotional gushers and the faint hearted, and indeed was a practical necessity for an organisation that relied on the limited time of volunteer members to do the supervisory work – as I realised when in later years I came to set up student regimes of my own.

After eight years' service I left the RAF in the Spring of 1956 and in September was enrolled at a teacher training college in Buckinghamshire, by which time I had advanced into the 3rd Degree. I could now get to meetings more easily, by public transport, although it entailed a five mile pushbike ride between Rickmansworth station and the college. It also meant that, as well as the monthly ritual meetings, I could now attend a weekly Wednesday evening discussion group. It was after one of these that I had a remarkable psychic experience on 6th February 1957.

At this particular meeting it so happened that, quite spontaneously, a former close associate of Dion Fortune was asked if she would chant a part of Dion Fortune's *Rite of Isis*. This turned out to be a moving experience for most of those present but it had an overwhelming effect upon me. I was publicly reduced to tears.

The words, even on the printed page, can be quite evocative:

> O thou that wast before the earth was formed – Ea, Binah, Ge.
> O tideless, soundless, boundless, bitter sea,
> I am thy priestess, answer unto me.
>
> O arching sky above and earth beneath,
> Giver of life and bringer-in of death,
> Persephone, Astarte, Ashtoreth,
> I am thy priestess, answer unto me.
>
> O golden Aphrodite, come to me!
> Flower of the foam, rise from the bitter sea.
> The hour of the full moon-tide draws near,
> Hear the invoking words, hear and appear –
> Isis unveiled, and Ea, Binah, Ge!
> I am thy priestess, answer unto me.

When chanted by a priestess who knows what she is about this can be mighty impressive – but if deep personal links are stimulated with the source from whence they came – then look out for fireworks!

On the bike ride back to college that night from Rickmansworth, on a road that runs due west, the great horned moon high in the sky before me began to appear like the headdress of a great goddess, who, to my inner eye, took up the whole sky beneath. Apart from the moon, which was physical enough, this was an imaginative vision but very clear and sustained. Yet what began to concern me was the appearance of what seemed a red jewel beside the crescent moon. This was no vision, it was plain to physical sight – so I began to wonder if I was hallucinating.

However it turned out that I was not. A newspaper cutting next day revealed that I had observed the astronomical phenomenon of a "lunation of Mars". It had been the red planet I had seen abutting the crescent moon. Which raises an astrological question. I have never been much of an astrologer but have often wondered about the synchronicity of this astronomical event (a conjunction of Mars and the Moon) with the psychic events of that remarkable evening.

The link was confirmed a few days later in a formal notification from the Pythoness of the Fraternity as dictated by one of the inner plane adepti – a high and unusual honour. It acknowledged that I had made a true contact with the Higher Self of the late Dion Fortune, which would increase my sensitivity and perception. However, I should not occupy my mind too much with this fact, but seek to improve and develop my current personality which was that of a young man.

I had also apparently made my presence felt a couple of months earlier by entering the presence of the Master Rakoczi with a kind of jocular insistence, wanting to "press on" with avidity. He had apparently spoken kindly to me, patting my shoulder and telling me that if I kept this desire, I would certainly achieve it later (*whatever "it" was*) but that I was very young in physical years, and must first "be a good citizen".

I must say I was quite unaware of all this hobnobbing with a senior member of the planetary hierarchy but felt I must be proceeding on the right track if, on the other hand, slightly put down by this "be a good citizen" business.

But such concerns were indeed pressing upon me. I had begun to realise at the training college that school teaching was really not for me, and the sudden exposure to full time higher education was also an unsettling experience. It raised ambitions in me to become a writer, and my English tutor, a highly charismatic poet, Harold Morland, gave me somewhat ill advised encouragement in this respect.

This was supplemented by a local writer James Reeves (who was almost blind and to whom I used to read) who went so far as to say *"if you want to write what the hell are you doing at that college?"* All of which raised my expectations no end, far beyond my likely levels of attainment. So I dropped out of college, and spent a few weeks labouring on a horticultural establishment run by John Hall, a fellow member of the Inner Light who later became my business partner. During this time I hacked out a play before moving to London with a fellow renegade from college, Russell Haley, who subsequently became an award winning novelist in New Zealand.

In the big city I learned how to touch type on a Post Office training course prior to working at Cable and Wireless sending overseas telegrams. The instruction in typing I must say afterwards stood me in good stead.

All this change was not without a certain amount of inner turmoil, and even caused me to drop out of the Inner Light for a matter of weeks. On my return I decided to change my mystery name, to *Verité sans Peur* – Truth without Fear. This may sound melodramatic if not vainglorious, but it reflected my extra-curricular excursions into modern French literature and existentialist philosophy back at the college. Whether any ancestral memory was involved in this choice of name I do not know, but I later discovered "Sans Peur" to be the motto of the Sutherland clan from whom I am descended on my mother's side. As the clan crest also figures a wild cat, my disrespectful family later chose to spell it "Sans *Purr*"!

However, the motive in moving to London, apart from the nearness to theatre land, was to be as close as possible to the Society of the Inner Light, for the time was approaching to contemplate advance into the Greater Mysteries.

3

Che Greater Mysteries
1959-65

As constituted in those days the Lesser Mysteries was divided into three grades. In terms of the Tree of Life it was in effect a journey up the central pillar of consciousness through psychical or magical toward mystical consciousness. In Qabalistic terms, from Malkuth up to Tiphareth.

Entry into the Greater Mysteries was a major step in an initiate's life as it involved making the Unreserved Dedication. Once that was offered – and accepted – from henceforth service to the Mysteries came first, over any other interest.

Progress through the Lesser Mysteries represented a gradual development from that of a simple desire to serve, through appreciation of the reality of the inner planes, to some kind of direct awareness of higher consciousness and the powers behind the Fraternity.

Many initiates never sought to go beyond this, and remained as "completed Thirds", or even content to remain in the 1st Degree, as dedicated "hewers of wood and drawers of water", attending the meetings and lending a hand with the office and domestic work.

Proceeding into the Greater Mysteries meant rather more than this, although did not transcend it. However elevated one's grade, one always remained at root an initiate of the 1st Degree. Earlier interpretations of the Unreserved Dedication seemed to imply that it was not far short of the vow of poverty, chastity and obedience offered in an enclosed religious community. Indeed, a nucleus of senior members at that time did consist of single, socially uncommitted individuals, living within the House of the Order, in single bed sitting rooms some of which also served almost as "live in" shrines or monastic cells.

However, beyond this nucleus, a wider group of Greater Mystery initiates had developed, with domestic commitments and social obligations in the world, who nonetheless had also offered the Unreserved Dedication, the exercise of which came down largely to a matter of individual interpretation and conscience. That was the condition to which I now aspired.

My initiation into the Greater Mysteries took place on 15th June 1959. On the Tree of Life this is equivalent to the central sphere of Tiphareth, which although one of harmony and balance, meant taking the principal part in a ritual drama of sacrificial death and resurrection. Whilst this could take the form of any of the many pagan gods in universal mythology – in the basically Rosicrucian tradition of the Fraternity of the Inner Light it was based upon the crucifixion of Jesus.

The fact that it is performed largely in the imagination, as those in the outer world might regard it, does not render it any the less harrowing or inspiring. Although no physical cross or nails are involved, to a trained imagination the experience is nonetheless vivid, standing in ritual conditions with arms outstretched for what seems a very long period in appalling circumstances. I had not realised before how the driving in of the nails splayed the fingers and also how much one felt the rocking from side to side as the cross was hoisted into upright position.

All was not grief and agony however. There came visions of the spiritual significance of it all. I seemed at one point to be looking down on the figures of Mary, Mary Magdalene and John at the foot of the cross – and feeling a sense of love and even compassion for them that they could not carry out the great and wondrous task that had fallen to me. Along with this came a feeling of thanksgiving that through me they might not have to – that my suffering made the Way easier for the rest – and I fully accepted the Crucifixion as necessary and good.

Then looking up, I saw the heavens open to the face of the Father with choirs of angels and great beams of light raying down upon the Earth, piercing the gloom around, and I felt myself as a channel linking the Most High to those gathered below and over the arid waste of Golgotha and thence to the whole Earth beyond.

Following this process came the descent from the cross to be laid out as in a tomb and left alone in the darkness. Here the very silence was alive. Indeed could hardly be called a silence. It was a time of review and yet also a time of rest. The crucifixion seen as a great climax – a thing of glory rather than of horror. Then the force gradually changed from Christian to Rosicrucian – that is, from love to wisdom, as I lay patiently waiting for the day to dawn when, the stone removed from the door of the sepulchre, I should be called by true initiates of the Order, to take my place with them in service to the world.

On entry into the Greater Mysteries one takes on a new mystery name. This time not of one's own choice nor a motto of aspiration, but directed by those on the Inner as an archetypal expression of the type of one's spirit. In my case this was *Son of Isis*. Indeed at the close of the ceremony and the symbolic resurrection I felt the touch of the goddess as I was called upon to arise and become a part of the temple.

In the clairvoyant report of the initiation the Pythoness observed:

> A tremendous figure of Pallas Athene (which was in some way linked up with Britain) built up on the South side of the Candidate. The face had a certain vague likeness to that of the late Warden and the figure was fully armed. The goddess form put her arm in protection around the candidate and raised her shield above his head in a protective gesture just as he was laid upon the pastos.

> In the Chamber of the Tomb the walls were covered with symbolic pictures in bronze relief – the one which stood out most strongly was that of Our Lord's body being taken down from the Cross. I saw the ladder, the dead body and the linen shroud very clearly. At the same time the figure of the Goddess presented the candidate with the Rose Cross surrounded by lunar rays. Great strength of Wisdom was predominant and it was Wisdom armed and fighting – not Wisdom and peace.

> An Aquarian sense of Christianity was felt – quite unconnected with any church – and a triad of great beams shaped like an arrow of white light spread out at the head of the pastos, representing the Way the Truth and the Life. It was a fine ceremony showing deep Aquarian contacts and especially that between the abstract mind and the normal mentality. I thought this ritual showed the spirit interworking with the mind apart from emotion or conventional sentiment. This is surely the true Aquarian pattern.

> As the candidate was passing the North a great figure of King Arthur built up riding on a white horse and turning to look down upon one of his younger nephews – Gareth or Gaheris – who was following close behind him.

There was an additional comment from the Chancellor:

> The wisdom of the Goddess is his best protection and armour. If he can take that great wisdom contact from Her, the best things in him will develop and flourish.

And, somewhat remarkably, from Dion Fortune, who appeared to the Pythoness as a priestess of Isis in a blaze of moonlight:

> To you I speak in my deepest self as a part of Eleusis of Britain. This is most possible for me to do when the hour of the high full moon draws near. The Rose Cross can come through me as well as through the solar teaching for

Christian Rosencreutz is the great androgyne. I am the power which works in the great Eleusis force yet I am not Demeter but the four-fold Isis – She who builds and destroys all of her three other aspects and it is in that manner that Wisdom works.

And, more significantly, which caused some puzzlement:

The young man who came in yesterday is my pupil – I shall not say how or what the reason is as yet.

Indeed it took the rest of my life to find out!

Two things were scheduled to happen after admission into the Greater Mysteries. One was an Esoteric Review, conducted by the Pythoness, and the other to write and perform a ritual based upon my new Mystery Name.

The Esoteric Review took place in the Greater Mystery temple, in almost complete darkness, face to face with the Pythoness, dressed in ceremonial robes. Mine were no longer the black of a Lesser Mystery initiate but gold, with a jewelled Egyptian style headdress, a Rose Cross lamen and red shoes. A tape recorder was permitted but as it chose to break down on this occasion, I had to remember all that was said and write it down later.

The system was for the Pythoness, having visualised a Tree of Life within my aura, to state her impressions of the conditions of each sphere. (I later discovered the technique to be described by Dion Fortune in notes I eventually edited and published as *Principles of Esoteric Healing*.)

Her general impression was of a very strong Isis contact, which was focused on the Goddess rather than on any human intermediary, together with a strong link between Essential Self and Lower Self in which there was a strange kind of "double barrelled" condition in that the inner levels were markedly feminine whilst the outer were obviously masculine. This somewhat puzzling remark was expanded upon not long afterwards in a remark attributed to the Master Rakoczi after the performance of my name ritual.

This brother represents the type of the New Age and <u>synthesis</u> is the essential key to his make up. He is masculine and feminine, he (without being pathological) is both mediumistic and intellectual. He combines the processes of past, present and future into one whole. In short, he is a human "synthesis".

She also had the impression of exceptional scientific ability, with a knowledge of atomic energy "bursting to come through". This seemed rather odd, because I had no especial scientific qualifications, apart from elementary atomic theory being part of the curriculum in my RAF lectures to radar operators. Although ever since seeing a film about Marie Curie and the discovery of radium back in 1943, quantum physics remained a matter of considerable fascination for me, and in later years I did indeed construct some rituals based upon atomic structure and the way that chemical elements interact with human life.

The Pythoness then went on to describe flashes of vision apparently from past lives. The strong Goddess contact she saw being first developed in Atlantis where I had been a worker in the Sun Temple – although not as a priest. Owing to the ability I showed I aroused the attention of a priestess of high standing in the temple (latterly Dion Fortune), who took an interest in my development. She felt that trying to get more detail on these early contacts would help my development tremendously.

There was also a glimpse of what seemed an important incarnation in medieval times. I was "in some kind of trouble" as she put it, in armour and chained in a dungeon. Whatever the circumstances, they had brought about a close contact with my Holy Guardian Angel, which had since been able to come into close contact with subsequent personalities.

There was also a Rosicrucian contact but in an Aquarian rather than medieval sense and contact with the Master Rakoczi – who had an interest in individuals likely to be of use in bringing in the Aquarian age.

She now became conscious of an immediate personal contact with the Master Rakoczi, accompanied by the Chancellor. The latter encouraged the development of the Isis contact, which he was at pains to point out was a high spiritual one and not to be confused with its more emotive side. That wherever I was – at any place or time – I had only to reach out to have contact with him. It might not come as a message in specific words, but he was always there.

I lost little time in preparing my "name ritual" which I performed on August 15th, an ancient Isiac festival that had been Christianised as the Feast of the Assumption. I used the occasion to try to give expression to some quite abstruse teaching that had recently been put through, via the Pythoness, from Dion Fortune. This was to the effect that the forces of the Heavenly (or "Uranian") Isis were little understood, but could be related to the Christian doctrine of the Assumption of the Blessed Virgin Mary, as well as with the Divine Androgyne, that implied a recognition of the feminine side of the Godhead.

Whether or not I achieved much of this, the ritual drew enthusiastic comment from a variety of inner plane sources. From the Chancellor:

> This was a very fine working indeed and so remarkably good for the first time that the fact of its being too long may well be overlooked. The magicianship was marked and the choice of setting and language excellent. This work makes one feel that the teaching behind has really taken root and I look forward to new work from this member. I congratulate him on an effective rite which brought through the power with efficiency and imagination.

The Master Rakoczi was also said to be watching, but from a remote distance, and his remarks have already been noted.

The Master Hilarion (sometimes known as the Egyptian Master) was also drawn by the strong Egyptian forces set in motion and declared it to be an Egyptian ritual such as he was glad to see again.

Whilst from Dion Fortune came the statement that she was able to be in contact with both myself and others present and help in the building up of the great power of Sothis, the Egyptian name for the star Sirius, perhaps recalling her own Rite of Isis that she used to perform:

> This was a real Isis working once more. I was in communication the whole time. The real Sothis condition did enter the atmosphere.

As it had been recommended at my Esoteric Review that I investigate my early links with Dion Fortune I spent a week trying to go back down the time track. For this I was assisted by Anne, Dion Fortune's previous close personal student, whose chanting from the Rite of Isis had stimulated my experience on the Rickmansworth Road.

She used a simple technique of asking just two questions, alternately put: "What had I done to Dion Fortune" and "What had Dion Fortune done to me?" I had to answer the first thing that came into my head, and whilst a great deal was no doubt fairly superficial, with the incessant repetition there came points when memorable and powerful visions seemed to take over.

One, that remains most vivid, seemed so far back as to be beyond time and space as we know it. Dion Fortune and I were simply geometric shapes, apparently residing in a retort shaped edifice built in a rectangular cavity in the ground, from whence we would emerge, to fly high up into the sky towards what appeared to be small pinkish coloured clouds. We would do a rapid kind of dance, resulting in what seemed a kind of copulation, from which a dark blue net or web would be produced, in which we would gather the clouds and bring them back down to the surface of the planet again. In short it seemed like some kind of aerial fishing trip.

The problem with this kind of vision is that there is no conception of scale. We might, by modern parameters, have been either vast creatures or alternatively of microscopic size, of physical solidity or abstract thought forms, or in some unknown dimension of space and time. The speculative possibilities are infinite.

A similar kind of vision, at another cosmic phase, concerned flying high over the surface of what looked like a new planet, generating between ourselves rays or cords which sank or reached down to the surface, thus seeding the globe in some way.

Advancing to more familiar conditions of space and time I experienced being some kind of local war lord in ancient times, somewhere around the north east coast of South America it seemed. Here I studied star lore from a tower and was at odds with some central power that eventually sent a punitive force to destroy me. I ended up with a spear through the heart, that led to an after death condition not unlike a Viking Valhalla.

I also recall having a long boat at the time, similar to the type we associate with Norsemen, and steering by a pole star different from the one we have now. This appeared to be Vega, which (although I had no idea of this at the time of recollection) had actually been the pole star some 14,000 years ago through the precession of equinoxes.

However, within a year, these speculative ancient links to Dion Fortune were superseded by a strong direct event very much in the present. At one of the Greater Mystery ritual meetings I became aware of a presence just behind me, which seemed to be Dion Fortune trying to make herself felt. It was quite without verbal content and seemed rather like having some kind of wedge pushed into the back of my neck. Nor did it go away, for upon leaving the house it continued with me back home, where it became ever more strongly felt, to the point of feeling I was being pushed out of my body altogether.

It became such a pervasive presence that even Roma (whom I had married just a month before) was aware of it as an overpowering atmosphere. The condition is difficult to describe – it was like being on the verge of losing my own identity. It felt quite insidious, as if my own consciousness were being pushed out and another pushed in. I must say that I did not much fancy my chances in a bout of psychic arm wrestling with Dion Fortune, if this was what it was!

However, I fought it off as best I could, and next day all seemed back to normal. Nonetheless I put in a strongly worded note to the Warden saying that dedicated service to the Mysteries was one thing, but being taken over, apparently by force, was somewhat beyond the spirit of the Unreserved Dedication as I understood it!

A lengthy reply, apparently dictated by the Chancellor, advised me to guard against encroachments of this sort. It went on to say that there was a desire on Dion Fortune's part to lay hold on the Fraternity and to keep power in her hands by means of psychic intervention, even to the point of "blotting out" my own legitimate force and inserting her own. There might well be karmic links and pre-historical ties between us but each soul had the right to work out a normal earth life, and it was not well to interfere with this right during the early years of incarnationary development.

If there was indeed a ruthless element inferred here on Dion Fortune's part, I have to say that I did not feel in a position to condemn her too harshly, for if the roles were reversed I would have had few qualms about acting in a similar manner – at any rate at that time. (An instance of a major principle of the mysteries, as I later came to realise, that you are likely to receive just whatever unpleasantness you are prepared to hand out!)

Whilst accepting the general advice, I was not entirely convinced by the detail, and in light of later experience, found Dion Fortune contacts entirely beneficial – even if she might come over a bit strong at times! I think she may well, at this period, have been aware of remarkable new developments that were pending in the Fraternity and also with regard to myself – and felt an urgent need to make a powerful contact – with which however I was not yet ready to cope – with the consequent negative reactions all round.

Certainly some major changes were about to be made!

4

There'll Be Some Changes Made!
1961-63

A prelude to esoteric changes afoot within the Society of the Inner Light was a physical change of location. By the late 1950s the Bayswater district had begun to deteriorate and the Society was fortunate to find an ideal new headquarters, complete with studios for group meetings, in North London.

Things carried on much as before for some time until a couple of senior members had some kind of Christian mystical experience in one of the upstairs rooms. It must have been a deep one for the place was set aside, draped in heavy purple curtains, and with allusion to the Last Supper, called "the Upper Room". All were invited to go and meditate there, but I have to say it did not do much for me. Indeed I found the atmosphere rather cloying and oppressive.

However, something big seemed afoot, for working in the library one day I was struck with a vision of my own. The figure of Jesus seemed suddenly to appear in the middle of the room, walk two or three steps toward me, and then disappear.

It was no more than a brief imaginative flash but so striking that I felt I must mark the occasion in some way. I rode up to a Hampstead bookshop on my scooter, bought a copy of *The Imitation of Christ* by Thomas á Kempis, and signed it and dated it – 27th September 1961.

I had no problem with an increased Christian emphasis within the group; after all, Dion Fortune had always pursued a broad line that included Christian mysticism along with hermetic philosophy, ritual magic and elemental nature contacts. However, this was the start of a major change of attitude in the Fraternity. The whole degree system was abolished and only one grade left functioning, that of the 1st Degree.

There was a down playing of the importance of psychism or mediumship, upon which the Fraternity had virtually been built since its inception. Despite her remarkable track record, and still at the height of her powers, Margaret Lumley Brown was relieved of her duties, and her place taken by Rosina Mann, called back from America for the purpose, who introduced her own method of inner plane communication, called "mediation".

Although this was said to be of superior accuracy, the style was very different from all that had appeared in the past, full of neologisms and convoluted syntax, even though allegedly from the same inner plane contacts. The emphasis was now on "Regeneration" – or more specifically "the Path of Redemption in Earth".

This was connected with what was called the Initiation of the Nadir, a concept derived from *The Cosmic Doctrine.* In traditional esoteric teaching, the life wave that comprises all humanity is seen as coming down the planes to the physical from the plane of spirit. This is the process of *Involution.* After due creative expression of spiritual principles in Earth it then returns up the planes in the process of spiritual *Evolution.* From this it follows that a successful turning of the corner, the bottom-dead-centre of the process, is absolutely crucial.

In practical terms, to pursue an interest in the higher worlds before the Nadir has been successfully reached and passed would be a retrogression and degradation of the soul rather than an evolutionary way forward. The implication was that the group in the past, with its emphasis on psychism and higher initiation, had been turning its back on life in the world.

The way ahead concerned the stewardship of the things of the Earth, and the immediate work for members of the Fraternity was very much a matter of self examination to achieve right living in the world rather than the traditional graded structure for developing magical techniques and psychic awareness.

I was prepared to go along with much of this but felt it incumbent upon me to try to mitigate some of the shock to outer members and far flung associates of the Society – tempering the wind to the shorn lambs, so to speak. I therefore started a little *Quarterly Review* from the library, (the first of many forays into small magazines), in which I tried to steer a middle course between the best of the old and the stark message of the new. There was indeed some considerable disquiet out there – as one old lady of long standing membership wrote in to say: "Oh I do hope the Society isn't going all High Church!"

This was hardly the case, although there was from now on a dedication of all rituals to some aspect of the Blessed Virgin Mary. There was, however, on the other hand a very strong emphasis on bringing things down to earth. This focused particularly upon the Planetary Being, the great generating Elemental within which we, and all our fellow species, live and move and have our being. In some respects, indeed, it could well be said that all this was a timely foreshadowing of latter day concerns with the planetary environment in what has come to be known as Gaia.

Certainly within the closer confines of the Fraternity it was apparent that the cloistered hot house atmosphere built up over the years was going to be a thing of the past. Senior members who had hitherto followed an enclosed withdrawn existence, or been regarded as superior beings, whether by others or themselves, were now expected to get out more into the world and meet people. As a first step this meant more socialising between those in the Society.

As a result Roma and I spent an interesting musical "at home" laid on by Richard Mallock and his wife, who were very much of the upper social set. Indeed Mrs Mallock's reminiscences of attending the first ever performance of Ravel's *Bolero* in Paris were fascinating. However the evening was mostly taken up with recordings of Wagnerian opera, which was not entirely to my taste, but the coffee was very good.

Arthur Chichester and Rosina Mann also came to visit us in our basement bed sitter where the highlight of the occasion was my cooking a stuffed marrow which was long remembered with wonder and affection by them both.

The really memorable occasion however was entertaining Margaret Lumley Brown to dinner, when she transported us with a fund of tales of other-worldly creatures she had observed through second sight.

The stories generally had to be coaxed out of her, perhaps because her remarkable psychism was now somewhat under a cloud. They were delivered in a matter of fact, slightly apologetic manner, of one who realised that all this must seem rather odd to those not gifted with her unusual faculties. There was a certain evocatory power about her that was not merely subjective, for when we returned to the room after she had gone, there was a strange stillness in the air, and all the candle flames were standing straight to a remarkable height. Nothing weird, but certainly impressive, and a fitting end to a memorable evening.

Another somewhat startling impression came when we walked her down to the tube station. I knew from previous conversation that she suffered some distress when crossing a busy street because she was sensitive to the traffic rushing through her aura. However, this seemed to have a positive side to it, for she walked straight out into the maelstrom of traffic at the busy junction outside Archway tube station, and looking neither to right nor to left, arrived unscathed at the other side, waving airily to us as she disappeared like some ancient goddess into the bowels of the earth.

By contrast the Wednesday evening meetings at the Society went through rather an astringent phase. The old readings and group discussion went by the board to give place to some rather forbidding exercises where we were paired off to "confront" one another. That is, to stare in each other's faces, whilst Rosina paraded around overseeing all.

I think this must have come from the armamentarium of assorted psychological exercises to be found in Scientology, which in one way and another played quite an influence upon the Fraternity. There never seemed to be any official tie up with the organisation although some senior members became quite deeply involved. Indeed Rosina Mann had gone off to America apparently to work close to L. Ron Hubbard, its founder, and in later years Anne, who had chanted the Isis ritual which had such an effect upon me, and who was later responsible for the Christ experience in "the Upper Room", left the Fraternity to work full time at Saint Hill, the Scientologists' headquarters in England.

For lesser fry within the Society the contact was relatively minor, although I was invited to spend a week being "processed" by Rosina, but not in any very intensive fashion. In retrospect I think it was a means of trying to gather how much of a potential problem I might pose to those in charge in view of my apparent inner affiliations to Dion Fortune. However, although I felt somewhat irritated at some of the ways in which things seemed to be going, I did not set up any major opposition, largely because it was announced that the current regime was simply an interim measure to provide a sound foundation for the Fraternity to be rebuilt after what was called a "three year plan".

Dion Fortune had indeed been much interested in forms of psychotherapy as an aid to the initiation process, and it was possible that such a means might well be found in Scientology. At any rate that was the reason why the system, if not the organisation, received quite enthusiastic endorsement in *A Practical Guide to Qabalistic Symbolism*.

One of the more endearing aspects of it was the Society's attempt to find some useful form of alternative activity for Margaret Lumley Brown now that her mediumistic and psychic gifts were no longer valued or employed. She was encouraged to lay on some elementary exercises for the benefit of individual members in her room. I found these quite enjoyable because I don't think either of us took them too seriously, but it was certainly a far cry from the evocatively charged Esoteric Review days. The exercises consisted of her telling you to look at the opposite wall, identify a spot on it, go over and touch that point, turn round and do the same with the other opposite wall, and so on. As an elementary exercise in taking control of a situation it had its beneficial side I suppose, although I felt the time better spent when she put on the kettle and got out the teapot, biscuit tin and jar of Gentleman's Relish and we could indulge in a bit of a chat.

There were other ancillary activities available that proved more useful. Such as acting as a guinea pig for a senior member, a qualified doctor, who was investigating various alternative therapies including the Alexander technique, a method of muscular re-education. This was to stand me in very good stead in later life, for when plagued with severe back pain, and prescribed nothing but pain killers and tranquillisers, all was cleared up by reverting to this remarkable system.

One interesting side effect of undergoing it was the coming into consciousness of what appeared to be injuries sustained on the battlefield in the 1st World War. This was entirely a subjective side effect and no part of the formal or official technique as practised or taught – as I discovered when I later mentioned these things to a highly effective practitioner, who had no esoteric background and who became quite frightened about it. There are times when you need to keep your own counsel about the inner side of things.

The esoteric background to this may have been accurately described in one of the Fraternity's earlier papers, which suggested that many who died in large numbers on the battlefield had reincarnated without going through all the usual processes of the after death condition. If so, did that explain why the age of 23 had seemed somehow significant to me? It was the age I made contact with the Mysteries in this life. Could it have been the physical age of my previous death? Because up until the age of 23 I could not settle to anything – it seemed that there would be no future after that time, that there was just a blank wall.

A speculative fancy? Possibly. But it had its relevance to some important inner work I was to do later on, with the Company of the Light of the Somme, towards the end of the century.

5

Gareth Knight and the Practical Guide

1961-62

But if things were on the move for the Society so were they for me. It began with a letter from America by a certain Carl L. Weschcke. Carl had recently set up as a publisher, and had bought up a small existing company, Llewellyn Publications, successful over many years as producers of *The Moon Sign Book*, which gave horticultural, agricultural and all kinds of other advice on living your life by phases of the Moon. It also had a number of astrological titles but Carl had wider ambitions – which included republishing some of Dion Fortune's old titles.

He had written to the Society and obtained rights on a couple of her books – my old favourite *The Esoteric Orders and their Work* and a volume of her short stories *The Secrets of Dr. Taverner*. Now he asked if a member of the Society would write an Introduction to each one.

No one fancied taking this on so the request was thrown onto the library desk, perhaps with some vague acknowledgement of my literary aspirations. I eagerly seized the chance and set about my first literary commission, a couple of essays entitled *The Work of a Modern Occult Fraternity* and *The Work of the Inner Plane Adepti*. In retrospect I think them hardly my best work but Carl liked them well enough. So much so that he asked if I would write a book on the Qabalah. This to be not only an update to Dion Fortune's *Mystical Qabalah* but an extension of it, for she had never got round to writing about the 22 Paths of Concealed Glory that join the 10 Sephiroth or Spheres of Emanation on the Tree of Life.

This was an unbelievable proposition. To my surprise, no objections were raised by those who ran the Society, who seemed to think it all rather irrelevant and even somewhat beneath their attention. Mr Creasy, the Treasurer, did wonder about the financial viability of the whole set up, and urged caution about getting too much involved. But as far as I was concerned Opportunity with a capital O was knocking hard at the door, and come what may, I proposed to answer it. Let old retired bankers purse their lips as they may!

My first task was to choose a pen name. With my precious literary ambitions, I wanted to preserve my own name for whatever fame and fortune might come from writing for the theatre. So for what seemed to me at the time no more than a sideline of writing occult books I decided to call myself – **Gareth Knight.**

After all, at my Greater Mystery Initiation, had not the Pythoness reported seeing one of the royal nephews, Gareth or Gaheris, following close behind King Arthur? And in the original story, Sir Gareth was not recognised for who and what he was. With the hubris of youth, I felt this reflected in some degree my own position in the Fraternity. For despite my acknowledged links with its founder, and being asked to write a major follow up to her work, I felt that I was being kept at arm's length and offered no help in undertaking what looked like a full time task.

This was no great problem as I buckled down to writing the first volume of *A Practical Guide to Qabalistic Symbolism*. It took me just six weeks, as it was largely a summary of well trodden ground, supplemented with extracts from Society papers. The Warden, or Spiritual Director as he was now called, was quite happy for me to use this material with the odd stipulation that I did not reveal the source! Israel Regardie later told me that he had been offered similar conditions with regard to the Golden Dawn but had refused to comply.

The second volume was a considerably greater challenge, involving a great deal of personal research on the symbolism of the 22 Paths that conjoin the 10 Sephiroth. There was very little about these in the Society's papers or on the Tarot. However, the library was a great help, where I turned up each day to work on the book. I could have done with some financial support however, having in a spirit of unreserved dedication given up my day job for the purpose.

The seventy pounds advance I received from Llewellyn Publications was sufficient to keep me going for a few weeks, and was a great symbolic milestone in my life. The first money ever received for writing something! In fact so unbelievable did it seem that, egged on by Roma, I drew it all out of the bank for the pleasure of throwing the notes up in the air to flutter down round our heads.

I continued hacking away at the book in the library, supplementing my diet with raids on the communal biscuit tin, my daily presence tolerated but otherwise ignored. Eventually a fellow member of the Society, John Devlin, a forthright Irishman whose name I record with gratitude, realised the situation and gave me enough cash to keep me going, refusing any suggestion of eventual repayment. However it was Roma's salary as a school teacher that really pulled us through.

In view of the almost complete lack of Tarot packs for sale in those days Carl suggested I design one to go with the book. He gave me a free hand in this and I recruited a Dutch astrological friend, the abstract artist Sander Littel, and spent a few convivial days, sitting on the pavement outside his warehouse studio in Dordrecht eating raw herring and discussing the project. We evolved a system whereby I would send him rough sketches of what I had in mind which he would paint up in full colour to be sent across to Carl in America. Nothing if not innovative, Carl decided that the dimensions of the finished cards should be those commonly used for poker decks.

He also thought about trying to issue a set of Aleister Crowley's cards, the designs for which had first appeared in *The Book of Thoth* in 1943. The originals had been painted by Lady Frieda Harris and Carl asked me to check out that they were all still in good condition. Roma and I spent a fascinating couple of hours at Lloyds Bank in Piccadilly examining all 78 paintings (plus one for the back design), which were of considerable size, brought up from the vaults on trolleys by puzzled, sweating and not best pleased officials.

Carl now asked for advice on a suitable British publishing company who might be interested in distributing Llewellyn books on this side of the Atlantic. The old firms of Foulsham and Fowler came immediately to his mind but I was beginning to get some business ideas of my own.

I had, by chance, recently met an unlikely new acquaintance in the person of Morris Kahn, a composer of violin quartets who had ambitions to set up as a publisher specialising in music. As a first step he had gone into partnership with a much loved and respected old representative in the book trade, George Averill, who had been running a part time publishing venture called Stanmore Press for a number of years, more or less as a hobby.

As Morris put it, publishing was a dead easy game. You just found an author, printed his or her book, warehoused and distributed it, and then with the money coming in published another book, and so on until fame and fortune was made. Needless to say, it is not quite so easy as that, but it is true to say that with a modicum of capital all you needed was a telephone to set up in business, as everything else in the game, from printing through to warehousing and selling could be done by others for varying royalties, commissions and percentages. Get the percentages right and what remained was profit or further working capital.

I had no capital to invest but I did have my link with Llewellyn Publications and so I suggested to Carl that Stanmore Press could probably distribute his books as well as anyone else. On getting his agreement to this I was welcomed as a partner into Stanmore, who hoped for a reasonable commission from handling the Llewellyn business.

Llewellyn had quite a sizeable list, at any rate by our standards, including some profitable looking titles. Admittedly they were somewhat down market from my own high flown pretensions.

They included *Thought Dial* by Sidney Omarr, who combined astrology, numerology and Jungian psychology to tap the "unconscious wisdom" deep inside everyone to find lost articles, pick winners and solve unusual and difficult problems. He enjoyed great popularity among TV and motion picture personalities – with a picture of busty film-star Jayne Mansfield to prove it. *Picking Winners* by Donald A. Bradley was for those of a speculative turn of mind interested in contest analysis, whether in football, boxing or horse racing. Whilst the *Moon Sign Quarterly* taught how to use the moon phases not only for successful horticulture but how to handle your husband or know more about women.

These titles and others like them were respectable enough (and saleable enough) at their own level, although Morris and I did have a few awkward minutes with a customs officer who pored suspiciously and disapprovingly over a copy of Ophiel's *Art and Practice of Astral Projection*. ("Many now separate the 'Self' from the Body. YOU are ready for THIS BOOK!")

The first lesson Morris and I learned about importing books was to get an experienced agent to do it. Turning up at London docks with a clapped out van and an Irish odd job man was not the best way of getting through the formalities.

Ophiel was remarkable in one other instance that showed the gap between the kind of occultism I was used to in the Society of the Inner Light and that of the popular market place. He was the type of respondent who liked to indulge in capital letters, exclamation marks, and triple underlining, all in green ink, and on writing with some enquiry to the Society had received a somewhat terse reply initialled by Arthur Chichester. Ophiel interpreted the AC as either from a disciple of Aleister Crowley or as a pentagram and came back with full force wanting to know exactly what was intended. On further rebuff, this time from Dick Mallock, Ophiel followed up by saying that if he ever visited England he would call at the Inner Light headquarters, and as soon as the door was opened, punch him right on the nose!

It is perhaps not surprising that the staid Mr Chichester viewed popular occultism with a somewhat jaundiced eye. Anyhow, this was the wider esoteric milieu with which I was now about to engage.

6

New Dimensions
1963

Involvement with Llewellyn Publications and Stanmore Press improved my financial lot as Carl began to send me a monthly cheque as salary for representing his interests, added to which was the unbelievable opportunity of launching a new occult magazine that he invited me to edit.

On the strength of this Roma and I were able to move out of our basement bed-sitter near Archway tube station, in a house frequented by jazz musicians that was bohemian and entertaining if somewhat cramped and noisy. We now found ourselves a large garden flat in relatively upmarket Hornsey Lane where the new magazine, *New Dimensions*, was born.

For the editorship I decided to use my own name although I also wrote an article for each issue as Gareth Knight to support the front cover design which featured a colour reproduction of one of the impending Gareth Knight Tarot cards. On the first issue was a picture of the Fool, and subsequent issues featured the Magician, the High Priestess, the Empress, and the High Priest. I have to say however that on occasion I was in such a state of nervous exhaustion with getting the rest of the magazine together that the quality of my own articles was not quite as good as I might have wished.

The magazine was to be bi-monthly, the first of which, for April/May 1963, duly appeared, printed in America but with a couple of thousand shipped over for distribution by Stanmore.

The high quality of the material I was able to commission surprised Carl Weschcke, many of the readers, and even me. The first issue contained:

EDITORIAL: *The Editor Thinks*, by Basil Wilby;
OCCULT EXPERIENCES: *The Mound on the Moor*, by W. E. Butler;
TAROT: *The Fool's Journey*, by Gareth Knight;
WITCHCRAFT: *A Witch Explains Witchcraft*, by Patricia Crowther;
CLAIRVOYANCE: *The Urwelt – the Elemental "Other-world"*, by Margaret Lumley Brown;
FOLKLORE: *The Twelve Brothers*, by David Williams;

The house in Hornsey Lane, London. New Dimensions *was run from the downstairs room in the corner turret.*

MAGIC: *Making Magick Work*, by Margaret Bruce;
MAGIC: *Introduction to Ritual Magic*, by Dion Fortune;
FICTION: *Murder at Malden Manor*, by Marc Edmund Jones;
POETRY: *Rosa Mystica*, by Harold Morland;
CARTOONS: *Nell*, by Roma;
BOOK REVIEWS: by Thomas Connor.

And I laid down a strong editorial campaigning policy from the start:

THE EDITOR THINKS that it is high time that the mystery was taken out
of magic, the superstition out of psychism and the pretentiousness out of
practical occultism. And this is one thing we hope to do with *New Dimensions*.
In these pages we are going to bring occultists, psychics, clairvoyants,
palmists, prophets and all the company of esotericism to explain their beliefs
and experiences in a sane and rational way to – we hope – a large and sane
and rational audience of readers.

And this is largely what readers got during the life of the magazine. I had
of course the advantage of my background in the Society of the Inner
Light, to whom I was grateful for being allowed to reprint articles by Dion
Fortune from the old *Inner Light Magazine*, despite their recent cooling
off towards her. All the more surprising as I chose a selection of articles
that made up a series on ritual magic – but perhaps I slipped under their
radar. In later years I was able to publish them in volume form with
parallel articles by myself under the title *An Introduction to Ritual Magic*
by Dion Fortune and Gareth Knight.

Margaret Lumley Brown was of course still a member of the Society,
and they were indeed quite supportive of my asking her to contribute
on the grounds of trying to make her more self-sufficient and open to
outside sources after twenty years of dedicated close confinement.

Ernest Butler was of particular interest to me, having been a member
of the Society of the Inner Light in its early days, joining in 1930 (the year
I was born). He had subsequently branched off on his own and recently
attracted attention with an informative little paperback *Magic, Its Ritual,
Power and Purpose*, followed by the more substantial *The Magician, his
Training and Work* and *Apprenticed to Magic*, obviously from the pen of
one who knew what he was writing about from first hand, and at a time
when little of worth was being published on the subject.

Roma and I were charmed by Ernest when he first came to see us. Our
first impression was that he might well have come out of a Gilbert and
Sullivan operetta, as "Mr John Wellington Wells, a weaver of magic and
spells". He was an affable rotund little man in his early sixties, with a three
piece chalk striped blue serge suit, complete with gold watch chain across
his waistcoat. Although we did not realise it at the time, he was to play an
important part in my future esoteric work as indeed I was in his.

I made my first witchcraft contacts almost accidentally when Morris
Kahn and I commissioned a book for children entitled *Let's Put On a
Show* for Stanmore Press from Arnold Crowther. Arnold, a delightful and
humorous professional conjuror and entertainer was married to Patricia
Crowther who ran a Gardnerian coven in Sheffield. They both contributed

articles to the new magazine and also introduced me to Gerald Gardner whose work I was also able to feature later.

Another important find from the north was Margaret Bruce, who ran a mail order business specialising in the supply of magical instruments, and ritual and devotional incenses, talismans, perfumes, medicinal and occult herbs, oils and magical robes, symbols and tools. I was later to have something of a shock when I went to visit her to discover that she had originally been Maurice Bruce, an ex-marine commando, who had undergone a sex change. This was almost unheard of in those days – so much so that the *News of the World* had taken an interest and been given a straight-from-the-shoulder interview in return for a contribution to charity. Whatever her gender, Margaret Bruce remained one of the most sensible and straightforward occultists that I ever met or had to deal with, whose articles were an epitome of rare knowledge and down to earth common sense.

David Williams had latterly been one of the students I supervised on the Inner Light Study Course and was to play an important part in my esoteric life some thirty years later. He contributed one or two articles on the secret lore in fairy stories which, along with Margaret Lumley Brown's first couple of articles had a longer lease of life than any of us could have expected. Years after, an American pagan group approached me, seeking help in tracing their origins, which they thought must be some ancient coven run by Margaret Lumley Brown. It turned out that their secret lore consisted of articles pirated from the first two issues of *New Dimensions*, that some hippy back packer of the time had come across and taken back home with him in order to found an esoteric group. This indeed had apparently thrived, which says something for the quality of the articles, although the initiates of the group that had grown from them felt disappointed that their roots were not of greater antiquity!

The fictional element of the magazine consisted of little detective stories based on horoscopes drawn up for the characters involved, written by Dr. Marc Edmund Jones, a distinguished American astrologer recruited by Carl Weschcke, who hoped eventually to publish the stories as a book.

To raise the cultural tone of the magazine I included some poetry from my old English tutor at college, Harold Morland, who turned out to be a far more highly regarded poet than I realised at the time. Whilst to lighten it, I featured cartoons by Roma, partly in a strip which featured a witch named Nell, and partly as visual comments upon some of the articles – with an occasional cutting edge to deflate some of the more pretentious claims that abound in occultism.

A major purpose of the magazine being to promote Llewellyn books, we featured an extensive advertising section, supported by book reviews written by me under the pen name of Thomas Connor. This name chosen because I owned at the time a couple of parakeets known as St. Thomas conures, being the nearest I could get to owning a parrot at that time. As a lonely child, brought up with a talkative parrot that a sailor uncle had brought back from one of his trips, I have ever had a soft spot for the species.

Despite our initial high ambitions, the magazine was never able to make it onto the general book stalls. As an executive from one of the leading distributors put it to me, there were some 90,000 retail outlets. How many did I expect each one to take, on "sale or return", at a discount of 55%? Plainly we would need to rely on drumming up private subscriptions and concentrating on the specialist market. I cannot say I was greatly encouraged at the response of Geoffrey Watkins, a leading occult bookseller in London, whose first response was "A new magazine? Oh not another one!"

Nonetheless he did stock it, but it set me thinking that what was needed was a specialist organisation that covered mail order work to support the magazine publishing. And fortunately the opportunity for this came about just at this time. The Society of the Inner Light, because of their change of culture, wanted to get rid of many of the books in their library that they felt to be unsuitable. "Occultism" along with "psychism" and "mediumship" were now almost dirty words. This meant that a large range of titles, some of them of great rarity (for it had been Dion Fortune's original intention to build up the best occult library in the country) were now marked for the discard.

Not sure of how to divest themselves of this load of condemned literature the Society were happy to accept my offer to sell it for them on commission. From my experience of servicing the postal side of the library it seemed to me that the time was ripe to launch a mail order book service to satisfy a growing demand for esoteric literature. For this I enlisted the help of fellow member John Hall, who had previously provided me with student vacation work, and who, disenchanted with the horticultural trade, was looking for an alternative business opportunity.

Thus Helios Book Service was born, its customer base culled from the mailing list of the Society of the Inner Light and subscribers to *New Dimensions*. With the help of the little Irishman and his lorry, the same who had accompanied me and Morris Kahn in our business at London docks, the discarded library books, carried in on his back in a blanket, were heaved onto the floor of our flat and stacked on hastily contrived shelves made up from pinewood planks and house bricks.

For the first few months of the business, John and Mary Hall did the mailing shots out of their home in Gloucestershire while I serviced the orders for second hand books from those piled up in my flat. Eventually all these were sold and John and Mary continued on their own, having established themselves as bona fide booksellers. This was not entirely easy, for some publishers, in deference to the established book trade, refused to deal with upstarts such as ourselves not in the Booksellers' Association. Nonetheless, even difficult sales managers would generally succumb to cash sent with orders, if need be, so gradually acceptance was achieved, all but one or two university publishers putting profit before principle and restrictive practice.

It is an ill wind that blows nobody any good but some members of the Society felt very bitter about the decimation of the library. One of its remarkable features, that reflected the deeper magical work of the past, was a large historical section and also one on science fiction. As I was later to discover in my own occult work, much of it is concerned with collective archetypes that figure in a nation's history as well in its myths and legends; whilst the science fiction was considered a means of stretching the mind to comprehend new cosmic vistas on inner as well as outer dimensions of reality. However, for better or for worse, the accent was now focused very much on the Earth rather than the stars, and on the present here and now rather than the past.

And so, for the moment, I was riding high on the prospects of authorship, editorship and business opportunity. But what goes up can also come down, and things were about to take a challenging turn. At the beginning of 1964 Roma announced that she was pregnant and in the same week Carl wrote to say that in the enthusiasm for all his new projects he had overstretched himself financially – or in short, run out of money!

7

Helios Rising
1964

Thus my salary and *New Dimensions* magazine were ended at a stroke. What is more, publication of *The Practical Guide* and of the Tarot cards were also abandoned. It seemed that cautious Mr Creasy had been right from the first.

However, all was not lost, thanks to William Elmhirst, a relatively new member of the Society of the Inner Light and obviously not hard up for a pound a two. He now stepped in as a generous benefactor, ready to bail out the typesetting for *The Practical Guide* from whatever financial maw it had fallen into, so that we could perhaps publish it at Stanmore Press.

This was not without its nail biting moments. Bill was very much a faithful member of the Society and anxious to observe to the letter the virtually *ex cathedra* opinions of its Spiritual Director. I must say that Arthur Chichester had been very helpful to me in writing the first volume of the book, which leaned heavily upon Society knowledge papers. He had read it with approval and made a few useful comments.

He was, however, not so keen on the second volume, which broke new ground and was largely the fruit of my own research. In particular he had reservations about the Tarot, nor did he like the word "occult". Therefore although the book had been advertised for a year in *New Dimensions* as *A Practical Guide to* **Occult** *Symbolism* he insisted that it should be called *A Practical Guide to* **Qabalistic** *Symbolism*. Apart from his word being law in the circumstances, I had to admit that this title was more accurate, if somewhat less appealing to the world at large.

However, a more vertiginous issue was whether he would approve publication of the second volume at all. For if not, Bill Elmhirst would never gainsay his wishes. After a sticky interview to discuss the matter it was finally decided that both volumes could go ahead. The accompanying Tarot cards however had to be abandoned, as apart from the lack of enthusiasm for them, four colour printing in those days was hideously expensive, even for someone with a very long pocket. It was the fate of Sander Littel's artwork to remain impounded for the next twenty years, without a penny piece going to him, until eventually the Tarot card collector and publisher Stuart Kaplan came to the rescue in 1984.

And thanks to Bill Elmhirst, *New Dimensions* remained in business, for he agreed to finance it through 1964. And so it continued without a break, divorced now from Llewellyn Publications, under the imprint of Helios Book Service (New Dimensions) Ltd, a new company that we hastily floated.

I think Bill was as much concerned for the welfare of Roma and myself as for the content of the magazine. He had also founded, encouraged by the new philosophy of the Society, the Homes Trust, which was devoted to providing a loan to any members who found it difficult to put down a building society deposit to buy a home for themselves. In those days long before easy credit (and the subsequent crash) quite demanding rules of credit worthiness were rigorously applied. Roma and I were certainly in need of a helping hand, and were fortunate to be around at just the right time to benefit from this opportunity.

It seemed to us that the time had come to abandon London (the magnet for all young provincials) and move to the country, hopefully to live more cheaply, but also to be near Helios, where John and Mary Hall had got the bookshop end of the business more or less established.

Much to our delight we received details of a charming 18th century cottage with a walled garden that had come up for sale on an old sacred site, the Mythe, just outside Tewkesbury. We had some concern however about finding someone to take over the lease on our expensive flat, which still had eighteen months to run. Finding another tenant proved something of a challenge, so – with a bit of heart searching I must admit – I got out *The Art of True Healing* and applied myself to the appropriate exercises, salving any qualms of conscience about "using the occult arts for gain" with the assumption that it was all in a good cause.

This little book by Israel Regardie had come to my notice some years before and completely amazed me, as it claimed to describe how to control or influence circumstances by esoteric means. In fact it was a

Mythe Cottage, Tewkesbury, c. 1964.

combination of New Thought principles, that had been around since the 1920s, and elementary symbolism taken from the Tree of Life. It certainly impressed me very much, although I did not realise that when I came to be an occult publisher it would be the first book I produced, or that when I came to be an esoteric teacher it would be the book upon which my first lessons were based.

However, whether or not assisted by Israel Regardie's exercises, we quickly had a taker for the flat, although, when the deed was done, I was tempted to ask the unanswerable question, would it have happened anyway? But I suppose much the same applies to those who turn their thoughts to petitionary prayer and it all comes down to faith anyway. The question is, faith in what? Or Whom?

The next problem was transporting Bramble the cat (so called from his wild temperament and sharp claws) along with our small three wheeled bubble car, from London down to Tewkesbury, which was not so easily accomplished by a few visualisation exercises.

I set off with Bramble secured in a large cardboard box on the seat beside me – there only being room for the two of us. By the time I got to the end of the road he had oscillated round inside with such frenetic energy that he had burst its bounds. Thereafter he clung like a scarf round my neck as we traversed the North Circular Road and thence the A40 out to the west country. It was an enforced non-stop journey, the two of us trapped inside the BMW Isetta, which ingeniously had only one door – the entire front of the machine, which hinged out, steering wheel and all. To attempt to open it would mean disappearance of cat – either into open countryside or under the wheels of some other vehicle.

We eventually arrived at John and Mary Hall's door, where their daughter Rachel soothed the cat and accompanied us the further few miles to Mythe Cottage. For the first night Bramble and I slept alone prior to the arrival of Roma and the removal van next day. Bramble slept in the airing cupboard and I on a camp bed close by. In the morning he showed his forgiveness for the disturbance by leaving a dead mouse for me to step on with my bare foot first thing next morning.

On Roma's arrival, now seven months pregnant, we set about the business of moving in. A big problem was having to cut up the great carpet that had covered the large main room in our flat so as to fit a number of small rooms in the cottage. To this end we had it stretched across the garden before attacking it with tape measure and heavy scissors.

We were still in the throes of this when called upon to entertain visitors – W. E. Butler and his wife Gladys. Ernest was a possible recruit to the Helios team.

John Hall, Ernest Butler, Gareth Knight and son Richard at Little Thatches, Ernest's cottage near Southampton, c. 1968.

Due to retire from his post as a laboratory technician at Southampton University he was somewhat concerned about his future, which sparked the idea of trying to incorporate him into Helios, for our thoughts had extended already to running a correspondence school. John Hall had been nagging me to provide some kind of practical course and in the end I found time to put together half a dozen lessons based upon Regardie's *The Art of True Healing*. However, that was the limit of what I felt able to do.

So we had it in mind for Ernest to take over supervising the students' work and to extend the course by writing further lessons in what came to be called *The Helios Course on the Practical Qabalah*. This is what Ernest did over the next few years, in the beginning just keeping a month ahead of the leading students, until in the end we were able to offer a course of no less than fifty lessons.

Thus the arrival of Ernest and Gladys hot on our heels at Mythe Cottage to stay for a few days while they looked around the district for a suitable place to live. This was not easy on their limited budget, but in the end a well wisher offered them a country cottage near Southampton on attractive terms, and we realised that distance need not conflict with Ernest's writing or course work for us.

However, the immediate concern as far as I was concerned was the design and production as well as editorial content of the new *New*

Dimensions. Presentation was much less brash and glossy but editorial policy remained the same.

Dion Fortune's long series on Ritual Magic continued right on through the whole history of the magazine as long as it lasted, culled from relevant articles in the old *Inner Light Magazine,* and would eventually be published as a book some thirty years later.

In keeping with my policy to keep the magazine open to all facets of responsible esoteric thought and practice there was also continued coverage of wicca and witchcraft, which was just beginning to come out of the closet at that time. The last of the American issues had featured an article by a leader of one branch of the movement, Gerald B. Gardner, who had been running a museum of witchcraft on the Isle of Man, but who alas became the subject of an obituary in the first of the Helios issues, written by Patricia Crowther. Other aspects of the movement came from anonymous writers, "Althotas", "Gideon Penman" and "Robert Cochrane" (the pen name of the appropriately named Roy Bowers, an important figure on that scene). One unlikely contributor on this front was Benedicta Chichester, sister of Arthur Chichester of the Society of the Inner Light, no witch, but an Anglo-Irish *grande dame* with forthright opinions of her own culled from experience of living in rural Ireland.

Elizabeth Higginson continued a ground breaking series that had just begun in the last of the American issues, *LSD-25, Door into the Unconscious,* which was not at that time the illegal "social" drug it was yet to become. And I was still able to attract American major contributors such as the astrologer Dane Rudhyar, Israel Regardie and the author of a definitive book on angels, Gustav Davidson.

I was no longer committed to producing articles on the Tarot Trumps, that project having fallen by the wayside, but I did contribute one or two Gareth Knight articles of my own – although in keeping with the spirit of writing *The Practical Guide* the material had its source ultimately in the Society of the Inner Light. *Towards a Cosmic Psychiatry* was an attempt to present some of the best of Rosina Mann's mediatorship into a reasonably attractive and readable form (not too easy I have to say), whilst *The Quest of the Holy Grail* was more or less a direct crib of one of the Society's knowledge papers, probably attributable to Margaret Lumley Brown. I followed this policy during this period whenever invited to contribute gratis articles to other journals. One such was *The Atlantean,* published by a new group of the same name founded by Jacqueline Thorburn (later more familiar as Jacqueline Murray and Murry Hope) to whom I gave space in *New Dimensions.*

Another contemporary magazine of this time was Marian Green's *Quest,* whose beginnings I aided with a small donation, which is perhaps the best investment I ever made, as I have been accorded a complimentary copy throughout its prodigiously long life of forty years and more.

Apart from former contributors who continued to write for *New Dimensions,* including Margaret Lumley Brown, Margaret Bruce and Ernest Butler, new offerings came from talented unknowns such as Mark Western and Alan Bain, as well as William G. Gray who would, as a Helios author, soon become very much known.

For by producing the magazine Helios had also become a publisher, as it occurred to me that if we had an established base of direct mail bookshop customers and magazine subscribers we could perhaps publish books they would like to buy. Certainly *A Practical Guide to Qabalistic Symbolism* was on the horizon, which I now decided to produce under the Helios imprint rather than continue with Stanmore Press, so in the meantime how about one or two small books to test out the ground?

My thoughts immediately turned to Israel Regardie, and I was absolutely delighted when my speculative letter not only reached Regardie but brought a positive response. Thus *The Art of True Healing* duly appeared under the Helios imprint in 1964, rapidly followed by *The Art and Meaning of Magic* and *The Art of Relaxation,* also by Regardie. As short monographs they required the minimum amount of capital to print, indeed just £150 in those days for a couple of thousand copies in hardback with two-colour dust jackets.

In the meantime our son Richard was born a couple of months after our arrival at Tewkesbury, and although Roma was able to go back to work at a local infant school fairly soon, a new problem arrived at the end of the year when Bill Elmhirst decided to pull out of supporting *New Dimensions.*

I cannot say I blame him as it was obvious that the magazine was never going to be self supporting, and he had been, and continued to be the soul of generosity in many ways. However, Helios Book Service, for all its comparative success, was not in a position to support more than one family, and that was the Halls, whilst revenue from the Course could barely reward Ernest Butler for his efforts.

Therefore, for all my bright ideas and seized half chances to get the Helios boat launched, I was going to have to be the one who jumped overboard to keep it afloat. Dabbling in small time publishing and relying on patronage was not going to feed wife and child or pay the mortgage. Time, I suppose, to heed what the Master Rakoczi had proposed, and "become a good citizen!"

8

Going it Alone
1965-69

Time in any case was running out for me. In the general business culture of the times if you were over 35 you were over the hill as far as job prospects were concerned, and I was just coming up to this age. Becoming some kind of representative seemed the most likely line and I placed a couple of small ads in *The Bookseller*. One was promptly answered by Cadness Page, a well known figure in the book trade, and until recently manager of the book department at Harrods. He had been coaxed out of retirement by the notorious Robert Maxwell who sought a respected establishment figure to develop his Oxford bookshop business.

Cadness was looking to build up the library supply side and sought a representative to cover the west country, quite an extensive territory, from Cornwall to the Scottish border, including Wales and the industrial Midlands. Thus I found myself salaried and solvent, working from home, and complete with a company car.

It turned out to be, however, a far from congenial occupation. Buyers in public libraries and the few booksellers who specialised as their suppliers operated a pretty conservative closed market which was very difficult to break into. It was also in a state of decline. The system was for a representative to turn up with suitcases stuffed full of dust jackets of books to be published in the next few months, which the buyer would sort through, picking whatever took his fancy. But as the information technology revolution began to bite, with computerised methods of ordering and stock control, this antiquated procedure was rapidly becoming redundant.

In the meantime, for any new representative trying to break in to the charmed circle, the only strategy was to keep cold calling in the hope that in the end, whether out of desperation or pity, or having been let down by a competitor, a buyer might put some business your way. This constant round of rejection could be soul destroying. I still recall my darkest hour, leaning against the wall of Wolverhampton Public Library, feeling physically sick at the prospect of going on. Nonetheless, I have to say that the Wolverhampton public librarian was a very nice man, even though he never gave me any business. Most of them were. And most of them didn't!

However, any enterprise in which Robert Maxwell was concerned was one in constant change. Senior executive life was measured in months – and within a short time Cadness Page fell from grace, and finding himself locked out of his office one day, decided to retire for good, devoting his last years to the more fragrant occupation of breeding pigs.

This turned out no bad thing for me, as I was asked to take over the promotion department at Pergamon Press on account of my somewhat limited experience of direct mail book selling at Helios and the fact that the last manager had either quit or been sacked. There were always vacancies turning up at Pergamon. Maxwell, despite being of great charm and energy, along with considerable ruthlessness, was not a man who delegated easily. He was quite capable of walking into your department and interfering at any level that took his fancy, from rewriting leaflets to summary dismissal of staff.

I soon tired of this game, which involved commuting from Tewkesbury to Oxford each day, but managed to get out on the road again in a more congenial role with a mobile exhibition unit, even though it meant giving up my company car for a Transit van.

Meanwhile I continued my membership of the Society of the Inner Light although becoming increasingly disenchanted with the way it was going. There seemed to be no sign of a regenerated group emerging after the promised "three year plan" and the quality of the material being issued to members seemed inferior to anything that had gone before. In other words, as far as I was concerned, the glory had departed. Consequently in the Spring of 1965 I tendered my resignation.

By coincidence my last position in office was at the initiation of a young man who was to become Warden twenty five years later, and invite my eventual return to the Society. David Williams had been a student of mine on the Inner Light Study Course and our fates seemed to be linked in some way. It was after a visit to his flat, when his wife Faith showed off their new born baby spread out on the hearth rug, that Roma's maternal instincts were roused into wanting one of our own. Hence Richard and subsequently Rebecca were born. David also had a minor input into the Helios project by producing a series of limited edition classic titles, such as *Kirk's Secret Commonwealth of Elves* and Barrett's *The Magus,* which we helped him produce and distribute, and he was also an early contributor to *New Dimensions.*

Resigning from a Society with which I had been so closely identified for twelve years was no light matter, and my inner life at first felt sparse and empty. However, I determined to do something about it. My only resource was to start from what I had, little as it was, much as Dion

Fortune had done. So I began with a small group at home – at first with just three of us, Roma, myself and John Hall.

The Pathworking technique as featured at the Society of the Inner Light seemed an obvious place to start, and so on 8th June 1965 we embarked on a working of the 32nd Path, led by myself. One of the lessons I learned from this small group was that you did not have to have had a lengthy training in order to function efficiently at this kind of work. It was more a matter of natural talent than training, and even John Hall, who showed no great ability at active psychic work, revealed himself to be what might be called a catalyst, apparently largely inert but about whom things tended to happen. But I found Roma to be highly gifted, possibly as a result of making up impromptu stories for infant school children. This freedom of imagination could equally well be applied to esoteric work without the need for a lot of metaphysical study.

A modicum of knowledge and experience was of course needful, but that could be provided by me. I recall that the first attempt or two proved somewhat shaky. On one occasion going on down, down, down, into ever constricting passageways until we came to a stop, at which I point I decided it was time for me to take over and lead us all back to the light and surface consciousness.

Another discovery was that effective path working did not require an elaborate ritual setting. You simply had to sit round as a small congenial group and get on with it.

That 32nd Path working (which I wrote up ten years later in *Experience of the Inner Worlds*) was the first of what was to become a long series of imaginal workings over some five years, becoming less rigidly structured in formal Qabalistic symbolism as time went by. Four early workings turned out to be minor Elemental initiations, though we did not realise this until the pattern of the four workings was almost complete. We also had occasional guests, including the poet Kathleen Raine, who spoke for years after in glowing terms about the experience.

However, my main focus of interest was ever on the esoteric scene, and throughout 1965 I kept *New Dimensions* going in my spare time. I did this by reducing it from a bi-monthly to a quarterly publication, typing it up myself in double page spreads on a long-carriage electric typewriter, and duplicating it off on the Helios office equipment. The task of collating the pages was performed by a team of volunteers, including W. G. Gray, marching round and round a long table picking up sheets in numerical order, to be finally stapled, trimmed and enveloped before being addressed and mailed. This was no light task as we aimed to give value for money by having no less than 100 pages per issue.

But at the end of 1965 *New Dimensions* (at any rate in its first incarnation) died the death, and in the last editorial I was drawn to express a certain irritation with the way things had been going at the Society of the Inner Light. However, the running of the Society was no longer a direct concern of mine, and apart from this farewell spat I maintained a cordial if distant relationship with them which worked to mutual advantage. I was able to keep *The Cosmic Doctrine* going for them when they lacked a publisher, and also to act as a mediator when they had a bit of bother with William G. Gray.

In 1968, although in no position to launch the magazine again, I felt it worth trying to keep the tradition going by publishing a bound volume called *The New Dimensions Red Book*. If successful, the proceeds of its sales could finance further volumes in various colours. It was also a means of nailing Dion Fortune's colours to the mast which I felt were in danger of neglect in the new Society of the Inner Light regime.

Subtitled *A Symposium of Practical Aspects of the Western Mystery Tradition*, it contained articles by Dion Fortune, W. E. Butler, Israel Regardie, William G. Gray, and old *Inner Light Magazine* stalwarts F.P.D. (Colonel C. R. F. Seymour) and S. F. Annett, along with four fairy poems by Joan Vigers. All this was typical old guard Inner Light material, which I garnished with a dedication to the memory of the late Dion Fortune, including a rare photograph of her given me by Mary Gilchrist, which I captioned with a quotation from *The Death of Vivien le Fay Morgan "...as the work has been good in standard, it will not die, but following seeming defeat will rise again in another manner."* A prediction that proved true enough, although it would have to wait a while for that.

In terms of earning a living I had by now realised that Pergamon was a company that served as a gateway to the publishing industry for beginners, for no one already in the trade readily went to work there, and anyone already in the company, given the chance, would take the opportunity to move on. Having eighteen months of experience under my belt I found a safe haven as a college representative for Longmans (established 1724!) and three years later was offered a desk job in Harlow, initially as promotion manager and subsequently as a publisher in their University and Further Education division.

However, on the verge of leaving Tewkesbury, a significant event occurred, which was the apogee of my literary aspirations – my play *The Pigeon Fancier* was professionally produced at the Phoenix Theatre, Leicester.

I had sent out the script to about every provincial theatre I could think of, about twenty two in number (some of whom have yet to reply!)

and was amazed and delighted to receive a telephone call from the Phoenix to say that they would like to produce it, and kindly would I furnish details of my agent. I had no agent but swiftly got hold of one with the help of the Society of Authors, and in the August of that year the play was duly produced for a two week run.

THE LEICESTER PHOENIX THEATRE

THE PIGEON FANCIER

It had, I suppose, a certain esoteric theme. It had been sparked by the sight of an old man who used to live at the bottom of Miranda Road where Roma and I lived when we first married. He used to litter the road outside his house with crusts of bread to feed the pigeons. Various neighbours took different attitudes to this. Some kind ladies donated their own scraps to the old chap for redistribution to the birds, others cursed him for encouraging the filthy pests to cover road and pavement with their droppings.

In the play, the old chap turns out also to be a saint, gifted with miraculous powers. He happens to restore the sight of the landlady of his lodging house, at which the other residents pester him to perform miracles for themselves, which develops into an unseemly and increasingly menacing squabble. At one point in an effort to retain the peace the old man leads the pigeons off to the local churchyard, rather like the Pied Piper of Hamelin. But in the end the demands of the other tenants become so out of control that they kill him. The pigeons then return to the filthy yard.

Headlined "a funny sad play" this met with a highly enthusiastic review in the *Guardian* but other critics, particularly the local hacks, were less ecstatic. We went through the usual theatrical emotional roller coaster ride as to whether it was going to transfer to the West End or die the death, in course of which I realised why it is that actors tend to be superstitious. It is the only thing that keeps them sane!

At the end of a two week run I was £35.50 better off from my share of the takings. Not a lot of return for all the effort, but my sympathies

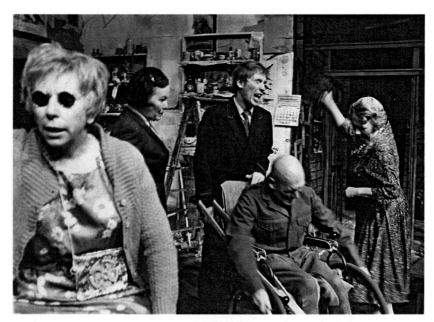

Left to right: Barbara New, Pamela Pitchford, Christopher Timothy (later to become a famous television actor), John Hollis and Peggy Ann Wood in the première of The Pigeon Fancier *at the Leicester Phoenix Theatre, August 1969.*

were for my agent, who had to make do with a mere £3.55! Altogether however it was an experience I would not have missed for worlds, but it also marked the end as well as the beginning of my long dreamed of dramatic career.

This same year our daughter Rebecca was born, who, looking into the future, was to show far greater dramatic and literary talent than me, and with remarkable gifts on the musical, esoteric and plant breeding scenes as well.

9

Magical Ritual Methods
1964-74

Our five years in Tewkesbury had been a very fruitful period, during which two important characters came my way, one a mystic, the Rev. Anthony Duncan, and the other a magician, William G. Gray. Each were great innovators in their way and I helped both of them on their way to successful publication and general recognition.

The redoubtable old occultist William G. Gray had already come to my attention by writing a fulsome welcome to *New Dimensions,* in which he likened its spirit to that of a great contemporary reformer who had just died, Pope John XXIII, who had proposed sweeping changes to the Roman Catholic church – not that I think that the Holy See and *New Dimensions* had too much in common!

As he lived in Cheltenham, I looked forward to meeting him on our move to Gloucestershire, although John Hall offered a note of caution, implying that he was not an entirely pleasant character to meet, and when we first met I soon found what John meant. Bill's bizarre practice on first acquaintance was to grasp your hand firmly in some kind of Masonic handshake, with two fingers pushed forcefully into your wrist, whilst fixing you intently in the eye with an almost hypnotic glare. It could be quite disconcerting. Nonetheless he was extremely knowledgeable about esoteric matters and obviously meant well.

A great deal was to develop out of a series of meetings he held at his house once a month to air his ideas to likeminded acquaintances. Not long after my arrival he began to read out a series of communications which he said he was "getting through" and which he thought were from Dion Fortune. It was an approach to the Tree of Life in an original, simple and thought provoking way, starting from the bottom upward as opposed to the more usual way of starting at the top – which was the method used by Dion Fortune in her *Mystical Qabalah.*

Nonetheless I had the feeling that he might well be right about this Dion Fortune contact. Indeed so convinced was he, that he went so far as to enrol on the Society of the Inner Light study course, although hardly in need of elementary instruction or meditation supervision.

This turned out to be a disaster. There were quite a number of West

Africans in London in those days as students of one kind or another and the SIL had a handful as members. Bill, who had strong racist views, did not realise this until he arrived and was immediately antagonised by their presence. He went through the initiation ritual in an attitude, as he told me afterwards, of psychic self defence, and as soon as he got home wrote a letter of resignation.

At first he had declined to accept the raft of knowledge papers that were proffered to him as a new candidate, but on being pressed by a somewhat disconcerted junior member at least to take them away and read them, did so with somewhat bad grace. Then, on discovering that the SIL had a very protective attitude towards its papers and was anxious to get them back, Bill in high delight refused to return them. Not, he said, in effect, until they asked him in the spirit of comradeship of fellow initiates! He rather resented what he considered to be their officious and standoffish tone.

In the end, although I had recently resigned from the Society, I was able to intercede. I asked Bill for the papers back, as one friend and fellow initiate to another, and at the request of a somewhat relieved and exasperated Arthur Chichester, duly burned them.

However, despite all this gamesmanship, I was much impressed with the quality of the material that Bill was "getting through" as he called it. Whatever or whoever the inner source might be, I felt it was just the kind of book we ought to be publishing at Helios. The problem was I did not have the money to do so. It would be a lot more expensive to print and bind than any of Israel Regardie's little monographs.

Bill suggested we try doing a ritual to evoke the money and after a lot of heart searching I agreed to give it a try. We duly performed it in Bill's ingenious temple downstairs. He lived in a narrow terraced house with a basement that led out to an area yard at the back. This basement could be walked through without anyone suspecting it to be anything other than a normal kind of scullery, but there was a trelliswork arrangement up in one corner which, when opened out, revealed an altar, and with the addition of some curtains and a floor cloth a temple immediately appeared.

Here my first ritual work outside of the Society of the Inner Light was done, and in a very different atmosphere. Bill could be very liberal with the incense, which in a confined space could be close to asphyxiating, and he was quite imaginative with other aids as well, including naphtha flares on occasion. He was also skilled in metal work and the fashioning of ritual objects. On the down side he did rather like the sound of his own voice chanting Qabalistic rituals of his own composing, which could go on a bit at times.

With Carr Collins (right) outside the Savoy Hotel, London, late 1960s.

Nonetheless, our work seemed to be effective, for having performed our ritual, within a couple of weeks I received an unexpected letter from Israel Regardie. He wrote that a wealthy American, Carr P. Collins Jnr, was about to pass through London and was keen on splashing his money about on what he considered good esoteric causes. Regardie felt that I was deserving some of this largesse and suggested I approach Carr.

Accordingly, I telephoned Carr Collins at the Dorchester Hotel, and charming and generous man that he was (he could well afford to be – being "Texas rich") he doled out £1000 – a sizeable sum in those days, equivalent to my annual salary at the time. Thus I was able to launch William G. Gray on his extensive publishing career, with his first book, *The Ladder of Lights*.

He shortly got stuck into another, even larger manuscript, apparently from the same inner source, and by going cap in hand to Carr Collins once again, I was able to publish *Magical Ritual Methods*.

This was an important radical text on magical philosophy and practice that got down to basic principles and completely ripped away a great deal of 19th century obfuscation that hampered the whole ritual field through most of the 20th century. R. J. Stewart has called it a revolutionary classic of 20th century magical literature and I would not disagree, for it influenced a whole generation.

I still fancy that Dion Fortune may have been the contact behind these two books, for I used to sense her presence vaguely in the background for much of this time. It was not until publication of Bill Gray's biography many years later (not inappropriately named *The Old Sod*) that I learned that he had once actually met Dion Fortune, back in 1927. He had rung the bell at Queensborough Terrace and sought admission to the Fraternity at the tender age of fourteen! In light of his persistence Dion Fortune had been called down to speak to the brat personally, telling him to try again when of a more appropriate age. Although as events transpired he never did. Like Ernest Butler before him, he joined the regular army in the interwar years.

Much impressed by what I read and published of Bill's work I felt it important to try out and carry through some of the principles that were described at length in *Magical Ritual Methods*.

To this end I constructed an eight foot square prefabricated concrete hut at the bottom of my garden and furnished it as a small temple. Building this, including clearing and levelling the ground, helped by my father, made me conscious of delving deep into the basic archetypes of the ancient Mysteries. It is not often that one is called personally to clear a site for sacred purposes and then erect a building on it, in however humble circumstances. It seemed to take me right back to the fundamentals of Solomon and Hiram building the original Temple of Wisdom.

It was just large enough for a central altar and for a seat at each of the four quarters on the four fold magic circle pattern as exemplified in *Magical Ritual Methods*. For three others to man those ritual positions I was able to recruit three local students on the Helios Course who had recently joined our little home group. Roma and John Hall did not care too much for this line of work, as much from a sense of antipathy to William Gray as for its methodology.

Bill Gray now decided more or less to take me magically under his wing, and I passed through a series of initiatory workings that he laid on for me until suddenly all this was brought to a halt by a most unlikely combination of circumstances.

I happened to be on the road in south west Wales and had put up at a small hotel for the night. Next morning I had ordered *The Guardian* with my early morning tea, but for some reason *The Times* was delivered instead. It happened to contain an article about ultra right wing publications and gave quotations from some of them, including readers' letters – amongst which, to my surprise I discovered one signed "W.G.G. Cheltenham". I already knew Bill Gray's trenchant right wing views but now felt that he had gone too far. I have no great concern with the political opinions of those with whom I work, but being actively engaged with the neo-fascist press was, to my mind, a step too far. Accordingly, I told Bill that although our business relationship might stand, as between author and publisher, I would no longer work with him magically.

His reaction was furious and I realised the truth of Dion Fortune's remark in *Psychic Self Defence* about some teachers who cannot bear to let go of their students. Nonetheless I was steadfast in my decision, even though Bill insisted that this was just a "test" to be expected by all who had received initiation, and it was important that I should not fail it. This cut no ice with me, as I considered my initiation into the Greater Mysteries of the Society of the Inner Light had greater power and validity, and that any that he had to offer were only ancillary.

He now insisted that I attend a ritual to take upon myself all the bad karma resulting from our association. This I naturally declined to do. Anyway, he went on to say, any initiation he had given me was invalid because the "lock word" had not been pronounced (whatever that is). Too bad, I thought, but I was a little concerned that I owed him a cheque for a small amount of royalties, as I suspected he might very well use my signature upon it as a link for some kind of magical riposte. However, I heard no more until a year later when a slim package arrived through the post. It contained a replica of my magical wand (representing my magical will), broken in two. End of story, more or less, except that I was somewhat amused by his cheek in writing to me soon after to request a duplicate cheque as the other had expired without having been cashed! Nice guy that I am, I provided it.

I should say that I was not alone in being roundly cursed by William Gray, for much the same happened to R. J. Stewart who more or less followed in my footsteps. He had been attracted to Bill's teaching by coming across a copy of *Magical Ritual Methods* in Bristol public library very soon after it was published. It is thus an interesting net that we weave between ourselves, and he and I were later to enjoy a very fruitful informal association although we had yet to meet.

William Gray, for all his faults, and he was his own worst enemy, nonetheless taught me – and by extension a whole network of readers – a very great deal about the principles and practice of magic, which I later passed on in practical workshops and to groups, as well as spelling it out in simple form in *The Practice of Ritual Magic* a monograph I published in 1969 and later in *Magic and the Power of the Goddess*.

Prior to all this, production of *A Practical Guide to Qabalistic Symbolism* had been dragging on, beset by numerous legal and technical delays, but eventually I received my first bound copies in the first few days of 1966. I proudly showed it to Bill, whose reaction, perhaps spurred by a pang of envy, was characteristically dismissive. "Oh!" he said, in a mixture of amused patronage and contempt, "you have used the old Golden Dawn attributions!" and on the strength of that dismissed it out of hand. He had, of course, worked out his own system of correspondences, which were no doubt valid enough, but I have to say that I have always found the Golden Dawn system to be an eminently usable one – if not the one and only true that some of its enthusiasts like to assume. But knowing Bill I did not take his strictures to heart.

Aware that, for all its pioneering record, Helios had its limitations owing to being run on a shoe string, I was happy in later years to see it act as a first step for new writers to get onto the publishing ladder. Larger publishers, in my view, seem particularly inept at spotting new trends and new talent. So in due time I gladly passed W. G. Gray along with *The Ladder of Lights* and *Magical Ritual Methods* to Aquarian Press where he and his books could get far better international distribution and exposure.

Aquarian Press had started off in much the same way as Helios, virtually a one man business in the hands of a dedicated bookseller and former publishing executive Frank Clive-Ross, who had been good enough to give me a few tips when I was starting up. When he retired the business was bought by a go ahead entrepreneurial partnership, David Young and his father, who went on to take over a number of other small publishers, and then to diversify as Thorsons, before being in their turn gobbled up by HarperCollins, a multi-national conglomerate.

However, in 1974 W. G. Gray and his works bounced back into my court. Although Aquarian had welcomed Bill Gray onto their list, he proved so cantankerous to deal with that, in exasperation, they simply put his books out of print and refused to have anything more to do with him.

As a result I received an unexpected letter from Bill, obviously written with gritted teeth, saying that I could little know how much it must be costing him to write to me in this fashion, but his inner contacts insisted that this was the only way to get out of his predicament. In short, he had an important new manuscript they wished to see published.

This turned out to be *The Rollright Ritual,* which I recognised to be unique and of considerable importance. It was an evocation of the spirit of a megalithic site in Oxfordshire known as the Rollright Stones. As well as providing fascinating theories as to its original function, Bill

One of the photographs from The Rollright Ritual, *showing William G. Gray (right) in action at the Rollright stone circle.*

included an evocative ritual that had apparently recently been worked, as demonstrated by a set of striking photographs. Accordingly, I lost no time in publishing it under the Helios imprint.

This led on to another new publishing venture and introduction to R. J. Stewart, who was Bill's latest acolyte. Bob, as he was then more generally known, was a much sought after performer/composer on the folk music circuit, and along with some friends had materially assisted Bill in a performance of the Rollright ritual, with evocative background music. It was proposed that I make this tape available to supplement the published book.

I went along with this idea, not without some trepidation, and completely ignorant of how to go about it. However, guided by Bob's technical advice I arranged for its commercial reproduction. These were early days for such a venture and I recall an anguished debate as to whether the tape should be made available on open reel (as had up until now been the vogue) or in these new fangled cassettes that were just then being introduced. Fortunately we opted for the latter – which have of course now died the death themselves in favour of compact discs.

To make up a viable package we added a couple more tapes, of magical songs written and performed by Bob, and another ritual, *The Rite of Light*, chanted by W. G. Gray.

This collaboration did bring about a temporary reconciliation with Bill Gray, if at arm's length, although our last meeting, to celebrate the results of our three part collaboration, verged on the farcical. I suggested taking them out for a celebratory meal in Bath, which proved easier said than done. We tramped with increasing frustration through rain soaked streets looking for an establishment where Bill would deign to eat. The trouble with a cosmopolitan town like Bath is that virtually all the restaurants are *foreign* – which was anathema to Bill. Eventually in desperation I offered to take them into the deluxe Royal Bath Hotel but Bob, in his casual clothes and long hair, did not feel inclined to enter that plush establishment. Fortunately we came across a more down market eatery that claimed colonial links – to Singapore – where Bill could dine on good British fare, the roast beef of old England, without completely deserting the flag!

In the course of time after I decided to run Helios publishing down, as it had more or less served its purpose, Bill had made closer acquaintance with Carr Collins. He was beginning to receive wider recognition as a result of his books and in time was invited to the United States and to South Africa in connection with the Sangreal Sodality, an organisation he founded, which probably became his lasting monument.

The alchemist Hans Nintzel, Gareth Knight, Israel Regardie and Carr Collins at a reception dinner, London, early 1980s.

We drifted apart again after that, in which time I learned from the psychologist Dr James Hall, a close friend of Carr Collins, that Bill had not a good word to say about me to anyone he met. However, whatever the reason, there was nothing I could do about this, although I drew some consolation from James Hall's opinion of him, which he summed up in one word: "paranoid".

The last I saw of Bill was at one of the big esoteric receptions that Carr Collins laid on in London which gave the opportunity to many practitioners on the esoteric scene on both sides of the Atlantic to mingle in common fellowship – and where I had the pleasure of at last meeting up with my very first author – Israel Regardie. Some meetings were not quite so "hail fellow well met" however, as I discovered with Bill Gray. In company with John Matthews, I happened to come across him in the cloakroom. He was leaning heavily on a stick which he banged on the floor at the sight of me, shouting abuse over some grievance that I could not make head nor tail of. To the best of my recollection he cried "I received your message! And I have sent it straight back!" I assumed he must think I was somehow still engaged in publishing or had given advice that was against his interests. God only knows. I simply left him to it. It was the last time we met.

In the long term, I think that between us we did quite a bit of good in the esoteric world. Certainly magic was never quite the same again. And there remains the query as to how much the spirit of Dion Fortune might have been involved!

10

Lord of the Dance
1964-73

There was an important mystical dynamic that ran alongside these magical developments. Before leaving London back in 1964 in response to the Christian emphasis in the Society of the Inner Light, and under the impetus of my vision in the library I felt the least I could do would be to discover what was happening in the Christian church beyond the confines of the esoteric lodge. To this end I sought some kind of formal instruction from the vicar of St Augustine's, Highgate. This was a very high church establishment, with candles, incense, even a representation of the Immaculate Conception of the Virgin, all of which I found quite congenial, although never much of an enthusiast for public worship after the blistering aridity of RAF church parades.

This endeavour was however terminated by the vicar. He conceded that I was the most fascinating heresiarch he had ever met, but he felt that I was not quite ready to join the church as the majority understood it. We parted good friends and with mutual respect, for as one of his acolytes had informed me early on, he was "a very *human* man". I am not quite sure what else I should have expected, but plainly it is not only the esoteric world that is prone to regard its leaders as plaster saints.

I still felt there might be a lot of common ground to be investigated, and on arrival at Tewkesbury it was not long before I was exploring the abbey, within which I had had quite a powerful mystical experience of sorts, some years before, in the company of John Hall. On that occasion we had both been struck by an incredibly powerful spiritual presence in a niche facing the Lady Chapel, which at that time was commonly used for confessions. Indeed the whole abbey fascinated me, in particular the story of the abbot advancing down the aisle in the aftermath of the battle of Tewkesbury in the Wars of the Roses, in an attempt to stop Yorkist soldiers from slaughtering Lancastrians who had taken refuge there. In fact when electing a place to live when leaving London for Gloucestershire it was the memory of the abbey that attracted me to the town.

On the abbey bookstall, my attention was drawn to a slender book of poems called *Over the Hill,* written by the new curate. The contents however, at first glance, promised to be a lot more exciting than the usual run of occasional verse, for the writer seemed to be something of a psychic.

> I am fey, so they say;
> I have seen the walking dead
> Hurry to Mass on a weekday morning.
> I have heard the doors go bang
> And have heard their footsteps hurrying.
> I have heard the solemn warning
> Through and beyond the bells' wild clang;
> The long, clear call from the tower.   [from "Elmbury Abbey"]

Indeed it said in the blurb that the author when on army service in the Far East, had become "deeply influenced by Eastern philosophy and religions". And as he was also said to have a literary interest in Yeats, Donne, Auden and T. S. Eliot, it seemed a good enough hint for me to seek out his view on things.

Anthony Duncan had originally been a regular army captain serving in Germany, where he was sufficiently offbeat to marry Helga, a local fräulein. As well as having a couple of boys of their own, they had also adopted a Chinese baby, a little charmer called Fifi. His military career came to an end when one day he had received an inner call to resign his commission and take holy orders. After passing through theological college and being ordained, Tewkesbury abbey was his first clerical appointment, shortly before my arrival there.

As a result of the conversations we had I discovered we shared more common ground than I expected, helped by the works of C. S. Lewis such as *Miracles, Mere Christianity* and *The Screwtape Letters*. At Easter 1965 I felt sufficiently confident to be confirmed into the Church of England at Tewkesbury Abbey.

All this was shortly before *A Practical Guide to Qabalistic Symbolism* at last saw the light of day. Having talked to him a lot about Qabalah in the course of our discussions I felt the least I could do was to present Tony Duncan with a copy of the book, although he had now moved on to become Vicar of Parkend in the Forest of Dean.

His reaction was in marked contrast to the grudging acknowledgement of W. G. Gray. He was absolutely fascinated by it. He read it through twice and concluded that the Qabalah was a remarkably profound and most profitable field of study – not least for him!

Then he launched into a deeply considered critique, based on reading it in light of being a mystic as well as a natural psychic, and a theologically trained one at that who was also familiar with eastern spirituality. This raised philosophical and theological issues of which I had until then been blissfully unaware, and I realised that he had raised some fundamental questions that could not be ignored. Indeed it was the subject of a number of long discussions between us.

In the end these talks stimulated him to write a book of his own, aided by various tomes I sent him from the Helios Book Service stock (ranging from Olive Pixley's *Armour of Light* to Aleister Crowley's *Magick in Theory and Practice)* that were unlikely to be found in other bookshops in rural Gloucestershire. Still less appropriately purchased by a local vicar!

When I read the manuscript he had written, under the title of *The Christ, Psychotherapy and Magic,* I was sufficiently impressed to want to see it published. I was quite willing to do this myself but felt that, to do it justice, it should appear on the list of a more general publisher than Helios. Accordingly I fixed up what is laughingly called in the trade a "profit sharing deal" with Allen and Unwin under whose imprint it appeared in 1969.

Nonetheless it did end up as a Helios book. The printer concerned went bankrupt after the first batch of copies had been bound and delivered, and in light of disinterest from Allen and Unwin I claimed the remaining unbound sheets from the official Receiver and put a Helios cover on them.

When in 1970 I bade farewell to Tewkesbury and moved to Essex, occult work went onto the back burner for a while, but was replaced by a vivid mystical awareness.

As I wrote to Tony Duncan at the time: *"I have been having some pretty shattering experiences of late. Yet they have been mystical. The occult has been as dead as the dodo, but every time I take the dog for a walk over the fields it's like Moses coming up against the burning bush. I get nearly flattened with "Immanence".*

At the same time, however, Tony Duncan's eyes were being opened in another direction, as the result of a remarkable conference in May 1971 on the holy island of Iona.

It had been set up by a number of Christian church people who were gifted healers, some of them highly sensitive in terms of clairvoyance and clairaudience. The sessions included one from two ladies who read "letters" from certain of the departed. Tony had always been dogmatically opposed to all that smacked of spiritualism (not without experience of its abuses), and so began listening, as he put it, "with all red lights flashing". But these were rapidly extinguished, he said, because the letters seemed so self-authenticating.

They had recently been published as *Letters from our Daughters* by the novelist Rosamund Lehmann and a gifted clairaudient, Lady Cynthia Sands, with whom Tony Duncan then engaged in long conversation. The whole conference seemed to open flood gates for him, and marked a turning of the tide for both of us.

Thrilled at the way in which the occult and his faith seemed to be coming together as parts of one unity, he left Iona with the conviction that things could never be the same again, were firmly set upon a new plane, and that we were at the beginning of a new epoch.

The first result came a couple of months later, in the form of a manuscript that really pinned my ears back. Called *The Lord of the Dance*, it was no cautious intellectual analysis like *The Christ, Psychotherapy and Magic*, but a straight "in your face" mystical contact.

It began with a vision of the created universe as a great dance:

> The whole creation is dancing; the whole universe – galaxies, nebulae, stars and their satellites – is engaged in the Great Dance. They turn, and come together, and draw apart, and come together again. And so it has ever been, and so it shall ever be through all eternity. Creation makes its own music. There is no created being that does not sing, and the music of everything that is joins together to make the great Harmony and Rhythm of the Dance.

and it ended with a direct call from its Creator, the Lord of the Dance:

> Oh Earth! Rejoice, for your sorrow is ended.
> Now shall your beauty be made manifest.
> Sing, O Earth! See: I dance to your music.
> You shall sing at my Wedding.
> Now is the Moment of Truth;
> now, behold, I AM.

He sent it off to Allen and Unwin who as rapidly batted it back to him, as I could have foretold. As I saw it, there was no chance any commercial publisher was going to take this on – still less any of the established religious houses.

The book seemed to me to be years ahead of its time and might indeed be the first spark of a much needed revolution. I felt that both the conventional religious and the occult apple carts needed to be sent spinning over in the near future. It might be a divine boot that provided the force, but Tony Duncan and I, willy nilly, were going to be rooting in the midst of the rough and tumble.

I suggested that rather than spend time hawking it round to publishers, knocking in vain from inn door to inn door, he bring the little waif to birth in my humble stable. In other words, have it published by Helios. And so it appeared, just six months later, in November 1972.

It caused no immediate revolution in church or state but certainly lit a fuse that led to some esoteric upheaval within the next six months.

It was promptly followed by another manuscript of an even more startling nature. This time nothing less than conversations between a clergyman and an angel! Entitled *The Sword in the Sun* it was a wise and often humorous dialogue with insight into several esoteric subjects, including the Qabalistic Tree of Life, the inner orders of angels and elementals, reincarnation and the evolution of consciousness.

At the same time Tony Duncan had written a more conventional looking work for the religious publishers Geoffrey Bles, called *The Priesthood of Man*. Without mentioning the heavenly visitant it nonetheless contained much that the angel had had to say – explaining how reincarnation, mediumship and other occult practices could be perfectly normal and acceptable elements of life – and were not necessarily counter to Christian belief and practice.

These assertions left the reviewer in the *Church Times* in something of a state of shock. However, closer to home, a greater shock was in store for some of my associates on the esoteric scene.

Whether because of his somewhat unconventional views (or his less known involvement in the ministry of exorcism), the Gloucester Diocesan office invited Tony Duncan to give a weekend of lectures at Hawkwood College, presumably as a kind of Christian outreach to those of an esoteric persuasion. The subject he chose was *The Two Qabalahs*.

This was largely a résumé of *The Christ, Psychotheraphy and Magic,* in which he sought to explain how there are two Qabalahs – not one – according to how we look at it. One is formulated by Jewish mystics to describe the nature of God – Creator of All. The other by Gentile occultists to describe the inner workings, or "psychic nuts and bolts" of the world – sometimes called the inner planes.

There is nothing wrong in either approach. In fact they complement each other. But problems occur if we confuse the two, and assume that God and the created Universe are one and the same.

In Tony Duncan's view, this monist philosophy had crept into modern occultism through the Hindu back door, and if taken to its ultimate limits, produced an Aleister Crowley, who by equating the universe with God, saw the Great Work to be raising himself to an infinite power – and thus *becoming* God. This was a far cry from earlier exponents of the Western

Esoteric Tradition – from the Renaissance through to the Elizabethan magi and the 17th century Rosicrucians up to the 19th century Eliphas Levi or Anna Kingsford – who had been Christian by religion and Platonist by philosophy.

To this more valid tradition, in Tony Duncan's view, the likes of Dion Fortune, Ernest Butler and Gareth Knight were the natural heirs. And this largely through a self-correcting element built into it by emphasis on **right intention,** encapsulated by the rubric impressed upon all candidates by the Society of the Inner Light:

Question: *"In whom do you put your trust?"* Answer: *In God.*
Question: *"Why do you seek to enter these Mysteries?"* Answer: *"I desire to know in order to serve."*

The calling of this weekend of lectures seemed to John Hall and me a good opportunity to introduce some of these considerations to the *Helios Course on the Practical Qabalah.* The senior supervisor was currently Dolores Ashcroft-Nowicki who had met Ernest Butler at the Society of the Inner Light. By a somewhat odd development of circumstances, on joining up with the Helios team Ernest had applied for readmission to the Society, not realising that John Hall and I were on the way out of it. Dolores had evidently also joined at much the same time, and being much impressed by Ernest, enrolled on the Helios course as well and rose to become its leading supervisor.

We therefore suggested to Dolores that she might like to come along to Hawkwood to see how these new ideas grabbed her. What we did not foresee was that she would invite a number of junior supervisors as well, who in the event proved hardly up to the challenge.

Apparently affronted by a Church of England clergyman lecturing on the Qabalah they assumed the slightest criticism to be a veiled attack. Indeed one or two seemed to have come in anticipation of seeing some clerical upstart being shot down in flames by Gareth Knight. So when I rose to admit the validity of some of the shortcomings of *A Practical Guide to Qabalistic Symbolism* that Anthony Duncan had gently pointed out, the atmosphere turned poisonous.

One of the supervisors buttonholed me immediately afterwards in a fury. "You do not know what you have done to me!" she hissed. She told me how she kept my book at her bedside as a source of inspiration and guide to life, and now felt betrayed by my saying that parts of it might be wrong! In fairness, she did write afterwards to apologise for what she realised had been an unrealistic attitude, and in later years went on to found a group of her own.

Nonetheless at the time, a right little vortex of spleen developed that even led to three of the supervisors trying to mount a psychic attack against the speaker. An act which, being a natural psychic, was not lost upon Tony Duncan, nor, in light of his experience and contacts, very effective. Nonetheless he was not too amused, and wrote with some asperity to me later:

> What a weekend! I fancy both of us went through a considerable initiation; yourself particularly, and painful to a degree.

> One thing is certain, …….. mounted a full scale occult attack on me throughout my last lecture, and on you too during your vote of thanks speech. But we had friends! The little man turned absolutely jet black in my vision during the course of the exercise, and I found myself thinking, "yes, I think you are, rather!"

> But as for the gathering as a whole, this set notwithstanding, I thought that they were the best audience I have spoken to for a very long time. There were some very good people there.

> I fancy we are both launched upon a continuing ministry in this field, but upon a higher level of initiation than before. (Can't think of a better way of putting it.)

He regretted that the Helios course seemed to have fallen into very wrong hands. I hastened to reassure him on that score, but it was plain to me that the Helios course was not suitable for the kind of innovation that I had in mind. I would have to think again.

Nonetheless, positive forces were already at work. When one door shuts another one opens. As the course broke up, I fell into conversation with a young couple, Brenda and Michael, who seemed sympathetic to what they had heard. I asked them if they would like to help me start a new study course based upon these lines, and they agreed wholeheartedly. Thus at tea time on Sunday afternoon, 15th April 1973, what was to become the Gareth Knight Group was founded, much of its future bound up with this remarkable college at Hawkwood.

11

Experience of the Inner Worlds
1973-78

Despite the ruffled feathers at Hawkwood all was amicably resolved. Roma and I along with our children Richard and Rebecca spent our summer holidays that year with Dolores and Mike and their family in the Channel Islands. Ernest Butler in the meantime wondered what all the fuss was all about. He considered that the background to all his own work had been a Christocentric mysticism which illuminated the whole esoteric scene. He felt he had been somewhat quoted out of context in *The Christ, Psychotheraphy and Magic* and also, as an ordained Liberal Catholic, felt a certain irritation about the established Anglican church "being by law appointed" – a favourite phrase of his in this context. So he certainly did not feel inclined to take too many lessons from one of their ministers.

As for the alleged psychic attack he felt that it was probably a case that the Helios students and supervisors, seething with suppressed indignation, had inadvertently unleashed a combined thought form, charged with emotion, that Duncan had perceived. Moreover he had since spoken to those who were at Hawkwood, who were unanimous in saying that they did *not* mount any such attack on anyone – indeed realised it would have been very foolish to do anything of the kind.

One indeed hoped so. Nonetheless the lady who had bitterly complained to me shortly afterwards boasted to John Hall, much to his disgust, that such a deliberate attack had taken place. Others felt less proud of the incident and tended to pass it off in later years as something of a light hearted joke. However, it was a dangerous game to play, and it seemed to me that at least a couple of those concerned suffered quite severe repercussions not long afterwards – if not specifically for this event then as a likely consequence of a tendency to use thought power maliciously, even in what they thought to be a good cause. The inner planes can be very reflective of our own attitudes.

However, all this aside, on the wider front, Ernest and I assured everyone in the next issue of *Round Merlin's Table*, a news sheet for course students I had launched, that all would go on just as before. The *Practical Guide* remained a basic textbook for the Helios Course, whilst I, in due course, would go on to launch a new course of my own. Although first I had to write another book upon which to base it!

This would turn out to be *Experience of the Inner Worlds*, which I had already started to plan, each chapter based on one of the powerful mystical symbols from Duncan's *Lord of the Dance*, together with a rubric taken from the angelic communications in *Sword in the Sun*.

- The Sphere of Light – *Secure within a sphere of Light, O Man, abide in peace and knowledge of my Love.*
- The Fiery Spear – *The spear which pierced my side shall run you through and make of you a reed through which my Grace shall flow.*
- The Serpent Flame – *The Serpent-tongue of flame shall rise in you and make you fit oblation for my Mysteries.*
- The Holy Grail – *A Chalice shall you be, a Holy Grail all emptied and receptive to my filling.*
- The Sea of Light – *The tide of Light shall rise about you like a Flood, and with its shining you shall be identified.*
- The Table Round – *A table round, and there, a place for you to come and go at will in Contemplation.*
- The Upper Room – *An upper room, symbolic of the world redeemed in which you shall abide in your redemption.*
- The Light of Christ – *A lamp is there for you to light your way, I am your Way, your Light, your Destination.*
- The Winding Stair – *A winding stair is there for you to climb, it is a symbol of your own true self.*
- The Dark Cloud – *And climbing, though you cannot see, the mist, the darkness, is my Radiancy.*

All this was quite powerful stuff, so before launching it into the public domain I spent twelve to eighteen months validating it with a small group of volunteers, some co-opted from the Helios Course.

I put a lot of historical research into the writing of it, on the development of the Western Mystery Tradition from its roots in ancient Greece to modern times, including coverage of some comparatively neglected areas of Qabalistic studies. I also included practical examples culled from work with my own small house group and garden temple over the past decade – including the techniques of path working and first steps in inner plane communication.

My coverage of the medieval Arthurian, Courtly Love and Templar traditions was stimulated by some mediumistic communications from a small group that John Hall worked with for a time – which we referred to privately as the Phaidon scripts, this being the code name of one of the communicators. Much of this was obscure but parts of it resonated strongly with one of the visions that came up at my Esoteric Review ten years before, at the Society of the Inner Light – of being in some kind of big trouble in the middle ages. It referred to my own involvement with events and personalities leading up to the 3rd Crusade, even to the point of naming names, although I later felt that the source of some of this remarkable detail might well have been a couple of recent historical novels rather than genuine psychic recovery. (*The Knights of Dark Renown* [1969] and *The Kings of Vain Intent* [1970] by Graham Shelby). Nonetheless there was sufficient stimulus to set me going on a number of years of personal research that led eventually to writing about 12th century faery lore in *The Faery Gates of Avalon* [2008].

In the meantime at a more mundane level the time had come to sort out the various directions in which the branches of the Helios venture were going. The publication side could be run by me from anywhere (all a publisher needs basically is a telephone and a source of credit) whilst the new course side would be taken care of by the couple I had met at Hawkwood at their home down in Chichester.

John and Mary Hall remained closely involved with the Book Service, run from their home, which shortly needed an annexe to house it, whilst the Helios Course – with fifty lessons to keep in print and student correspondence to service – had begun to be quite a burden on their facilities. It seemed therefore opportune to pass it over to Dolores and Mike Ashcroft-Nowicki in the Channel Islands under Ernest Butler's overall direction. This was duly put in hand and the new organisation, named the Servants of the Light, came into being in November 1973.

Unfortunately, Ernest was not entirely happy with these new arrangements, for reasons that were not immediately apparent. It later transpired that he felt that the change was due to my trying to oust him from Helios for esoteric reasons. This was far from the case, for I was the one who was making my departure although I could see how a certain sense of resentment arose. In the earlier days of his taking over writing the course he took a little time to find his sense of direction, so that I got the call from John Hall on a couple of occasions "I think Ernie is waffling a bit" with the expectation that I do something about it as diplomatically as I could.

However, the main cause of resentment came later when I felt that a completely flat bottomed course of fifty lessons had its limitations, and suggested that some kind of degree structure could perhaps be bolted on to it, perhaps with the more promising students introduced to the kind of work that I had pioneered in the hut at the bottom of my garden along the principles pioneered by William Gray. Ernest found this idea complete anathema however, and so I backed off. It was left to Dolores in later years to provide the necessary degree structure with initiatory grades.

For some time however, he warned his supervisors of my supposedly Machiavellian tendencies – completely unbeknownst to me – although I was conscious of some kind of barrier put up toward me. This did not worry me too much however, as I had plenty of other concerns on the go. One of these was to launch, in 1973, a new series of *New Dimensions*. This was a somewhat different beast from the ambitious project that had folded eight years before, as it was aimed at a fairly limited readership from which a future esoteric group of my own might be drawn. It was simply a couple of dozen A4 sheets stapled together at one end, hammered out on my faithful long carriage electric typewriter but now reproduced by offset litho – a considerable advance on the messy old duplicator stencils.

Nonetheless it was with great joy that I was able to declare "*New Dimensions* is back!" in the first issue of this new incarnation and even to indulge in a rare burst of verse:

The Phoenix
A wonderful bird is the Phoenix,
With singular passion so hot,
A marvel of occult eugenics,
The one that begets is begot.

Editorial content was much the same as before, but without the need to spread topics over so wide a general readership. I was concerned to keep the old Dion Fortune flag flying, largely with articles culled from the pre-war *Inner Light Magazine*. The Society raised no objection to this, even if they noticed, for they tended to keep themselves to themselves, and – as far as I was concerned anyway – to follow a policy of live and let live. I think perhaps they might even have been glad of my taking unreconstructed Dion Fortune enthusiasts off their back.

Within these limits I pursued a pretty broad editorial policy that catered for Christian and pagan approaches together with articles on magical technique. The pagan approach to things has never given me a problem, it is simply that I regard it as somewhat incomplete without the Christian dynamic. Just as the Christian loses a great deal by standing off from the pagan.

I reprinted an early series of articles by Dion Fortune on The Guild of the Master Jesus, which she had floated since 1934 as an appendage to her occult fraternity, along with a series *Children of the Great Mother* by her staunchly pagan colleague of the 1930s Colonel C. R. F. Seymour. Israel Regardie chipped in with a magical analysis of the Dionysian Greek drama *The Bacchae* and the techniques of *Opening by Watchtower*. Newcomers such as Alan Richardson, W. G. Gray and R. J. Stewart also provided articles, and have come to greater prominence since – although one stalwart contributor, Philip Senior, who faithfully provided copy on a variety of practical topics for every issue, seems to have disappeared from public view. Arthurian and Grail traditions were covered by some old lecture notes culled from old senior Inner Lighters, a former librarian F. C. G. Gough, and Margaret Lumley Brown from back in the early 1950s.

In 1975 *Experience of the Inner Worlds* duly appeared and the course could go live. It consisted of a series of ten small booklets with supplementary notes to the textbook and to Gray's *The Ladder of Lights* which I used as an introduction to the Tree of Life from a fresh perspective. I sent a copy of the new book to the Society of the Inner Light in the hope that it might prove of some assistance to them in resolving the divide they appeared to feel existed between mysticism and magic. However, beyond a polite acknowledgement from Rosina it obviously cut little ice within the hallowed precincts.

A singular event now occurred in relation to Margaret Lumley Brown which in the longer term melded past with future. It came about through an astounding coincidence. Roma was out shopping with our five year old daughter Rebecca when an old lady collapsed in the street just in front of them. They were first on the scene and Roma was amazed to find that the little old lady was none other than Margaret Lumley Brown! What was the former Arch-Pythoness at the Society of the Inner Light doing in our small country town? And collapsing at so opportune a place and time?

It turned out that she was no longer living at the Society of the Inner Light headquarters, which had provided her with residence since 1943, and was looking for somewhere to live whilst staying with a niece who lived nearby. We were delighted to greet her as a neighbour and invited her round to dinner. There were no more candle phenomena as at the previous occasion in London some years before, but she delighted us with the priceless remark, said in all seriousness, that she quite liked the town, (which was situated on an old crossing of Roman roads), but sometimes found it rather hard to sleep on account the of noise of marching legions! Soon afterwards she moved away, to live with an old Inner Light member, in whose care she died the following year. When I last saw her she gaily professed to being "nearly ninety!"

Towards the end of her stay in Braintree, she arrived unexpectedly on my doorstep and presented me with a small bundle. It contained a black plaster statue of a goddess of extremely primitive aspect, and a somewhat inefficient but very evocative looking brass thurible ornamented with swans and roses. Along with these artefacts were a number of letters and press cuttings, an old sketchbook of psychic impressions, and three little printed books, two of which she had written herself. Thrusting these into my hands she declared that she was appointing me her literary executor.

Oddly enough, after her death, on the strength of this appointment I began to be nagged by a persistent thought that I should demand the right to publish much of the Inner Light knowledge papers for which she had been responsible, on the grounds that they were her copyright as much as theirs. Nonetheless, I resisted this line of action as being too much of a hassle, probably counterproductive, and anyway beyond my current means.

It was not until after my return to the Society of the Inner Light years later that I was able to do some justice to her by compiling *Pythoness – the Life and Work of Margaret Lumley Brown,* which was published in the year 2000, followed later by a re-issue of her novella *Both Sides of the Door.* She had claims, in my view and others who knew her, to be regarded as perhaps the finest medium and psychic of the twentieth century, despite being sidelined after the 1960s new regime was introduced at the Society of the Inner Light, when still at the height of her powers.

The first public evidence of having a group of my own in course of development came at a meeting in a church hall in Trumpington Street, Cambridge on July 3rd 1976, in conjunction with student groups from the Universities of Oxford and Cambridge. We each put on a practical session, the Oxford students on *A Qabalistic Understanding of Ritual,* the Cambridge students *The Principle of Three* and the Gareth Knight Course people *The Magical Imagination.* For some reason the most vivid recollection I have of the event was Mike Harris turning up all the way from Wales in his best suit for the occasion. Later to become well known as author of *Awen, the Quest of the Celtic Mysteries,* and co-author of *Polarity Magic,* leader of the Company of Avalon and organiser of the e-publisher RiteMagic, and of the Dion Fortune seminars at Glastonbury – but back then a squeaky clean recruit to the *Gareth Knight Course in Christian Qabalistic Magic.*

Soon after, in the beginning of 1977, it felt time to take a more concentrated approach to my magazine publishing, and so I brought *New Dimensions* to an end and started in with *Quadriga,* which was focused principally at my students. My course had now got to the point where I had established 1st and 2nd Lesser Mystery grades and by October 1977 I was able to open up a 3rd degree and hold a meeting of senior students at The Royal Hop Pole in Tewkesbury.

In terms of numbers my course was pretty small beer compared with the Servants of the Light which, particularly after Ernest Butler's retirement in 1976 had, under the leadership of Dolores and Michael Ashcroft-Nowicki, by 1978, grown to an international organisation with some 1200 students on the books. Dolores in particular was tireless in trotting the globe, as far afield as Australia and New Zealand, to say nothing of some hair raising adventures in Israel and an enthusiastic reception in Greece by a group led by early students of the old Helios course.

It was almost certainly due to the increasing spread of the Servants of the Light course that I was now approached by Donald Weiser, doyen of esoteric publishing in the United States at that time, to licence an American edition of *A Practical Guide to Qabalistic Symbolism.*

In October 1978 the Servants of the Light held their first annual conference at the Kenilworth Hotel in London, where Dolores successfully conducted a Qabalistic path working with no less than 150 participants. Magical activities had certainly externalised since the early days! As main speaker on the occasion, I gave a talk on *The Golden Ass,* the supposedly erotic novel by Apuleius which I was convinced revealed much of the ancient Mysteries of Isis. It later formed a staple part of a very popular book of mine which has been through three changes of title in the course of its life, first as *The Rose Cross and the Goddess* [1985], then revised and expanded as *Evoking the Goddess* [1993], and finally reprinted and retitled as *Magic and the Power of the Goddess* [2008].

As we entered 1979 however, little suspected by any of us, a remarkable new development was about to occur. This was a series of remarkable public workshops spread over the coming years at Hawkwood College. It all began with a tentative invitation to me from its Principal, Bernard Nesfield-Cookson, to give a weekend of talks on any subject that took my fancy.

This was the start of a sequence of events that, to a number of people, are now regarded as legendary.

12

A History of White Magic
1977-79

In the spirit of the old *New Dimensions* magazine I had always kept a weather eye on the broader publishing front; of books with serious esoteric content intended for the intelligent enquirer in the general public rather than the already committed student.

I had already ventured into this field with one of the little primers I published in 1969 under the Helios imprint. *Occult Exercises and Practices* had been a complete beginner's guide to practical occultism, giving exercises in development of clairvoyance, clairaudience, relaxation, meditation, magical visualisation, spiritual exercises and prayer. Divided into sections, it allowed the student to develop upon whatever level happened immediately to appeal – the physical, etheric, astral, mental, intuitional or spiritual.

It was inspired by a classic title, *Your Psychic Powers and How to Develop Them*, written by veteran psychical researcher Hereward Carrington in 1920 and I rather ambitiously sought to do in 68 pages what had taken him 380! His book was virtually unobtainable at the time and if I had had the money I would have been happy to republish it myself. It has since been reprinted by others many times, but it is no good being a visionary if you lack the wherewithal to follow through. Nonetheless my little 1969 primers *Occult Exercises and Practices* and *The Practice of Ritual Magic* were later taken on by Aquarian Press, from which exposure they were soon translated into a number of European languages.

In the course of writing *Experience of the Inner Worlds* I had also trailed through a great deal of the historical development of the magical tradition and now Morris Kahn, who had been somewhat disappointed at my publishing the *Practical Guide* with Helios, asked me if I would like to write a general introduction to occultism for him to publish at Stanmore Press, which was now known as Kahn and Averill.

Called *The Occult, an Introduction*, it provided a brief introduction to the occult for the open minded and enquiring lay person with no knowledge of the subject but interested to discover if there was really "anything in it". It was divided into two parts: the first a survey of the occult in historical perspective spelled out the history of the Western

Esoteric Tradition; and the second in the form of an illustrated glossary covering various aspects of the occult scene, from Alchemy through to Yoga.

At much the same time I was approached from an unexpected direction by the educational department of a religious publishing house, Lutterworth Press. They were producing a series of school books aiming to inform children about various other religious faiths and looked for an author to write one called *Meeting the Occult*. Their intention was hardly to seek recruits but rather to appraise them of the dangers of the subject. They had first approached Tony Duncan on the strength of his reputation for knowing something about it, but for whatever reason he had passed them on to me. I hesitated about taking this on, but then thought that I might as well, using my own name rather than Gareth Knight. At least it would avoid some bigot denouncing or distorting occultism, and I could give a fair coverage of what it was all about, whilst providing advice on how to avoid going about it in the wrong way. I borrowed heavily from Dante's *Divine Comedy* and within the prescribed limits didn't do a bad job of it, I think, although I had to defend myself from the objections of a strait laced publisher's reader who was horrified when I compared some Christians to Biblical Pharisees.

It was my turn to be horrified, however, when copies of the book arrived! I found myself described as *"an Anglican writer who at one time was caught up in the occult. Under a nom-de-plume he even wrote a book about it 'from the inside'. Then he was converted to Christianity and writes now from a different angle."*

I rang up the commissioning editor straight away to protest about this farrago of half truths – which I considered verged on the libellous. But in the face of his bewildered naïvety I drew back from demanding they pulp the edition. It was after all, I felt, only a school book, and if it might do a little bit of good I was prepared to live with the patronising misrepresentation on the cover. After all, the blushes would be on their side if they knew the full story! Far from being a snivelling convert from unspeakable practices, I was about to produce another couple of books all about the occult "from the inside" – *Experience of the Inner Worlds* and *The Occult – an Introduction,* to say nothing of *A Course on Christian Qabalistic Magic*!

All this passed off without further ado, apart from some bewildered occult enthusiast who had come across a copy and – as is the way with the conservative in any branch of belief – considered I had betrayed the cause. You cannot please everyone. In the course of life I have felt that if I am lambasted from opposing sides I am probably getting things about right.

I was now approached by another religious publishing house with an unexpected commission. Apparently, Richard Mulkern, the Managing Director of Mowbrays, had looked into his shaving mirror one morning and been struck with the thought of publishing *A History of White Magic*. Goodness knows where that came from! His search for someone to write it probably came by way of Anthony Duncan, and his friend and spiritual advisor, the Benedictine monk Dom Robert Petitpierre, and ended up with me.

I had reservations about this offer, bearing in mind my experience with Lutterworth, and was still undecided whether to accept an invitation to meet Richard Mulkern when I began to receive a strong and persistent psychic impression to consult the I Ching. I am not given to frequent use of divination, finding that my own intuition sees me well enough through most vicissitudes of life. However, so strong did these impressions become that I dusted off my copy of the I Ching and cast the oracle of yarrow stalks.

The result was the hexagram Ts'ui, "Gathering Together", which has as its general interpretation: *"Success. The king approaches his temple. It furthers one to see the great man. This brings success. Perseverance furthers."* This was encouraging enough for me and so I went forth "to see the great man" and duly signed his contract.

A History of White Magic duly appeared in January 1979 and attracted more general interest than any of my other books so far. I was invited to talk about the book on BBC Radio 2, on Anglia TV and at a number of local radio stations. One clerical gentleman (who had not read the book) wrote to say how appalled he was at its publication by a respectable religious publishing house – but it was very well received in the esoteric field, and even compared to Dr Bronowski's famous television serial *The Ascent of Man*. I would not have put it in that class myself, but it had its influence and was translated into French and Greek and later had an American incarnation as *Magic and the Western Mind*.

When it was in course of production I came across a photograph of Bill Gray in the *Gloucestershire Echo*. He was sporting a Stetson hat and had just returned from America graced with an honorary doctorate apparently from the University of Texas. This was obviously the work of Carr Collins, to whom I now wrote, suggesting that if such academic prestige could be laid on for one of my authors, a similar recognition might not be out of place to the publisher who had discovered him. This all the more importantly because I had been commissioned by a respectable Oxford publishing house to write *A History of White Magic* – a worthy cause which might be furthered if its author had a handle to his name!

Carr, ever willing to oblige, did me proud, granting me not only a doctorate, but the award of Outstanding Humanitarian for 1976 from the Sangreal Foundation, a trust he used for his esoteric promotional activities, whilst his psychologist friend Dr James Hall chipped in by appointing me Consultant in Archetypal Symbolism to the C. G. Jung Institute in Dallas, Texas.

MR. WILLIAM GRAY

The doctorate was not however quite as prestigious as I had supposed. The degree did not emanate from the University of Texas but from Carr's Sangreal Foundation, and when I asked just how far the University might be involved was advised that it would be politic not to claim that it had been awarded *by* the University – although awarded *at* the University might possibly be acceptable. Presumably in the street outside!

I used the honorific in publicity for *A History of White Magic* but quietly dropped it after that. Although the granting of degrees by non-academic institutions is perfectly legal, my daytime job in higher education hobnobbing with real doctors and professors precluded me from appearing to debase the currency of educational qualifications.

The book also had its pay off some years later when a producer from Border Television invited me to appear and contribute my views on the Elizabethan magical revival in a series entitled *The Gnostics*. In the event this meant being called at short notice to sit in the corner of a borrowed office with a camera almost rammed up one nostril while I was grilled at short range for about an hour. The outcome was edited down to a couple of minutes to select what the producer wanted to prove, that possibly Shakespeare had Dr John Dee in mind when writing the character of Prospero in *The Tempest*.

Much like my experience with the theatre, it was a fairly exciting episode, with lots of emotional ups and downs, and marginally better rewarded – with £50 and a free drink. The series was quite well received but the experience did not particularly impress me as a way of getting my own ideas across. At least not without becoming a producer. Too many middle men at work. As an old fashioned author and publisher I liked to keep things more under my own control. Which is, more or less, what I was able to do in the burgeoning "esoteric workshop" movement.

13

A Tree Grows at Hawkwood
1979

Hawkwood College, a Cotswold manor house set in the heart of spectacular Gloucestershire countryside was founded on principles inspired by Rudolf Steiner, but was not limited by them, for a wide range of people were invited to run their own courses, seminars and conferences. It was the location for that memorable weekend back in 1973 when Anthony Duncan, talking on the Qabalistic Tree of Life, caused such a fluttering in the esoteric dovecots and brought the Gareth Knight Group to birth.

When I was invited to put on a weekend of lectures over the Whitsun bank holiday of 1979, it seemed a good opportunity to go back and talk about the same thing. To see how things had moved, and if they had not moved, at least to give them another shove. So under the title *The Tree of Life – Universal Symbol of the Mysteries* I set out over much the same ground that Duncan had covered. It was attended by a mix of my own students and those of the Servants of the Light along with a number who were neither.

Tony Duncan had drawn attention to what he called "two Qabalahs" – one the original Jewish mystical conception as expounded in the Zohar and other early traditions. I covered this with a session on *The Tree of Life as Image of God*. The other was the Christian interpretation of the Tree of Life in the Renaissance, with its angelic, stellar and mundane correspondences in a 3 tier universe. I spoke on this as *The Tree of Life as Pattern of the Universe*.

However, I did not intend to be limited by this basic dividing line. I went on to talk of *The Tree of Life and Initiation*, the use of the Tree by alchemists, Rosicrucians and Freemasons, and *The Tree of Life and Psychology* – its application to 19th and 20th century comparative religion and mythology.

The Saturday night was illuminated by a magic lantern show – *The Tree of Life and the Tarot* – with the help of a set of evocative colour slides produced by Josephine Gill, a student of the Servants of the Light.

So much for the theory. On Sunday morning I introduced some practical work – a directed visualisation of a traditional view of the heavens – in *The High Medieval Christian Tradition and the Tree of Life.* Instead of the usual pattern of the Tree of Life as a series of triangles drawn on a page I presented it as a series of crystalline spheres, one within the other, with the Earth at the centre. The idea was that by visualising ourselves starting on the Earth in ordinary mundane consciousness at the centre of things, and then expanding consciousness outward, we could experience the powers of each of the surrounding heavenly spheres, the Moon, Mercury, Venus, the Sun, Mars, Jupiter, Saturn, the Fixed Stars, the Primum Mobile, until we burst out into direct spiritual awareness and the clarity of the Limitless Light.

This was the great conceptual image of the universe held by the ancient world, right up until late medieval times, when it was recapitulated in Dante's great vision of the *Paradiso.* The sequence of heavenly spheres in exactly the same order as on the Tree of Life.

This pre-Copernican vision may no longer be considered a very accurate model of the universe according to physical science, but that does not invalidate it as an accurate model of the *inner* universe – the one that is perceptible to our inner senses. For each and everyone of us is a spiritual centre of perception, currently based upon Earth, in a multiplex universe of rings and rays. And it is ultimately dehumanising, and indeed unrealistic, to think of ourselves in any other way.

At all events, this journey through the spheres went very well. Such was the joy that some experienced that they were in tears. Happy and surprised tears at touching the supernal heights. Their first truly spiritual experience perhaps.

It seems worth noting that this pattern, and indeed the technique, had been readily available for years in cheap editions of Dante's *Divine Comedy.* So what price the much vaunted occult secrecy beloved by our forebears? Magic is where you find it. In effect it was exactly what Dion Fortune used guardedly to refer to as "rising on the planes", although she never published much detail on this practice – such was the concern for occult secrecy in her day.

Then having broached the practical applications I went on, in *Principles of White Magic and the Tree of Life,* to show how the traditional magic circle could be applied to the Tree of Life. And in *British Racial Archetypes and the Tree of Life,* with a little esoteric model making and castle symbolism I described how the Tree of Life could be aligned with images from Arthurian legend, building on principles that Ernest Butler had demonstrated on the Helios/SOL course. And on the Sunday evening, *Path Working on the Tree of Life* was an opportunity to conduct a traditional guided visualisation of the 32nd Path working from Malkuth

With Roma at Hawkwood, 1983. 　　　　　　*(Photo by Mike Omoleye)*

to Yesod, the first that I had ever experienced at the Society of the Inner Light, and later (greatly daring) conducted for myself with my own little house group back in 1965. I had, more recently, published an account of it in *Experience of the Inner Worlds*. The technique was obviously workable in a far different ambience from how I first experienced it in the secrecy and temple surroundings of an esoteric lodge. The Western Mysteries were in process of being "externalised".

On Monday morning I concluded the weekend with a talk on *Patterns on the Tree of Life,* looking at the Tree of Life in various ways but with particular emphasis on the "invisible" sphere of Daath. This had been a particular focus of interest in the Society of the Inner Light back in the 1950s and duly featured in *A Practical Guide to Qabalistic Symbolism* with a chapter of its own. The suggestion was that the most practical way to come to terms with it in other than Christo-Judaic terms was via the mythology of Isis – in short, the mediation of the Divine Feminine.

And so my first Hawkwood came to an end, this time with none of the problems that had accompanied Tony Duncan's presentation, although I covered much the same ground, albeit with a lot more besides. In the intervening six years we had all moved on a bit. Dolores, who was also present on this occasion, wrote up the event in fulsome terms:

> May 25/28 saw a weekend devoted to lectures on the Qabalah given by Gareth Knight. Mr Knight, an expert in his field, made it a weekend to remember for some fifty students – some from the Gareth Knight course, some, including three young Americans from North Carolina, from SOL, and some from other courses or schools, along with a few interested newcomers.
>
> If I thought after many years in the occult field that I knew a lot about the Qabalah – I soon found that there were avenues I had neglected, and some which needed a new viewpoint. In ten marvellous and sometimes shattering lectures Mr Knight took his audience from the earliest, purely Judaic system of the Qabalah to the glyph as we know and use it today.
>
> Along the way we took in two deeply effective pathworkings that I think will keep working in many of us for quite a while.
>
> Gareth Knight is planning another series of lectures next May. Judging from the remarks made by departing guests I would suggest booking as soon as possible. Certainly I would highly recommend that both students and supervisors try to attend.

At this weekend Dolores also revealed something of her natural psychic abilities which were to feature quite strongly – and disconcertingly – on future weekends. She asked me "who is the small tubby man in a Greek outfit with a snub nose? He kept flitting in and out of my side vision throughout the weekend. He seemed to be with you."

She recognised him instantly when I showed her a photograph of a statue of Socrates – a strong inner contact of mine back of my early house group at Tewkesbury in 1965. The validity and origin of such contacts and impressions and whether we should take them at face value is a matter to which we shall return. This particular contact featured strongly in Dion Fortune's esoteric career, and indeed was largely responsible for her metaphysical treatise of 1923/4 *The Cosmic Doctrine*. The first inkling of my own contact with it had however been low key to the point of the ridiculous.

At one of the Wednesday evening discussion groups back at the Society of the Inner Light the Warden had suggested a little practical exercise of visualising opening a book and seeing what was on the page. What I saw was an old man leaning on a cudgel, who reminded me of the Scottish comedian Harry Lauder and invited me to step into the page with him. The Warden, who was not without a sense of humour, responded that he thought he knew who it was, and if I did not show a bit more respect might well get a clout from that stick. He said no more and it was some years before I realised it was the Master Socrates he had in mind. He was sometimes called the "cosmic midwife" – one who helped bring things to birth – which in my publishing and somewhat maverick esoteric activities seemed perhaps to be also very much in my line!

14

Dion Fortune and the Sea Priestess
1980

Invited back with enthusiasm to Hawkwood for the Whitsun weekend of 1980, I decided to keep the Dion Fortune banner flying with *The Occult Work of Dion Fortune*. I intended not just a résumé of her life and work, which was pretty well known to most people, but to discuss some elements that had never been revealed, and to challenge some aspects that had been abused or taken for granted.

A general survey of her life and work more or less sorted itself out along the lines of the books she had written. First, in *The Cosmic Background to Dion Fortune's Thought*, a look at the highly complex and abstruse metaphysical philosophy, *The Cosmic Doctrine*, mediumistically received by her from 1923 to 1925, and then her later classic, written in her own words, from 1931 to 1934, *The Mystical Qabalah*.

Then in *Training for the Ancient Mysteries in the Modern Age* we discussed the two introductory books she wrote when founding her esoteric school in 1927 to 1930, *The Training and Work of an Initiate* and *The Esoteric Orders and their Work*. I also included another vintage work of hers, *Sane Occultism*, a collection of 1920s articles that expressed her trenchant no-nonsense approach to many pseudo-occult pretensions, and succeeded in upsetting a number of major occult figures of the day.

At the same time I chose to soft pedal her early works *The Esoteric Philosophy of Love and Marriage* and *Psychic Self Defence*. The first because, based on her early mediumship before she really found her stride, it is badly dated, almost to the point of levity. The latter because, despite its biographical interest it tends toward the credulous and sensational. Like her early fiction, it was written with a view to drawing attention to occultism rather than to explaining it. Thus it misrepresents rather than reveals what the subject is really all about.

This left Saturday evening for a run through Dion Fortune's works of fiction: a collection of short stories, *The Secrets of Dr Taverner*, inspired by her first teacher, Theodore Moriarty, plus the sequence of novels intended as a way of teaching some of the practicalities of occultism, *The Demon Lover*, *The Goat-foot God*, *The Winged Bull*, *The Sea Priestess* and *Moon Magic*. The first of these was an early occult "blood and thunder" but the others, written after her work on *The Mystical Qabalah,* were an attempt to provide practical illustrations of the theoretical teaching at a time when such matters were felt to be highly secret.

As with the previous year I devoted the first session on Sunday morning to practical work – a directed meditation on aspects of the Glastonbury legends evoked in Dion Fortune's *Avalon of the Heart.* This little book, written at much the same time as *The Mystical Qabalah* was in effect a love letter to the town as much as a tourist guide or esoteric text. Not entirely accurate as to facts, she nonetheless beautifully evoked the many aspects of Avalon – of Arthur, of Merlin, of the Abbey, of the Celtic Saints, of Chalice Well, the Tor, Wearyall Hill, Pons Perilous, Beckary, of Joseph of Arimathea, of the Holy Grail and the Holy Thorn and so on. Indeed I have found it possible over the years to use extracts from it, virtually straight off the page, as an effective directed visualisation or as the basis for ritual work.

For the rest of the day I launched into lesser known elements of Dion Fortune's work. In 1941/2 she had produced a series of inner communications known as *The Arthurian Formula.* This was an analysis of Arthurian archetypal characters against a background of Atlantean tradition and, supplemented by Margaret Lumley Brown, had been a staple of the Society of the Inner Light's higher level work throughout most of the 1950s. This was a little before my time but the Warden, who was not ungenerous to keen young initiates, had given me a copy which I found of great fascination. Indeed I was to delve into it more practically at the following Hawkwood, with some quite remarkable results.

Then for lighter relief I read extracts from *The War Letters of Dion Fortune* which provided a useful picture of her as an active down to earth occultist in real life. When the Second World War put a halt to many of the Society's activities in 1939, with restrictions on public meetings and difficulties of travel, she kept in touch with students and associates through a series of weekly letters that effectively formed a widespread meditation group, in the course of which she gave out a deal of practical information that otherwise might have been withheld.

In these letters much of the real woman comes across. One of my favourite passages occurs after bombs had recently fallen on Queensborough Terrace. Her letter of October 27th 1940 begins:

> In our last letter we asked our members and friends to invoke for the protection of 3 Queensborough Terrace, and in this letter we have the ironical task of informing them that we have been bombed out of it, though without casualties; so it may be maintained that the invocation was at least a partial

success, though your Leader and her Librarian look like a couple of sweeps owing to a difference of opinion with the roof, which fell in on them, but tactfully refrained from hitting them.

It has often been alleged that Dion Fortune was Black Occultist, and we regretfully admit that the allegation can no longer be denied; however it is hoped that soap and water will restore her to the Right Hand Path and her students will once more be able to hold up their heads before a world always too ready to think the worst.

Reading out these letters at this point in the weekend was a deliberate preliminary to some important practical work that I intended to do in the evening on the subject of *A Priestess of Isis* – the heroine of Dion Fortune's last two books *The Sea Priestess* and *Moon Magic*.

Few people knew, although Dion Fortune had given some indication of the issues in her introduction to *Moon Magic*, that the character Vivien or Lilith Le Fay Morgan had taken on an almost independent existence, to the point of virtually dictating the events of the second book. This is of course by no means unusual in any work of the creative imagination but in Dion Fortune's case the character seemed to be possessed of information and ancient lore that was completely unknown to the author. In which case she might well have been an independent inner plane entity. She might also be said to have had quite an influence upon Dion Fortune herself, who at the time of writing *The Sea Priestess* was given to dressing in the same way as her – with large floppy brimmed hats, long cloak, furs, and chunky jewellery.

Moon Magic was not published until 1956 and an odd sequel to this melding of author with character is that shortly after this an increasing confusion developed in readers' minds between the author and the character. In my view this was in part exacerbated by the lack of photographs of Dion Fortune, and was one reason for my having published one in the front of *The New Dimensions Red Book*. Apart from this there was another side to the problem, in that the fictional figure being identified with Dion Fortune was proving something of a handicap and embarrassment to the latter's ongoing inner plane work. Thus Margaret Lumley Brown had been encouraged to make a sustained contact with the post mortem Dion Fortune in order to help bring things to a natural close. The result was a piece called *The Death of Vivien Le Fay Morgan* in which the character made her final departure. Although announced as "an epilogue to *Moon Magic*" it never appeared in the actual novel but only in a volume of Dion Fortune articles, *Aspects of Occultism*, in 1962.

What also concerned me was the effect this confusion between author and character could have upon a vulnerable and credulous type of reader. I was already aware of a young woman who had identified with the more outlandish aspects of the Sea Priestess and drifted from glamorised fantasising into abuse of drink and drugs – all of which, it must be said, were a far cry from the abstemious rectitude of the fictional character. With this in mind, and whether the figure was an actual inner plane entity, or no more than a thoughtform, albeit ensouled by a certain degree of elemental essence fed by enthusiastic readers, I determined to do something about it.

Accordingly, by means of directed visualisation, we went off to the end of Bell Knowle and put it to Miss Le Fay Morgan that whilst we much appreciated her past services, the time had come when their usefulness was over. Much had been achieved in the liberation of sexual mores and knowledge of the Mysteries since 1938, and it was time for her to get on her boat and sail back to Atlantis.

This seemed to go according to plan, indeed she went off like a lamb, albeit seemingly somewhat remote and entranced, although one or two sensed a certain reluctance. As one participant said to me later "She didn't really want to go did she?" and thought it no end of a lark. However, rather more serious issues were at stake than esoteric power games.

Anyhow, I was going to have plenty of this kind of thing to deal with in the future, not only at the series of public Hawkwoods, but with my own group. In this respect, the episode with the Sea Priestess was a preliminary skirmish in a line of service balancing up various neuroses in the collective psyche. All on a much wider and deeper basis than I dreamed possible at this time.

15

The Return of the King
1981

The Whitsun Hawkwood weekend had now established itself as a regular annual festival on the calendar, and for 1981 I decided to take Dion Fortune studies a little further – which may not have been readily apparent from my chosen title of *Arthurian Archetypes.*

I had however long been intrigued by *The Arthurian Formula,* a script that had once formed the mainstay of advanced work in the Society of the Inner Light and had been one reason why, when I was a Study Course student, a requirement had been to read Sir Thomas Malory's *Le Morte D'Arthur* from cover to cover. However, by the time I made it into the Greater Mysteries it had ceased to be actively worked with, although the Warden was kind enough to furnish me with a copy.

The Arthurian Formula had been mediumistically received by Dion Fortune in 1941/2 in rather unusual circumstances, when she had met up again temporarily with her old Golden Dawn mentor Maiya Tranchell-Hayes. It was later expanded by Margaret Lumley Brown during the 1950s when the group worked consistently with it.

It covered heady subjects such as the role of Merlin and Faery Women in the birthing and training of Arthur – and the function of other semi-human or supernatural beings, such as the Lady of the Lake and the enchantress Morgan le Fay, along with dynamics from the Atlantean tradition. It had never been released to the public, although many years later I was able to arrange its publication with additional material by Wendy Berg.

I had been doing some individual research on Merlin a couple of years previously when in August 1979 I made a trip to the Prescelly Mountains in south west Wales to investigate the origin of the blue stones, which according to tradition had been transported from there by Merlin to build Stonehenge. Whatever the truth of that, one thing I experienced on that occasion, and have never been able to explain, was the freak weather conditions that sometimes occur when working with ancient Arthurian dynamics.

Just as we reached the top of the bluestone outcrop after a hard climb we were struck in the face by the most severe storm that had been experienced for years. Indeed, it wrecked the famous Fastnet yacht race with some loss of life. Within seconds, despite waterproofs, we were drenched to the skin. It was a virtual baptism by total immersion! Oddly enough, as I was only to discover in later years, my close esoteric friend Robert Stewart, who later initiated a great deal of Merlin research, was actually in the middle of it at the time, bearing the brunt of it on the high seas.

On another occasion it snowed in April to herald a visit I made to the Merlin stone on Alderley Edge, whilst as I shall later relate a freak storm sprang up in New York when I was evoking the storm theme in Chrétien de Troyes' *The Lady of the Fountain*.

Whilst I had *The Arthurian Formula* in the background of my thoughts and intentions for the Hawkwood weekend, I structured the initial talks more or less on the grand old academic classic from 1921, *The Morte D'Arthur of Sir Thomas Malory* by Vida Scudder, several copies of which had been in the Society of the Inner Light library. On this basis, after *An Outline of the Arthurian Cycle* on the Friday evening, we spent all day Saturday progressively on *Merlin, the Faery Women and the Coming of Arthur; The Fellowship of the Round Table; The Cult of Romantic Love;* and *The Quest of the Holy Grail*. All this as a preliminary to some ambitious practical work on the Sunday.

There was a rather odd practical element that intruded onto the first Saturday lecture however, wherein I covered the role of Merlin in the Arthuriad and his relationship to semi-human or supernatural beings such as the Lady of the Lake. During this, a gentleman who evidently possessed some degree of psychic sensitivity reported being aware of the figure of a woman walking about the place singing. He was even able to transcribe the words and music for me:

SONG OF NIMUÉ

I hear your voice again, still singing that sad refrain,
A song of love, enchanting me, and drawing me to you once more.
How strange a mystery, to hear your voice again,
Enthralling me, enchanting me, and calling me to you again –
To you again – to you again.

Entitled *Song of Nimué* I have not to this day been sure from whence it came or to whom it was addressed. I have to say I found it quite evocative at the time – although the tune has been criticised for its sentimentality. Not that this bothered me too much, having something of the musical taste of a cocktail bar pianist.

However, insofar that it was a Whitsun weekend, or Pentecost, when Arthur's court always awaited some kind of adventure, it seemed possible that something out of the ordinary might be expected to happen. Although this turned out in the end to be far greater than I or anyone else anticipated.

I commenced the practical sessions on Sunday with a directed meditation on *The Vision of the Grail*, which involved a trip to Sarras with the three Grail winners on the ship of Solomon and back again.

I then decided to try out an exercise in ritual. This was quite a revolutionary step in those days, so I took the precaution of it being somewhat disguised. We did not do any dressing up – thus it appeared more in the nature of a formalised reading by students of mine sat in four parts of the room – with the invitation for others to visualise the images rather than just listen to the words. Otherwise it was much like a Degree Catechism working such as I had experienced years before in the Society of the Inner Light.

The *Catechism of the Grail* seems quite low key stuff nowadays, and has subsequently been published in a collection of my articles, *Merlin and the Grail Tradition*. However, at the time it was sufficiently impressive to be copied and worked at other public workshops that were beginning to be set up by other people. I must say I have no great objection to this, even though I did not know about it at the time. Imitation is the sincerest form of flattery – and as long as the work is being done without too much distortion it means the light is being spread, which suits me well enough.

However, the real kick on this Pentecostal Sunday came in a completely unexpected manner. After an afternoon lecture on *The Human Tragedy of the Passing of Arthur* on the roles of Arthur, Guinevere, Lancelot, Gawain and Mordred in the break up of the Fellowship and of the dynasty, I thought a fairly routine marrying up of literature with occultism might be appropriate. I aimed simply to read a piece of relevant poetry in the context of a directed visualisation. My aim was to reproduce the effects of a minstrel upon an assemblage of people which, in medieval times, would have been the means of passing on or even creating these living legends.

It all started innocuously enough. Everyone was sat around the hall in a great oval, by candlelight, as I read out the famous story from Tennyson's *Morte D'Arthur,* of how Arthur and the sole surviving Round Table knight, Bedivere, arrive at the Lake after the Last Battle. The King is mortally wounded and commands Bedivere to cast his sword Excalibur into the Lake. After twice failing to do so for plausible but specious reasons Bedivere finally does so. An arm rises up and takes the sword, and as if this were a signal, a barque with three mourning queens arrives to take the wounded King to the Isle of Avalon.

The sequence ends with the point that Bedivere now, as sole remaining knight, holds within himself the whole Round Table. And the last words of the King are to ask that Bedivere should pray for him.

As soon as I said this, it became plain to me what I should do. I told all present to identify themselves with the Round Table and also to pray for the King.

And as they did so, so I became aware that a great Round Table had formed on the imaginative level within the room, or possibly even the etheric, for it seemed almost palpable, and extended out to the very seats of all present.

I then took up a hunting horn I had by me, and blew three long blasts.

As soon as I had done so it seemed as if, to the eyes of vision, great doors opened in the West, together with a waft of sea air, and even spray. A mighty figure of the King came through the doors, crowned, with short golden beard, robed, and with the great hilt of the sword Excalibur very prominent, impressive with its jewelled work, and in its mighty runed scabbard.

With the King came Queen Guinevere, Lancelot, Gawain, Tristram and all the knights and ladies. Larger than life, they took up their positions about the Table Round. In the centre rose a column of incense smoke with astral rainbow colours manifesting the powers of the Grail, the Cauldron, Merlin and Nimué.

To my surprise, although I was seated in the East, the traditional quarter of rulership, the great throne of the King, with the Queen's beside it, built up opposite me in the West, where Dolores was placed.

The power within the room was intensely strong. So much so that the small table altar with the two candles and incense burner upon it seemed to be wavering up and down as in a heat haze.

Somewhat nonplussed as to what to do now, I decided to let the powers continue running overnight, and suggested that all present leave quietly, independently and in their own time.

One by one, all left until there were but three of us left, myself, Dolores opposite me in the west, and one other, a somewhat inexperienced young man who was perhaps intent on making an endurance test of it. We sat for some time, and at one point Dolores rose to go – but was forced by a strong impulsion to sit down again.

Finally, she turned and in stern tones that brooked no argument, commanded: *Man! Leave us!*

The young man, realising he had overstayed his welcome, scurried out. Whereupon, apparently entranced, Dolores announced across the empty hall:

You have done well, priest.
As a result of this work new doors will be opened for you.
A light has been rekindled tonight that has for too long been extinguished.

Then coming to the central altar, and exchanging a salute, she turned and left. At which, after ensuring the power flowing into the place was stabilised, I extinguished the candles and followed her.

Although somewhat shaken by the experience, Dolores soon recovered her composure, and declared that never before had she experienced a psychic contact quite on a par with this. Oddly enough, none of us yet realised who or what it might be that had "come through" in such dramatic fashion.

Nothing like this had been a conscious part of my plans for the evening. Although I did have a half suppressed inkling that something unusual might be expected, for when packing for the weekend I had a strong impulse to take the small hunting horn with me. I resisted the thought as there seemed only one purpose for using it, and I did not fancy the presumption, the responsibility or the possible consequences. However, I was quite firmly nudged to include it, and so I took it with me. Much the same kind of inner debate took place minutes before I went down to the hall. I saw no reason to take the horn with me, but in the end had the strong feeling that I should do so, and so put it into my box file.

The significance of all this did not occur to me until driving home, when I realised that only one person could have talked through Dolores in such an utterly imperious although not overbearing tone, and that must surely have been the King! But then, who did we mean by that? I did not know. Nonetheless, whoever the original Arthur was, whether 5th century Romano-Briton or the Titanic god Albion, what I did know was that the living experience had been vivid, and one of reality, if not of this world.

It was what I would now call an objective Archetype – which is a far cry from the psychological conception that is popularly confused with it. And the inner dynamic that was coming strongly through it was:

The King lives. Long live the King!

The power stirred up by the weekend carried on working with a number of others who had been present, who began to have realisations and contacts of their own. No sooner had I arrived home than John Matthews rang me to say he had sensed the following message that seemed important.

The sword is unsheathed and should be kept on the altar in that way.

This sparked a realisation in me that somehow these forces of the King were indeed abroad in the land and that all who had been present should be told.

Until this had been achieved I was under intense subliminal pressure – my neck and shoulders tense as if carrying a great yoke. But as the word spread so this condition eased. And indeed it appeared that others also had been picking up message in various ways.

Yet there was also a lighter side to the ongoing contacts that expressed themselves as the days passed and the immediate power gradually faded out. I found myself being accompanied on country walks with my dog by a character who purported to be Sir Gareth. It seems he found it easier to make contact in a country environment and also in the company of animals. He saw the landscape very much in the tactical terms of a cavalry commander and I felt slightly inadequate in his company, conscious of my inability to ride a horse.

However, as a counterbalance to this, other knightly characters turned up, who evinced a high respect for me from the way I handled my car! They were enormously impressed with this "flying chariot" and my bravery and skill in using it at such speed as they sat in the back.

They also had some strange technological ideas, and insisted on calling the accelerator "the spur", along with a not too accurate but superficially plausible theory that the gear stick was a sort of magic wand or rod of power that conjured one horse, two horses, three horses or four horses beneath the bonnet!

To this day I do not know what to make of all this. In the interests of accuracy I record it, however ludicrous it may seem. For it indicates some way of the working of the magical imagination when under impress from Archetypal forces. And at the very least it gave a certain welcome relief and gradual let down from the previous portentous proceedings.

The ripples out from the weekend also produced a more material response – for on the strength of it I was contracted to write a book on Arthurian legend by Aquarian Press. The result was *The Secret Tradition in Arthurian Legend* (1983) – later translated into French and Italian, and which incorporated most of the content of *The Arthurian Formula* along with a number of ideas of my own and from other sources.

16

A Rosicrucian Adventure
1982

I now had to decide how to follow all this for the Hawkwood event of 1982. In searching for a topic I recalled W. G. Gray once saying that if anyone was looking for occult experience they had only to try working with a 17th century Rosicrucian document entitled *The Chymical Wedding of Christian Rosencreutz*. And I remembered that the first time I ever heard of Hawkwood College some years before was when a couple of ladies associated with it issued a commentary upon this work – albeit from an anthroposophical point of view. So I decided it might be appropriate to investigate its complex symbolism to see if W. G. Gray was right. And as events proved – he certainly was!

The Chymical Wedding describes a symbolic journey spread out over seven days during which the hero, Christian Rosencreutz, is invited to a wedding at a mysterious castle full of wonders and strange rites. As part of the wedding ceremonies a royal couple are beheaded and then restored to life, spiritually transformed, through an alchemical process in a seven storied tower. However, there is a strong hint that the wedding is the hero's own, and to the goddess Venus who sleeps in an underground chamber.

If this sounds somewhat fantastical it was nonetheless the essence of 17th century spiritual alchemy. The secret in working with these quaint old texts, however, is not to speculate intellectually about their meaning, but to enter wholeheartedly into their evocative imagery. That is to say, the pictures which accompany them are not so much illustrations to an obscure text, but gateways to inner experience.

In for a penny, in for a pound, I intended to present a whole range of these images taken from the background of contemporary spiritual alchemy. This included the anonymous *Rosarium Philosophorum* (1550); *The Hieroglyophic Monad* of Dr John Dee (1564); *The Amphitheatre of Eternal Wisdom* by Heinrich Khunrath (1609); *Atalanta Fugiens* by Michael Maier (1617); *The Macrocosmic Monochord* of Robert Fludd, (1617); *Lumen de lumine* by Thomas Vaughan, 1651; *The Clavis or Key* to the works of Jacob Boehme (1575-1624) by William Law (1714).

If this sounds somewhat scholastically demanding, it is much less so when focusing on the evocative diagrams – and I added a practical element to seven of the talks with a visualisation based on each of the Seven Days of the Alchemical Wedding. So it was quite a practical weekend magically speaking. What is more, it turned out to be a natural continuation of what had been evoked last year with the Arthurian Archetypes – the Archetypal theme being no less than *the return of the King* – although after another manner.

I capitalise the term Archetype to distinguish a cosmic Otherworld power from popular psychological usage.

However, the Archetypes as expressed in Arthurian legend have a certain legendary distance which means they do not impact too uncomfortably on the modern world. Similar Archetypes in a 17th century context are a lot closer to home! What is more, these were Archetypes in conflict and embodying sacrifice to their cause in the process.

One Archetypal conflict of that time was between democratic ideals opposed to principles of "divine" rulership through blood lines and the ownership of land, which brought about a Civil War between King and Parliament. This ended up with the beheading of the king, consequently hailed as a saint and martyr. Then after a decade the "Return of the King" with the Restoration of the monarchy – to be closely followed by "the Glorious Revolution" when the Catholic Stuarts were sent packing and the Protestant Hanoverian line enthroned. If all this seems somewhat obscure and irrelevant history, nonetheless the consequences festered on for over three hundred years. First with the 18th century Jacobite rebellions under Bonny Prince Charlie and beyond that, up to the present seemingly intractable "troubles" in Ireland.

It was perhaps then a significant coincidence that on this particular weekend, the Pope of Rome was making an official visit to England for the first time since the Reformation – although his visit was almost cancelled at the last minute on account of the country going to war with Argentina, a Catholic country. As we met at Hawkwood, British troops were storming the Falkland islands.

So in this year, at the climax of one of the workings, it was not romantic figures of Round Table knights who came streaming in – but killed and maimed soldiers, sailors and airmen, both British and Argentinian, straight from the battlefield, presumably attracted by the light of our working. (And for added synchronicity one of the horrors of this conflict was the conflagration of the frigate *Lancelot*).

This influx from a current battle ground was a heavy burden to bear, and indeed the psychically sensitive Dolores, who was once again at a key point in the west, left the hall, not only in floods of tears but with loud cries of grief, to the surprise, discomfiture and even disapproval of the some of the Hawkwood staff. But whether we liked it or not, or understood it or not, we were involved in some very deep Archetypal dynamics concerning blood sacrifice, rulership, and religious conflict.

There was another element in this weekend of what I might call the Falkland factor. The Falkland Islands conflict had been far from my thoughts when I chose as an Archetypal focus for part of the weekend a 17th century character, Lucius Carey, who also had, by coincidence, the title of Lord Falkland. I had chosen him as a paradigm of mediation between contending forces, for he was a figure with a foot in both camps of the Civil War.

At the time leading up to its outbreak he had mediated between the Cavalier and Roundhead sides, being known and trusted by the King yet also respected as a Member of Parliament. Alas, his mediation was not sufficient to reconcile the contending forces, and when civil war broke out, torn between conflicting loyalties, he acted with such foolhardy valour – some said in a mood of disillusionment bordering on deliberate self sacrifice – that he was cut down by musket fire at the Battle of Newbury.

A friend of Ben Jonson and one of his companions at the Mermaid Tavern, this young cavalier was untypical of his time in founding a kind of Neoplatonic academy, which included women, at his estate at Great Tew in Oxfordshire. I was later to experience a strong archetypal presence of this character for some weeks.

Whatever the significance of all this, the key working for the weekend was held on the Sunday evening, a directed visualisation based upon the *Lumen de Lumine* of the English Rosicrucian, Thomas Vaughan.

This involved climbing a magic mountain guarded by wild beasts, to enter a cave and then proceed underground to find a Rosicrucian vault. This vault was a replica of the famous description in the *Fama Fraternitatis* of the seven sided burial chamber of Christian Rosencreutz himself, but this one was that of Frater I. O., the first of the original Rosicrucians to die, and that in England. So this was not only an update but a localisation of the Rosicrucian tradition.

The concluding atmosphere of this working was once again profound, and I found myself alone in the hall with an entranced Dolores, who had however been knocked slightly off contact by being jostled as others left the hall. However, she was still able to announce, from some undisclosed contact, in awed and hushed tones:

Priest, you know not what you have done!
You have made a Grail of this place!

Who or what may have been the origin of this statement, and indeed what precisely it meant was a matter for conjecture, but it certainly seemed something to be taken seriously. I mentioned it discreetly to the Principal, Bernard Nesfield-Cookson, who whilst treating, as I did, the statement with some caution, was inclined to believe that something of great significance had occurred.

Whether or not Hawkwood had become a "Grail" I was able to help the place out in a very practical way that year. Bernard needed to find some cash to repair the roof of the stable block. In meditating upon this problem he had been directed to lay it before me, which he did with some circumspection. I had nothing like the £5000 that was needed, a substantial sum in those days, but I still had my contact with Carr Collins, who, blessed man, although not able by the terms of his Trust to come up with the full amount, helped considerably in the refurbishment of the building. By perhaps what might be a law of good karma, the stable block was to become the virtual home of the Gareth Knight Group for many years to come.

As had occurred the previous year, there were ongoing experiences for some of those attending. One very powerful vision concerned a return to the magical hill and underground vault, where, instructed by a guide, the stone was lifted again and the uncorrupted body of I.O. taken up a steep stairway formed by an extension of the axis of the Earth to the green/white flaming splendour of the Pole Star. With the planet still clearly visible, hung below like a beautiful living jewel, the body of I.O. rose up, and pointed to the Earth below with the words:

This is the jewel in your crown.

In those days, prior to any great concern for the well being of the Earth, there was more significance to this message than first met the eye. Indeed, it was a foreshadowing of the important work of R. J. Stewart, his *Underworld Initiation,* which was to feature importantly, and for the first time, in the Hawkwood meeting of the following year.

At another level, many at Hawkwood were intrigued by the pregnancy of Princess Diana, who was herself a direct descendant of the Stuarts. The birth duly came about on June 21st, the time of the Summer Solstice, when Prince William, who included Arthur in one of his given names, came into the world. What is more, his ascent to the throne would bring about, in part, a restoration of the Stuart blood line. Irrelevant in the modern age? Not, it seems, to those on the inner side of things! But whatever consequences there may be in all of this remain for the future to reveal.

In contrast to the heavy dynamics that had gone before, the weekend concluded quite light heartedly, but when I got home I had the house to myself for a couple of days as Roma was visiting relatives, and a strange period it turned out to be. I began to feel deeply lethargic. The feeling is hard to describe, I was as much out of this world as in it. It was like being in some kind of after-death condition. (Dolores later reported feeling in much the same way.) Then I became aware of a strange strong Tibetan influence. My mind kept being drawn to my dog, a Tibetan terrier, and to a Tibetan rug we happened to have.

I mentioned this on the telephone to Bob Stewart, who had also been present at the weekend, who told me that there was indeed reckoned to be a close link between Tibet and the mysteries of Britain. These inner matters were very recondite and part of a tradition known only to a few associated with the remarkable English adept Ronald Heaver. All of which led me to investigate some of the elements of Mahayana Buddhism over the next few months – thus following in the tracks of the American scholar Evans-Wentz who began by writing *The Fairy Faith in Celtic Countries* but went on to translate some key Tibetan texts, the study of which stood me in good stead when I came to write *The Rose Cross and the Goddess* (1985) – latterly *Evoking the Goddess* (1993) and *Magic and the Power of the Goddess* (2008) – which has proved to be one of my most successful books over the years in its various incarnations.

One important contributor to it was however Roma, whose burgeoning powers were responsible for the concluding chapter with its oft quoted final paragraphs:

> The wisdom of the heart is all important. For wisdom is unbalanced and distorted when held only at the intellectual level. The silver wisdom of the head must be changed to the golden wisdom of the heart by the warmth of human love.
>
> Tend the fires of love and understanding most carefully, for without the glow of their light and warmth, there is not only no wisdom to be had, there is no point in having the wisdom at all. The greater vision of unity lies in the transformations of the Goddess, the dancer at the heart of the rose.
>
> Reflect upon these deep things. And thus may the wisdom of the stars shine in your brow, the grail of love flow from your heart, the waters of life encompass your loins, and the stones of Earth support your feet. This is the image and function of redeemed humankind, the new Adam and new Eve, conjoined in the new Heaven and the new Earth, the new Avalon where the green apples have turned to gold.

One practical application of the above occurred at about this time with the temporary loss of my wedding ring. It had become too tight for my ring finger and so I had taken to wearing it on my little finger where it was a tad too loose. Consequently, whilst out walking the dog in the park one evening it slipped off somewhere along the way. On discovering the loss, Roma went straight out, singing what she called her "finding song" and duly came back with the ring, having found it in the long grass somewhere along my mile long route. True love will find a way – perhaps with a little help from inner friends. And it turned out to be a significant step when she elected to attend the next Hawkwood event, in which she became a key figure and in those that followed.

In attempting to sum up the significance of this weekend, the obvious conclusion was that the Rosicrucian mysteries are profound and complex ones containing powerful feminine and underworld dynamics. The figure of Venus in a guarded and concealed vault in the depths of the mysterious castle is a key to the whole process – along with the prospect of her awakening – which can occur on a personal or a social or even on a world wide level. That which we know as Gaia.

17

The Mysteries of Isis
1983

If I had learned anything from the dynamics of the Rosicrucian weekend it was that there were deep feminine issues involved, and so for the 1983 Hawkwood it seemed appropriate to broaden out the theme into *The Mysteries of Isis*. This was of course still Dion Fortune territory. Back in the late 1930s she had laid on semi-public Rites of Isis, parts of which were indeed incorporated in *The Sea Priestess* and *Moon Magic*.

In a spirit of broadening things out I also invited Dolores and Bob Stewart to contribute to the programme. They had both helped out in the 1982 event by taking part in a panel discussion along with Christopher McIntosh, author of a recent book on the Rosicrucians, and the alchemical expert Adam McLean. If Hawkwood was attracting talented participants it seemed a good idea to take full advantage of what they could contribute.

The events were also attracting some unexpected support from a group of regulars, mostly in the London area, who had banded themselves into what they liked to call the Hawkwood Survivors Club. Although this was all done quite openly and with the best of intentions it eventually brought home to me a cardinal rule in running a magical group (which is what the Hawkwood events had virtually become) – that all should be "of one mind and in one place."

In an open public event this may seem difficult to achieve but is quite manageable, given good leadership. However, if some decide to form a sub-group within the overall group – even with the best of intentions, it can rock the boat quite disconcertingly. I suspected the worst when I noticed couples pairing up and sitting in significant positions in some practical workings, and exchanging significant looks with one another.

This did not faze me too much at the time, for it must be said that some couples within that group could be very helpful. Certainly John and Caitlín Matthews proved their worth in contributing ideas and supporting action before or after an event. Unfortunately the same could not be said for all, some of whom had a penchant for "polarity magic" and spontaneous trance mediumship. Combine this with inadequate training and doubtful motivation and you have a dangerous mix.

However, as far as broadening the official programme was concerned I invited Dolores to open the proceedings with a directed meditation she had put on to considerable effect at a recent Aquarian Festival. Entitled *The Sorrows of Isis*, it covered the basic myth of the Egyptian Isis seeking the dismembered parts of her husband Osiris. This had apparently upset some of her original audience, but I reckoned that the Hawkwood company was made of sterner stuff. And indeed they took it very well.

I made use of the talents of Bob Stewart by sharing a joint talk with him on *The World of Faery in Oral Tradition* – which although I did not realise it at the time would burgeon forth later with considerable research by both of us into this important territory. I also gave him a free hand on the Saturday evening for the first public working of his now celebrated *UnderWorld Initiation* – a powerful system of tuning consciousness by undertaking a journey **into** the Earth rather than away from it, using the ancient wisdom contained in ballad lore.

It was a revolutionary way of going about things in those days, going down within the Earth rather than upward and away from it as a source of inspiration, as indeed I had done in my "rising on the planes" exercise at the very first Hawkwood. Both systems, let it be said, are obviously valid. What Stewart's initiative did was to show that going "down" was not necessarily a venture into a dubious underworld of phantom shades, unbalanced force or agents of evil as some earlier Qabalists tended to believe. That there were, on the other hand, deep and beneficent forces within the Earth itself. Hence his unusual spelling of "UnderWorld" to differentiate it from common conceptions of the word. His point was adequately proved to those who were present on this first occasion, which for most was a revelatory experience – discovering "the stars within the Earth".

However, there were those present who had their minds and hearts on other things, so Bob, aware of this suppressed emotional disturbance, but not sure of its origin, decided to cut the session short. At least it had the benefit of allowing some free time which was pleasurably filled by an impromptu musical entertainment in the lounge, where Bob played his psaltery and Caitlín Matthews sang.

This was an evocative combination to say the least, and particularly so to Dolores, who began to feel strangely disturbed and quietly left. Someone noticed her a little while later coming down from her bedroom, clad in ceremonial robes and proceeding down the corridor toward the lecture hall, but thought no more about it.

The one who did shortly know all about it was me!

I also had left the music for the prosaic task of arranging chairs in the hall for the next day's work. As I was busy with this I noticed Dolores had entered – dressed up as if for a ritual, but looking somewhat distrait.

Having plenty else to do I paid no great attention to her until she suddenly called out:

"Merlin! What do you want with me?"

She then began to wander about, as if in a daze, and looked as if she might even try to walk through one of the plate glass windows. I then realised that she was in some kind of somnambulistic trance.

Somewhat at a loss as to how to deal with this bizarre situation, I managed more or less to get her attention and tried to reassure her, quoting from Julian of Norwich "All will be well, will be well, will be well," before leading her gently back to where others were, where she collapsed on a settee and gradually collected herself together to tell her story.

It appeared that she had become obsessed by the consciousness of a young girl who had been sacrificed and bound to the place, presumably in Neolithic times. With a feeling of desperation and need to get to someone who could help, she was aware, as this young girl, of wandering into a strange faery like hall with lights, where a man who could help her was moving strange wooden shapes around. (This was the lecture hall with me shifting chairs.)

She wanted desperately to speak to this man but did not know his name. But "Merlin" had been used to refer to him in a ritual rehearsal that afternoon, when she must have been vaguely present. Still aware of the trees of the ancient site, she could not find her way through them, whilst in vague consciousness of the present she was disconcerted by strange walls of cold air through which she could not pass, and beyond which great stars seemed to be lying on the ground. (These were the lights of Stroud in the distance below, observable through the plate glass windows.)

She was a young girl, not a virgin, and with bad memories about this – a lot of pain and fear and a wooden staff that caused the pain. But a feeling of pride in being someone special, and of lying on a cold flat stone, and the pain and flash of a flint knife that had ripped her open. She was still afraid of the man who had done this, and feared he might still be lurking in the woods.

But listening to the man in the faery hall, distrusting his voice a little but needing its authority, it suddenly became clear to her – she did NOT have to stay any longer, she could just GO!

This was quite enough unscheduled evening's work for anybody and provided plenty of conversation pabulum as all retired for the night, looking forward with some trepidation to the day ahead and three very ambitious practical projects scheduled for it.

The first working on Sunday was to be an excursion into the world of Celtic faery, the second a full scale ritual evoking the powers of Merlin, and the third a deep working into uncharted territory contacting ancient Atlantean dynamics! The culture at Hawkwood had developed over the past three years to the point where I felt I could be quite open about ritual procedures, despite some rather askance looks from the domestic staff.

The first event however was to be a simple directed visualisation – *Across the Ford of the Moon*, based on an article by Colonel C. R. F. Seymour, a former colleague of Dion Fortune and great enthusiast of the pagan Green Ray. It featured some evocative poetry by W. B. Yeats – a great champion of faery tradition and former member of the Hermetic Order of the Golden Dawn – and resonated well with Bob Stewart's *UnderWorld Initiation* in featuring a descent into the Earth by climbing down an inverted tree whose leaves and branches led to a faery world underground.

However, as we were all assembled and about to start I was somewhat disconcerted to find that Dolores had not turned up! I was relying upon her to take the Western pole position as she had a great sympathy for the work of Seymour and indeed later edited a collection of his articles under the title *The Forgotten Mage*.

It turned out that her absence was due to an outbreak of the emotional disturbance that had cut short Bob Stewart's *UnderWorld Initiation* session the night before. A young man, recently engaged in some kind of polarity working with a fellow member of the Hawkwood Survivors Club, had apparently lost all self control. After making obscene remarks at the breakfast table about what he would like to do to his former magical paramour, he had taken to wandering up and down the drive shouting expletives. Something else to faze the Hawkwood staff when Gareth Knight was around!

This however was where Dolores came into her own. She took him aside for a heart to heart talk and a motherly shoulder to cry on. In the meantime, however, I needed to get on with the work in hand. I therefore decided to leave the Western position open, and unexpectedly found it more of an advantage than a handicap, for it felt that the faery powers evoked had a gate through which they could flow unimpeded out into the world.

The second event of the day was a full dress ritual, the rehearsal for which we had conducted the previous day, as witnessed by the little Neolithic maiden. Entitled *The Maze Dance of Merlin,* and tacitly based upon the magical dynamics of a remarkable ballad *The Weaver's Song* by Bob Stewart, I wrote it to celebrate the release of Merlin from his legendary imprisonment – a tradition which to my mind was largely misunderstood. Even Tennyson had distorted it into the tale of a besotted old man outwitted by the wiles of an unscrupulous faery, tired of his attentions.

My view was based upon a powerful contact I had received at an inner gateway where oak and ash and thorn had come together in fields near where I live. It seemed that the tale of the enchantment of Merlin by Nimué was at root a great cosmic myth of the star wizard and the earth maiden, in which were compressed the history and destiny of the planet and all the lives upon it. According to this source, Merlin was the archetypal wizard or master of the wisdom whose function is to guide human evolution and establish patterns of civilisation. He thus appeared at various moments to guide, warn or advise or take action at critical points – such as at the birth of Arthur or the endowment of the Round Table.

Part way through the story, he disappears, apparently enchanted by a faery woman. He is never seen again, though there are reports of some who say they have heard his voice in the forest, imprisoned in an invisible tower.

"What will become of the human children, deserted by Merlin in his fascination for Nimué?" I asked at the hawthorn gate.

"When Nimué, the earth maiden has learned all the star lore of Merlin, and Merlin has learned the earth lore of Nimué, then the two will go hand in hand in a cosmic marriage to the stars taking the children of earth with them," came the answer. With this came a strong image of the dark mantled Merlin in his robe and tall hat of stars, and the young floral and earthly maiden simply clad in the natural colours of earth.

So to my mind, not only was Merlin's original withdrawal into the Earth intentional and to good purpose, but also the time had come for the forces he represented to be celebrated in the wider world again.

The evocation of Merlin coming out of a hawthorn tower and treading out a spiral dance was a memorable experience for me, and one that others found extremely moving. I felt a valid and powerful contact had been made and a major work been completed.

Alan Richardson, an informed and down to earth esoteric commentator and biographer, was present, and in his book *Spirit of the Stones,* described his own experience:

Gareth Knight is a magician. He has been practising High Magic of an essentially Christian kind for an exceedingly long time, now. His many books on the Qabalah, on Ritual Magic, Merlin and the Holy Grail will prove in the decades to come to have had a subtler and far greater impact on the spiritual life of the late twentieth and early twenty-first centuries than current observers realise.

I first saw him working magic at the Hawkwood College in the mid-1980s. And during the rite, when under the full flow of the Merlin archetype, he looked at me. He looked right at me and into me, and through me. But it wasn't Gareth Knight from Essex behind his eyes. It was, I *knew*, the Merlin himself. The Merlin of Britain. And I saw forests and wild lands, and hidden glades, and forgotten worship, and felt the staggering sense of age, and Ages stretching backwards, and I was startled by the sense that this blunt being behind the mortal eyes was not quite human, or more than human, and that it somehow knew me, from a long time ago.

The whole performance was felt to be a great success, and culminated in the formal purification of all present with water and with fire, giving them an accolade with the sword and presenting them with a gemstone memento of Welsh jasper.

It also led on to some follow up work at the sacred site of Dinas Emrys where Bob Stewart experienced a contact that led to him organising a series of Merlin conferences in 1986 and beyond, a series of books and a unique Tarot set designed by him on the theme of Merlin.

And so we proceeded in the evening to the third, and somewhat risky, working – *The Mystery of the Moon Ark*. This was another ritual of release, but aimed at some ancient forces not quite so beneficent as Merlin.

The Moon Ark is a vessel of supreme purity. It looks like a luminous orb of milky light cupped in two hands, similar to the three phases of the moon: waxing, full and waning. A Grail like power, it can act like an energy transformer or blood purifier as a clearing house for psychic debris and can be meditated upon quite safely. Chaotic energies transferred into it may be purified and made usable again.

Such was the intention with regard to some of the ancient Atlantean forces that had been locked up under the ocean since the fall of the legendary continent. Nonetheless some seemed to have been seeping through from time to time to retrogressive effect – in effect a kind of communal "ghost" – a drag from the past. Possibly even the source of master race theories or religious fundamentalism of various persuasions.

Implicit in this was also the contacting of an extremely ancient sea goddess, typically depicted bare breasted and with double fish tail – called

The Moon Ark, as depicted in William Blake's Jerusalem, *1804 (top) and Jacob Bryant's* A New System of Mythology, *1776.*

by some Posula. She was perhaps the origin of many or even all mermaid legends or of fish or serpent tailed faery women that have come down to us in somewhat degraded form. With origins even before Atlantis she worked directly under the aegis of the Moon Ark, the sea cave of her origin being below the Moon Temple where the Moon Ark was housed.

Bizarre as some of this may sound, it was the consequence of considerable esoteric research by Roma and myself, with invaluable support from John and Caitlín Matthews in the few weeks running up to Hawkwood who had been providing me the details of some ancient and in some ways disquieting contacts they had been receiving.

The work in hand was to make contact with these ancient powers, to re-consecrate the submarine temple of the goddess and its link to the stars – typically the constellation of Corona Borealis – which should help restore order and balance and release some of the pent up Atlantean powers in an equilibrated manner.

At the same time it was not without risk and so I was moved to keep the bulk of those present well clear of the focus of the working, and had them ranged up at the back of the hall, in rows, more or less like an audience, looking on at the focus of operations which was toward the eastern end of the hall.

Here, seated at the east, I intended to work directly with Roma, who faced me at the central point, where otherwise an altar would be, in the traditional station for a pythoness. I placed three female officers immediately round us at south, north and west, to form a triangle of support, thus providing an extremely rigid psychic structure able to withstand very high pressure.

In the event, toward the end of the working, the circuits blew wide open to startling effect, causing many afterwards to say that it was the most upsetting rite in which they had ever taken part.

As the work proceeded I began to sense that something was not right with Dolores in the west, who had elected to arm herself with a strange looking staff. I asked her if all was well with her, at which she rose to her feet, apparently completely possessed.

Obviously she had been taken over again, this time by some dominating male figure, and evidently all was not well with *him*! He badly wanted to take over the show. After uttering a series of hardly coherent but obviously displeased remarks, Dolores turned and rushed down the hall and out through the door. Indeed had the guardian not thrown it open just in time she might well have crashed straight into it!

I closed the working and everyone left the hall, some, in a state of confusion, to rush outside and link arms around a tree. Others gathered to discuss what might have happened and try to interpret what the uninvited guest had said. It seemed to have been a confusing mélange of archetypal claims:

"I was a king who died in the forest, and spilt his blood on the chancel steps. I was killed at Agincourt. I was Harry's friend and he sent me to my death. I stood on a cliff and watched the pride of Spain's men go down. I brought the thorn to this land and planted my staff. I made a bridge without nails..."

There was a general feeling that something had gone wrong, although just precisely *what* was not easy to fathom. To my mind it had "gone wrong" with a purpose. One or two felt me rather callous in not attending too much to Dolores' condition at this point, having "given her all" for me. However it was not to me she had given her all but to some inner interloper. I also had other things on my mind as it occurred to me that the work was still only half done. Roma now came into her own and declared that we had to go back in, just the two of us, and finish it.

I have to say this was a daunting prospect that I would have given quite a lot to avoid. But Roma showed her true mettle, both in intuition and courage, as we went back into the hall, on our own, to go through it all again – contacting the ancient submarine sea goddess powers, building up the temple there, and aligning it to the stars. Our close friend Kurt sat outside on guard, and reported feeling great waves of power seeping out, as if the very waters of the Atlantic ocean were about to break through the door and inundate the place.

Some mooted the theory that the work was perhaps intended to have gone in two parts. Perhaps. Perhaps not. We can never be sure of all the inner dynamics in a situation like this.

Whether or not all had gone according to plan, Dolores later told the anthropologist Tanya Luhrmann that she felt that she had experienced an initiation into a higher grade of practice. Indeed after this event she withdrew from further Hawkwood meetings and began running her own at Runnings Park. A number of people were quite pleased at this development and duly attended both!

What we finally realised about this weekend as a whole was that ancient Atlantean powers, so beloved by occultists of a previous generation, need no longer be regarded as the root and power base of traditional wisdom. They could be sloughed off from the bottom, so to speak, to give way to a new foundation – one that was based on Celtic myth and legend. An impetus was thus given to the native traditions of Britain, and the power points to be found at ancient trackways and sites.

With this in mind a number of us felt called to go directly to the Uffington Horse complex, where a Celtic horse figure is carved in the chalk, and to visit Wayland's Smithy nearby, just along the ancient Ridgeway track, one of the oldest roads in England. Here, some powerful faery contacts were sensed, particularly of a kind of Green Roads patrol along the ancient ways, and a place was also found for the little Neolithic girl who had been released from Hawkwood on the Saturday evening, who seemed very happy to be accepted as a minor guardian and guide to the benevolent forces of the whole Uffington complex.

On the debit side, just to show that we had not been forgotten by the forces of misrule, our car was broken into and Roma's handbag stolen while we attended to these higher things so the weekend ended up with a visit to Faringdon police station. However, the powers of light finally restored the balance as the thief was eventually apprehended!

Further work developed out of all this later in the year when volunteers from the Hawkwood event, including Caitlín and John Matthews, Bob Stewart and members of my own group, gathered for an outdoor ritual meeting on Dinas Emrys in North Wales, where Bob Stewart confirmed a Merlin contact that led on to much else.

As after previous Hawkwood workings, some people found themselves contacted by beings or archetypes of one kind or another. One, which came to a leading member of my group, seemed some kind of priestess straight out of Atlantis. She no doubt intended to be quite helpful but tended to have her own ideas about how to go about it. This was based upon some kind of spider morality, as she offered to demonstrate how to deal with rivals and enemies by some species of kundalini magic, and to give instruction on ritual incantations for the binding of souls.

In the course of time she was persuaded that this might not be the best way to go about things in the modern world, of which she had so recently become aware. This episode, which was not entirely easy to cope with, was a practical example of how such contacts should be handled – not by passively allowing them to take over psychically, or impose their will with vastly outdated ideas, but gently and firmly to seek a way of mutual instruction and compromise.

Unfortunately we also had a vivid example of how not to go about such situations. A couple of people who were also members of the Hawkwood Survivors Club turned up at Wayland's Smithy, where they showed every evidence of having just formed a very close relationship. They later telephoned to say they needed to see me urgently, and could they come round to my house? When they arrived they put into my hands a large sealed envelope prominently inscribed *"These seals must only be broken in a sealed place."*

Not being too impressed by portentous occult strictures I took it straight up to my office to read there and then – and was not best pleased with the contents.

It was an account of their emotional relationship, which they reckoned to be of high esoteric significance. This would normally have been their business rather than mine except that they linked it up to aspects of my Hawkwood work – and even regarded themselves as surrogates for Roma and myself. At the recent Moon Ark ritual they considered that the heavy handed interloper who took over Dolores was no less than Merlin, who had thus deliberately broken up the working into parts so that the two of them could perform sex magic in their room at the same time that Roma and I were going through the work again in the hall.

Returning downstairs to express my distinct lack of enthusiasm for this interpretation of events, I discovered that the young lady had fallen into a trance, apparently taken over by some kind of Atlantean dominatrix, and was declaring imperiously that the place was now to be a chalice for her powers.

It is one thing to have one's ritual workings hijacked, quite another to have one's home and family invaded and imposed upon. So after advising them to focus more sensibly and responsibly upon this world rather than the antediluvian one, they were ushered to the door – the priestess still more or less breathing fire and her hapless companion somewhat embarrassed by it all.

He indeed wrote a few days later to apologise for their untoward behaviour and to thank us for our calming influence, promising to think again about their assumptions. This was not the last I was to hear of this couple however, who proceeded to compound things even further at a later Hawkwood, and served to point up how high levels of esoteric power can play havoc with even the most intelligent and well intentioned of people. And also, it seems, that some people never learn!

It seemed not entirely inappropriate that Dolores had presented me with a joke T-shirt at the commencement of this weekend, emblazed with ONE KNIGHT AT HAWKWOOD IS ENOUGH. A big laugh at the time, but one which in retrospect was more appropriate than many realised, and contained much wisdom!

18

Hellas and the flaming Door of Celtica

1984

The May 1983 Hawkwood event on the Mysteries of Isis was a major watershed in more ways than one. The most important element of the programme had been the ritual "freeing of Merlin", or rather a re-stimulation of the forces for which the great Archmage of the British Isles stood. At the same time it was the sloughing off of a stratum of primeval "Atlantean" dynamics to give place to a new foundation for the modern mysteries, rooted in Celtic myth and legend.

It seemed appropriate therefore to devote the 1984 event to the Celtic mysteries, under the title of *The Flaming Door*, in recognition of an important book written back in 1936, subtitled *the Mission of the Celtic Folk-Soul.* The author, Eleanor C. Merry, although a lady of independent mind, was much influenced by the teachings of Rudolf Steiner, and so it also seemed appropriate given the anthroposophical background of Hawkwood College itself.

There was a fair amount of preparatory work involved in all of this, in so far that the Mystery streams of Europe were a context for ancient Celtic traditions that led in turn toward the Mysteries of the Holy Grail. This involved a couple of weeks in Greece for Roma and me, picking up on some ancient contacts of our own, as well as revivifying a general inner link between Hellas and Albion.

I also felt it advisable to lay on an additional Hawkwood event in the December of 1983, under the title of *Inner Realities behind Material Existence* which aimed to provide a modicum of basic instruction on what magical ritual was all about and how best to conduct it. This event, insofar that it did not involve the deliberate evocation of Archetypal forces, went off quietly and efficiently, although an impressive synchronicity occurred when I concluded with a working using candles and mirrors. It so happened that the women of the anti-nuclear-weapon peace camp at Greenham Common had organised a demonstration featuring candles and mirrors at the same time. This had been completely unknown to me, so it seemed that, low key intentions or not, someone on the inner planes was pulling a few strings.

Our preliminary visit to Greece was at the invitation of Iamblichos – a Greek group that had trained itself along SOL lines but which now operated independently with SOL's blessing. One or two of its leading members were originally on the old Helios Course before it became SOL. They were now intent on translating *A Practical Guide to Qabalistic Symbolism* into Greek, which they followed up with *The Cosmic Doctrine* and *A History of White Magic.*

Their dedication was very high, to the extent of making no charge for admission to a public lecture I gave in Athens, despite the high cost of hiring a hall. This, being free, attracted a large audience and I gave it in English with one of the group translating sentence by sentence as I went on. I based my talk on *A History of White Magic* although it was only partway through that I realised that there might be some difficulty in getting some of it across as the Greeks had not experienced the Renaissance as we had.

However, this was the least of my concerns as I was only too pleased that we had not all been run in by the police, for one of the group had been arrested in the night for fly posting notices of the coming event. What concerned me particularly was that European elections were about to take place which featured a great poster of the prime minister Andreas Papandreou holding out his hand in a histrionic gesture. Our intrepid fly poster had been unable to resist the temptation to paste the details of my lecture into this outstretched hand as if it were endorsed by government support!

The group were unstinting in their efforts to entertain us and transport us to the main esoteric sites, giving us the benefit of a somewhat battered car (all cars were battered in Greece in those days) which nonetheless did not prevent us from being booked for speeding. The rest of the group tended to follow along in a convoy of two wheeled machines, generally scooters for the ladies and high powered motorcycles for the men, which were sometimes ridden three up, without crash helmets, and irrespective of the amount of retsina consumed.

There were several significant high points in our visits to the sites. It was still possible at this time to visit the remains of the cell where Socrates was administered the hemlock as movingly described in Plato's *Phaedo*, which had recently been discovered by American archaeologists. Roma found a dried snake skin nearby which she scattered on the site. His ambiance was also strongly felt near the Acropolis, where he used to speak, and again at the Theatre of Dionysus where a fallen old Silenas type of statue brought him to mind.

We both had a remarkable feeling of *déjà vu* at the Agora, the civic centre and market place of ancient Athens, which seemed greatly familiar

to both of us, and where, to the surprise of our guides, we were able to locate the joint temple of Hephaistos/Athene, seemingly by ancient memory. This contact was later to prove of considerable significance back at Hawkwood the following year.

It would be tedious to recount all the major and minor contacts that we made at the various sites, of an unexpected Asclepian contact at the Temple of Poseidon at Sounion, or of a sustained Merlin contact at the Temple of Apollo at Delphi and at the little visited Stadium right at the top. Again in an unexpected appearance at the lesser known oracular site of Triphonium, where we were led to blow into a crevice in the rocks as a means of reawakening very ancient Mysteries represented in part by a group of water nymphs in a dried up pool. Here Roma was nudged into looking into a crevice in the rocks, to find a silver bracelet.

The climax for me of the whole trip seemed to be at Mycenae, site of the ancient House of Atreus, with its lion gates and colossal sophisticated bronze age architecture built when even Stonehenge was young. Close by, at a peak where a rowan tree grew near a thorn I was moved to clasp the rowan to make contact through its physical and etheric roots via all the thorn and rowan trees of Albion and Hellas. As I did this a sudden wind sprang up physically around me, and feeling surrounded by air and other elementals and I was urged to run down the mountainside toward a special sacred spot, only to find myself suddenly dropped by the elementals who were guiding my feet, and so fell, badly spraining my ankle and breaking blood vessels in my foot. The sudden pain seemed to act as a seal to the union of the forces. Here I planted one of the red Welsh jasper stones left over from the previous Hawkwood.

I was able to continue walking that day, but my foot later swelled so badly I was incapacitated for the rest of trip, by which time no less than three of us were limping for one reason or another. I was reminded of a species of ritual laming I suffered immediately after attempting my own first Qabalistic pathworking at the foundation of my small house group on leaving the Society of the Inner Light. Ostensibly it was the result of a bad mosquito bite but it also marked an important initiatory beginning with resonance to the lamed god evoked in that sequence. It drew attention too to an important link with Asclepios (also a lamed god) who showed up again strongly at his major centre of Epidauros. Oddly enough this phenomenon was to afflict me for a third time many years later on my first visit to Troyes in search of contacts with the Arthurian romancer Chrétien de Troyes, the subject of my book *The Faery Gates of Avalon*.

In addition to its healing sanctuaries sacred to Asclepios, I was particularly attracted to Epidauros on account of its ancient theatre, still in occasional use, not least for an evocative modern rendering of the Oresteian trilogy, part of which I later utilised to good effect in a workshop in New York. Its acoustics are so remarkable that it is possible to whisper in the centre of the open stage and be heard anywhere in the vast open air auditorium.

Ancient Greek tragedies were always accompanied by farce, which tend in modern times to be acted out by the troops of tourists who seem to be compelled to enact the worst of nationalist sentiments in them. It was one thing to be assailed by a group of Spaniards raucously singing *Viva España* centre stage, but my toes curled in embarrassment when a lone English lady decided to sing *Land of Hope and Glory*, egged on by an American friend, who bizarrely remarked, apparently quite sincerely, *"How appropriate!"*

I was rather thankful that my Greek friend Notis was not present, who distinguished himself at Delphi by telling the character and fortune of a party of German tourists who admonished him for stepping over a public barrier. "Whose xxxxxx country do they think this is?" is the most polite way of reporting his sentiments.

The final important site for powerful memories was Eleusis, sacred to the ancient mysteries of Demeter and Persephone. The sacred way of which was instantly recognised by Roma, whilst one of the bas-reliefs of initiation taken from this site gave off hair raising vibes to me in the National Museum at Athens. Here at Eleusis I came upon the strongest Demeter contact I have ever experienced at a natural throne-like place up a flight of steps, and later I found our Greek companions gazing in wonderment at Roma, who had wandered off to sit at this same point where in her white dress she seemed an utter personification of a Greek goddess – not only in superficial appearance but in the charisma that shone about her. It was a place full of beautiful ancient forces and memories, and I was reminded of a picture postcard I had long treasured (of the Demeter of Knidos) that seemed to me to encapsulate the spirit of Dion Fortune. An opinion that was confirmed by Arthur Chichester of the Society of the Inner Light who had once closely worked with her.

So all in all, our visit to Greece was a time of renewing deep ancient contacts for Roma and myself and an inkling that our present partnership probably had its origins at Delphi at the time it was sacked by the Celts in 279 B.C. More immediately, although we did not yet realise it, it was a preparation for elements of the Hawkwood meeting of May 1984 on *The Flaming Door*.

Eleanor C. Merry's book had expressed what she saw as a growing interest in the native traditions of the British Isles along with the belief that they would form the foundation for the Mysteries of the future. The gist of which could be summed up in a phrase from her final chapter: *"The Celtic Mysteries of old are the signature of our immortality. They are a ladder upon which the Christian faith may mount to the stars."*

On the Friday evening and Saturday morning I followed her line by outlining the context of the Celtic Mysteries in the four Mystery streams in Europe, along with the roots and then the development of the Celtic Mysteries, leading up in the afternoon to the modern heritage of the Celtic Mysteries in the Holy Grail Tradition.

Following this preparation the main purpose of the weekend was expressed in two practical workings. On the Saturday evening a guided meditation by Roma on *The Crystal Boat*, which was in some respects a Celtic halfway house between the latter day Holy Grail traditions and the ancient Moon Ark that featured in the previous year's Mysteries of Isis.

There did indeed remain a certain element of ancient or interloping forces at this point in the proceedings. In the middle of Roma's working Bob Stewart became aware of a tall presence standing behind him who demanded *"Where is the woman?"*

And on asking what woman was meant, the reply came *"The Woman of Sorrows."*

Bob now realised it was Dolores who was being sought, whose name means "sorrow", and who had opened last year's proceedings with *The Sorrows of Isis*, and later been overshadowed by the interloping figure. Upon making this connection he felt a ridiculous urge to stand and grow very tall, which was really the last straw as far as he was concerned, having been plagued with vaguely menacing astral interference since arriving at Hawkwood. Rather than allow himself to be "taken over" he told the entity to clear off in no uncertain manner, which it promptly did, although not until after similarly approaching and being rejected by Caitlín Matthews.

At this crucial point Roma departed from her script to pick up on a spontaneous vision of a triangle of power between a Smith, a Child of Light, and a Rose and Lily Wand, at which Bob felt as if a bag had suddenly been lifted from his head. At the previous year's event he had received a firm instruction to "seek the Mysterious Abbey and enter therein" and later was given a ritual by those in the Abbey to awaken the Smith at Wayland's Smithy. This had apparently been very successful, but now the appearance of a Child born out of the Earth was a new and significant development.

Marian Green, doyenne of the Green Circle, also found Roma's working, and especially her digression, to be very important. In her eyes it managed to bring together a whole set of images, symbols and pieces of the complex Celtic maze of myths which had long been the basis of her own studies. Not only did it focus some of the patterns of the past but clearly showed the direction for future study, with a great deal of work still to do on the Smith and the Child, who must have come forth from the blending of two streams, the red and the white, within the heat of the forge. The image of the Smith had also recently cropped up in a new set of Tarot cards from the USA – as the maker of things anew, the forger in the fires of experience, an image in which could be found a unity of all alchemical work.

With this influx of realisations it seemed to me that an inner link between Hellas and Albion had been forged or renewed.

This set the tone for a full scale ritual on *The Transformations of the Grail* which we rehearsed and performed on the Sunday.

As Marian Green remarked, the Sunday rite was extremely potent too, for it again brought together much of the legends from Bran to Arthur, along with the Irish and the Welsh Celtic. In this respect the work was a melding of pagan and Christian mystical traditions – and as was later remarked, to general approval: *"it was extraordinary that so many people of differing beliefs and 'ways' could come together as one to perform a given piece of work without any feeling of dissension."*

In keeping with the Celtic traditions of the apple orchard I concluded the work by giving an apple to each person present. As I did so, I felt as if I were sowing the seeds for many apple orchards. Some ate them there and then, others gave them to the horses in the adjoining field, others kept them to try to preserve and germinate the seeds or for other ritual purposes – each apple core indeed reveals a pentagram when cut crosswise.

As John Matthews remarked, the meeting seemed to have been a quiet one on the surface (which indeed is how things should be in well regulated magical work!) but was not without its more energising side (which is also the principal aim and effect of responsible magical ritual.)

He went on to say: *The ritual on Sunday was splendid, and light and full of good things. The apple imagery was very apt to us, as I think it was to everyone. I think when you said 'I seem to be planting many orchards' you spoke truer than you knew. Many seeds will blossom forth from that beginning. The son of Merlin's apple trees is strong in my mind as I write, and after a weekend in Glastonbury I can feel the beginning of many new things awakening with the earth. This is truly an amazing time in which to live! Nor can I forget that we travelled home from Stroud in a train pulled by an engine called Albion...*

Indeed the weekend may well have sparked the idea for a highly readable and practical helpful book *The Grail Seekers Companion* by Marian Green and John Matthews, published in 1986. The weekend seemed of major importance to R. J. Stewart as well, who seemed to undergo a quite harrowing initiatory experience during the main ritual, that caused him to arrive home very weak and exhausted yet convinced that it had been very successful. I like to think it may have helped to initiate the important books and seminars on Merlin that followed shortly after – *The Mystic Life of Merlin* and *The Prophetic Vision of Merlin* in 1986, the series of Merlin conferences from 1986, followed by *The Merlin Tarot* in 1988 and *The Way of Merlin* in 1991.

It thus appeared that we had worked through a great deal of turmoil and turbulence over the past six years of Hawkwood events and all was set fair to continue on the foundations we had laid.

19

Drake and the Dawn Treader
1985

For the Hawkwood of May 1985 I turned to the works of C. S. Lewis whose popular theology books had been a great help to me in my discussions with Tony Duncan. Apart from this, from reading his science fiction trilogy *Voyage to Venus, Out of the Silent Planet* and *That Hideous Strength*, and his set of books for children *The Chronicles of Narnia*, I was absolutely convinced he must be a closet occultist. At any rate by a close analysis of his work I now intended to find out for sure.

In the event, it turned out I was wrong! Despite being attracted to the occult in his youth he had been badly frightened off it by the psychological disintegration of an elderly acquaintance through an unholy mixture of alcohol and spiritualism. Nonetheless, he remained fascinated by the subject, if at arm's length, and absorbed a great deal of knowledge about it from his friends, the occult novelist and Rosicrucian mystic Charles Williams, and Owen Barfield, a keen advocate of the teachings of Rudolf Steiner. He also shared a deep and long standing interest in myth and legend with his Oxford colleague J. R. R. Tolkien.

The weekend began somewhat disconcertingly when I was confronted after the first lecture by an elderly lady who had enrolled on the course assuming it to be a more conventional devotional Christian weekend. Some people just do not read the big print, let alone the small print!

"*I saw the name C. S. Lewis,*" she said, "*and felt I just had to come!*" To give her her due, she struggled gamely on through most of the sessions, which included three powerful magical workings, but it did point up the problem of holding public meetings such as mine at Hawkwood – apart from difficulties that came from psychics out of their depth.

I based each magical working, quite loosely, on one of the novels of C. S. Lewis. I developed the first from Lewis' science fiction novel *That Hideous Strength*, a story of the physical resurrection of Merlin to fight against powers of evil in the modern world. In my hands it became an evocation of planetary powers and the elevation of the Planetary Being from a "dark planet" to a sanctified one through the mediation of Merlin as a star walking Lord of Light.

And the third magical working was developed in part from the final

Narnia story, *The Last Battle,* where the children and all their animal and otherworldly companions elect to go "further out and further in" in planetary terms. This developed into a moving spiritual "mass" of the seven continents, a balancing and dedication of the forces of the national angels and those whom they govern, the Principalities and Powers world wide.

However, the weekend was most memorable for the second of the magical workings, on the Sunday evening. This was originally inspired by Lewis' *The Voyage of the Dawn Treader* in which the children embark on an initiatory sea journey by entering a picture hanging on the wall of their magician uncle's house – an invitation to directed visualisation if ever there was one! But for reasons which are difficult to explain it developed into an evocation of Tudor national archetypes of royalty (via the Virgin Queen, Elizabeth I), magicianship (Dr. John Dee), and world discovery, (Sir Francis Drake as circumnavigator of the globe).

Their relevance to Hawkwood started to become apparent about a week before the event when John Matthews sent me some fascinating material that was coming through from a contact who was ostensibly one of Drake's "powder boys", Tom Hailes. The lad seemed uncertain of much that he relayed – as it came from a much more powerful source beyond his own knowledge. Some was simply presented to John in pictures that had to be "translated back" into modern speech and concepts.

> They say that Drake's Drum resounds in the world again, for in the times that are coming he, like Arthur before him, will be needed. The ancient trio of Arthur-Guinevere balanced by Merlin form a triangle. They are felt in the later images of Elizabeth I, Drake and John Dee. Drake is important because he was a discoverer and because it is from the sea that the new energies will come – flowing, they say, from the gates of Atlantis… For when Atlantis was to be sunk under the seas, a great store of energy was "sealed " in a special "house" and when the continent sank it sank also – but a time was set for it to open again and the resources it contained to flood out once more upon the world at a time when they were needed. This may take the form of a new energy source – actually a rediscovery of the force which was ours long since. The beating of the Drum, which will be heard by many, will be the signal for this.

Parts of this impinged strongly on the Moon Ark material of the year before.

> *The voyages of discovery which were made by Drake form a pattern in the grid of the world.* He understood that the energies of the earth lay beneath the sea and that by passing across them he was able to channel the soul of

his own place to that of other lands... The interfacing of the mighty angelic hierarchies with those of Atlantis form a new matrix in which the globe becomes a natural torch for all the heavens... the world is now turning to a new phase and certain important points of influence will be felt, raying out like a star from the polar regions. *Look for the ways of our great captain and you will see how the pattern fits...*

The key to this was in the first and last sentences that I have italicised above. And with it there came an intuitive realisation on how this pattern might be explored and presented in a magically effective manner.

There was no need to dress up and have all the accoutrements of a full scale ritual, but as with the earlier Arthurian archetypal contacts of 1981, simply to evoke, in the semi-dark, the outline of Drake's ship, as once the Round Table had been described. Although for this occasion I stationed a trusted member of my group at each of the four quarters, Philip to represent Dee at the prow in the west, Jenny to represent Queen Elizabeth to port in the south, Kurt to represent Drake to starboard in the north, with myself as pilot in the east.

The set up demonstrated that powerful magic could be done with the minimum of resources. It simply needed the appropriate basic elements to provide a framework for the creative imagination of the participants (who were of course present on the inner as well as the outer plane.)

The power of this could act in quite bizarre and unexpected ways. For instance, when Kurt and I laid out the mirrors and candles to outline the ship some time before the event, it felt as if the floor of the hall was rocking, just like a ship at sea. It was indeed quite difficult for us to keep our feet! Obviously there was no such physical motion in the hall itself, it was all imagination – projected upon us by the forces that were being evoked.

So when sceptics say that magic is simply "all imagination" they are of course correct. Where they fall short is to assume that imagination is simply subjective and illusory. It is real enough on its own level – with effects on other levels beside – believe me!

The anthropologist Tanya Luhrmann happened to be present on this occasion, and wrote it up for her doctoral thesis, later embellished and published in 1989 as *Persuasions of the Witch's Craft*. We therefore have a record of events from her perspective from the moment I came in to conduct the work:

Knight lit a candle near him, at the stern, he said, and then one at the equivalents of starboard, port and prow, setting the candles down abruptly on square mirrors. Then he took his seat, and told us in detail the story of Drake's voyage, of his trip around Cape Horn, and his discovery of passes that no Western man had ever known. He described Drake's trip up western North America, where ice had caked the mast-head and forced him back along the California coast. Drake and his shipmates were treated as gods when they landed, he said, and they named the land "the new Albion", and put a brass plaque upon a tree with a sixpence behind it to dedicate it to the Queen.

Knight continued in this way for perhaps half an hour, the listeners sitting, eyes shut, in the dark. At the end, when he had spoken of Drake's death at sea, and the solemn burial, he read Newbolt's chestnut about Drake's drum: "Take my drum to England / Hang it by the shore / Strike it when your powder's running low." After a short silence he stood up, walked across the room, and beat a furious drumroll from the covered instrument. He drew the sword from the scabbard that was lying on the table (he had spoken of swords earlier, of Elizabeth knighting Drake, Dee hovering in the background) and held the sword aloft, saying "Let the sword that was broken be mended here on earth anew". He replaced the sword on the table, resumed his seat, and faced us. There was a short silence. Then, in a throaty voice, he said, "Ye can open the door, Mr Dunbar, and let 'em all ashore."

"What was happening in this ritual?" Dr Luhrmann goes on to ask. And well she might! Although I doubt if anyone present, including myself, could give a complete answer to that question.

The hoarse voice at the end was no play acting on my part. It was as if I were overshadowed, at the very least, by the figure of Drake himself. Although it is important to distinguish between effecting a strong inner contact and maintaining conscious control, and falling into complete domination or possession by it.

Once again, as in previous workings, the Archetypes evoked tended to hang about for a week or two, offering advice or asking questions – and in the case of Drake – who I think thought me a bit of a wimp – causing me to drive my car with more than accustomed verve!

I went on record at the time as saying that this ritual, and indeed weekend, was one of the highlights of my magical career and so it seemed at the time, and that all was set fair for the Hawkwood events to go on from strength to strength. But events of the following year would show that all might not be plain sailing. As we headed into deeper waters we would have to contend with heavy ocean swell and sudden squalls.

20

The Fellowship of the Valar
1986

Having done so well with the works of C. S. Lewis in 1985 it seemed appropriate to base the May 1986 Hawkwood on the work of his close friend J. R. R. Tolkien. Tolkien needs no introduction to most because of the remarkable success of his trilogy *The Lord of the Rings*, both as a book and subsequently as a phenomenal event in world cinema. His more significant work however, was to be found in the source material for it, much of it published posthumously as *The Silmarillion*.

Tolkien did no less than construct his own mythology and body of legend from a vast store of Anglo-Saxon and other early literature, but his apparent neo-paganism was entirely compatible with his deep Christian faith. From this body of private myth and legend he drew stories of many different kinds, including a creation cycle, where the Creator of all is called Ilúvatar, whose body of sub-creators, the Valar, are easily identifiable as either archangels or pagan gods, according to taste.

Indeed in a formal ritual setting I invoked not the traditional archangels of the quarters or their pagan god equivalents but relevant Valar (or shining ones) drawn from Tolkien's imagination. The consequence was perfectly satisfactory, which confirmed to my mind that intention is at least as important as form in magical work. In short, that it pertains to a creative art more than to the traditional repetition of medieval formulae.

The main and final working of the weekend was to build a rainbow bridge to the legendary Islands of the West, so that a form of reconciliation and cooperation could begin between the human and the elven worlds. The bridge was opened, in much the same fashion as the calling of Arthur in 1981, by the blowing of a horn. This indeed did seem to have the desired effect, although eliciting different reactions and personal challenges.

As one report has it: *When the Undying Shore was built, the magnetic force emanating from it was so strong that it was almost impossible not to let go and cross over the bridge and disappear into that golden land for ever. It would have been so easy, and it took a definite act of will to create the cords of restraint.*

Another: *As I looked to the West, to that point of star light, certainly a wisp of something gradually formed from that star, across the sea to my feet. I felt an urge to walk onto that bridge but 'nerves' got the better of me – but the desire was there. However, the star seemed to get larger as a wide 'halo' formed and this formed into a number of beings that seemed to wrap themselves round the star. One of them turned and looked, and then extended his hand right across the bridge – I reached out, took hold, and was gently taken across. The beings were working on some design, but I knew that I was only there by grace and that I had very soon to return. I thanked them and took my leave and as I stood on the shore the arm withdrew but the bridge remained.*

Whilst another: *I realised how important one's own 'Shire' is. I didn't even wish to cross the rainbow bridge – though I was happy to welcome any who crossed it to my side! I realised that in a way the 'immortals' have a different relationship with Earth than man. Man knows he must one day die and leave behind these things which he loves; what he calls beauty; what he calls home. Because of that every day is magnified, every beauty seen with greater clarity.*

A number also felt afterwards that the contact with 'elven' beings was still near, if they wanted to take advantage of it.

However, the weekend had a sting in its tail, the reasons for which remain debatable. One of our regular stalwarts at the Hawkwood weekends decided to turn up with a facsimile of the notorious Ring – the one that caused so much trouble in *The Lord of the Rings* trilogy and had cost so much to destroy. He had apparently had it specially made for the occasion, and was showing it around as an amusing curiosity.

I did not feel too happy about this. Having a replica made of an object of such potential evil for a bit of light hearted frisson at Hawkwood did not seem to me very helpful. We were not just playing fantasy games, but were in a magical environment where any symbolism evoking an imaginative and emotional reaction could act as a magnet for inner forces that felt attracted to it. The presence of "One Ring to rule them all" – thus seemed not best calculated to keep the forces of misrule from the door.

However, faced with the situation, I felt the best I could do would be to incorporate it into the final working, passing it around the group, each person present formally eschewing its power. Indeed the "ring bearer" had also brought along a replica of one of the eagles of Manwë, which was certainly a force for good, and to which the ring was now attached. So far, so good.

However, an indication of there being something untoward came a few hours prior to the working, when I was informed that some kind of sub-group activity was being set afoot. It turned out that at the root of it was the young lady who had laid on such a spectacular private show as an Atlantean priestess at my house after the 1983 Hawkwood. During the afternoon she had fallen into a state of semi collapse, apparently because of the presence of an inner plane contact of hers whom she referred to as "the Companion". She felt it her duty to represent this character in the work ahead and approached a few others to support her in this cause.

I was not best pleased with this turn of events, and could find time only to have a brief, slightly strained, conversation with those immediately concerned, repeating my general admonition about the unacceptability of organising sub-groups in ritual conditions. I did indeed have half a mind to cancel the work ahead, but was loth to do so as the intended ritual was an important one, for which the whole weekend had been heading. Nor did I want to bar anyone from attending, which would have caused ripples of resentment and concern, disrupting the carefully prepared atmosphere.

I carried on with the working anyway, which was largely unscripted, though I discreetly kept the power levels down commensurate with maintaining its effectiveness. All seemed to pass off well, as the above reports testify, but immediately after the weekend the full brunt of unbalanced force broke forth. It would be tedious to go into details but many harsh words and accusations and denials flew back and forth about the validity of this inner "Companion" which our friend had felt possessed by, and who had in spite of my strictures spent time "beaming" the forces of the ritual to another centre dear to her heart.

This might have been well intentioned, but apart from the bad esoteric manners and attempted hijacking of the work, I was more concerned about the nature of these inner plane beings who showed an inclination to take over passively psychic people and use them for their own purposes. Not that such powers were necessarily evil. They might have been highly motivated according to their lights, but their methods, in my book, were desperately out of date, and insufferably high handed. In short, typically "Atlantean" in the worst possible sense.

However, whatever the cause, as reports came in I discovered that others had been the butt of unpleasant experiences at this Hawkwood weekend. This included bouts of depression and psychological malaise, even a case of physical injury, and a new member of my group, a young Canadian, whom we had initiated this weekend in a private ceremony apart from the main events, suffered something of a kickback for some time to come.

One question now came to mind. Was all this a consequence of the presence of the facsimile of the Ring? The intentions had apparently been high of the one who brought it, seeing it possibly as a symbol of redemption for all that it had once stood for. Maybe. But it seemed to need handling with a long spoon! In the end he became increasingly unhappy about it and, at my suggestion, it was smashed up and thrown into running water – perhaps appropriately, the River Isis!

Whatever the issues behind all of this, what came over loud and clear was the truth of the old adage that, in terms of esoteric hygiene, it is essential that "all be of one mind in one place." And when it comes to high powered work, "near enough" in this respect is simply not good enough. Perhaps indeed this was an indication that the levels of power that had come to characterise the Hawkwood events were now self-defeating. My immediate reaction was that the public Hawkwoods as currently run would have to come to an end. It had been a fascinating experiment in bringing magic out into an open arena, but the power generated had reached such a pitch that it was becoming too much to handle safely.

Nonetheless some positive elements did develop from the occasion. An individual named Michael Beechey who had been at the event was recommended to contact me on the grounds that he claimed to have been in contact with Tolkien elves to the point of their wishing to set up some kind of organisation.

He was indeed so much into the Tolkien world that his first letters to me were written in elven script! They transliterated well enough into English but it was a labour I could well do without, so I prevailed upon him to modify his enthusiasm in this respect.

On the face of it this looked like the work of an unbalanced nerd who sought escape from life in fantasy fiction. However, there was a sense of quality behind the façade, and so with a handful of trusted associates I set about evaluating what was coming to hand. Opinions varied. The most negative felt that it came from someone "mad, bad and dangerous to know" whilst others were cautiously sympathetic, but felt no wish to get involved themselves. However, I set out with a panel of three experienced colleagues to look into it all and see where it might lead.

The proposal was to set up a loose organisation entitled the Fellowship of the Valar, featuring a set of meditations and rituals for common use, the long term aim being the establishment of seven groups of seven people each of whom had a personal dedicated crystal (or *palentír*) that was dedicated to one of the Valar – that is to say the equivalent of an archangelic or traditional god form. Each group of seven (or "Star") would have a group stone, or Nienna stone, to which the personal stones would be attuned, and these Nienna stones to each other.

A system of individual rituals were in effect simple ceremonies of dedication that opened up to a series of path workings that eventually gave entry to the next level (or traditional "grade") of "Flames of the Stars of Varda". Beyond that it was presumed a similar system would operate giving access to a third grade, that of the "High Airs and Winds of Manwë". All this added up to a standard pattern of esoteric grouping and grading. I saw no inherent difficulty in the material having a fictional source, for Tolkien obviously based his work on a valid base of general mythology. The remaining months of 1986 were spent evaluating all of this, to which end a private event was laid on at Hawkwood in October, which in effect became the first annual meeting of the Fellowship of the Valar.

A set of three rituals was deemed to be important, based upon events in *The Silmarillion:*
i)   a Rite of the Unmaking of the Oath of Fëanor;
ii) a Rite of Healing based on a pathworking to the Gardens of Lórien;
iii) an all inclusive Rite of Reconciliation.

The aim of the first of these was to take the heat out of the situation that had driven things to disaster when the Noldorian elf Fëanor had sworn an oath of implacable vengeance, the consequences of which had rattled on down through the ages. The creator of magical crystals filled with star light, he had made the Palentíri, or "seeing stones", and the three Silmarils filled with the living light of the Trees of the Valar. These most beautiful gems became a curse because their power and beauty were so ineffable that they corrupted even high spirits close to the throne of God, who desired them for themselves at any price. This was the start of the great conflict which was still being felt at the time of *The Lord of the Rings*.

The second rite, one of healing, was an evocation of Lórien, a domain named after one of the Valar, the Master of Dreams, that consisted of golden gardens in the Undying Lands where great spiritual beings came for physical and spiritual restoration of their powers, in the centre of which was a lake that contained an island of Este, the Healer.

It is important to point out that although we were dealing with imagery whose immediate provenance was in fantasy fiction, back of it all were profound metaphysical dynamics to be found in other mythopoeic, religious and legendary traditions.

With these elevated dynamics in mind I was prepared for possible trouble, but despite one or two minor technical difficulties that arose from inexperience, I was relieved to find how well the whole thing went off. The conclusion of my report of the meeting sums it up:

Certainly my general remembrance of this weekend will be considerable amazement at the way the Forces of Light dealt themselves a winning hand from the bottom of the pack! It would not be too much to say that this weekend was the culmination of the whole series of public Hawkwood meetings that have attracted so much attention over recent years. Fëanor's sword point in the candle flame marked the end of that phase. It remains to be seen what new beginnings bring. If all concerned can maintain the dedication and purity of motive demonstrated on this occasion then the possibilities for this group are high indeed.

Whilst a close colleague put it even more dramatically and succinctly:

I was impressed with the whole thing really. If they can keep their feet on the ground then this lot are going to be a force to be reckoned with. What a delight to be hoodwinked once again by the inner! You think you are going for a hike and then find you have taken a stronghold by marching in unopposed.

However, what also become apparent was that whatever the potential or the importance of the Fellowship of the Valar it was not an organisation that was going to be led by me, and by August it had become clear to me that my involvement was not intended to be permanent.

Although I was appropriately referred to by the elven powers as "the Instigator" of the group, this was also a perceptive summing up of what my whole occult life was about. I *started* things. What some have rather dramatically termed "an arsonist". Or as Dolores Ashcroft-Nowicki once prosaically put it – I prepared the ground and sowed the seed and then left someone else to hoe it!

Nonetheless there was plenty of new ground awaiting the sowing.

21

Inklings and Archetypes
1987-99

As a consequence of the Hawkwood events based upon C. S. Lewis and J. R. R. Tolkien in 1985 and 1986, John Matthews urged me to follow up with a book, to include their close friends Charles Williams and Owen Barfield. Thus was *The Magical World of the Inklings* conceived.

The Inklings were a small group of individuals, who each in their way set out to explore the myth making element in imaginative fiction. Their works made a profound impact on the contemporary world, and in my book I tried to show how each created a "magical world" which initiated the reader into hidden and powerful realms of the creative imagination.

However, to concentrate my mind on the quite intellectually demanding fictional and poetic work of Charles Williams it seemed no bad idea to devote a Hawkwood weekend to him and I set this up for August 1988, which in John Matthews' opinion was the most *spiritually* powerful one I had ever conducted.

For this most of the credit must go to Charles Williams himself, whose breadth of mind successfully covered both mystical and magical dynamics, in the context of a profound Christian belief. His magical interests tend to be played down by latter day enthusiasts of his work but he was a member of a magical fraternity run by A. E. Waite for a number of years, and the titles of his novels speak for themselves, *Shadows of Ecstasy, War in Heaven, Many Dimensions, The Place of the Lion, The Greater Trumps, Descent into Hell,* and *All Hallows Eve,* and are probably the most profound of any in the genre ever written.

His poetry, *Taliessin Through Logres* and *Region of the Summer Stars,* is rooted in Arthurian tradition, and although something of a challenge, for even T. S. Eliot described it as "difficult", it contains some highly original work on the Arthurian legend and the Holy Grail. To help me tackle this I enlisted the help of John Matthews, who was a poet and Grail expert in his own right.

I then wondered whether to run a Hawkwood weekend on Owen Barfield but decided against it, for it would rather have been like carrying coals to Newcastle. To lecture on a leading expert on the thought of Rudolf Steiner, at a college closely associated with Rudolf Steiner would, I thought, only lead to the audience being packed with Steiner enthusiasts who knew a great deal more about the subject than I did! However it seemed there was no escape from some kind of confrontation when I learned, somewhat to my disquiet, that the publishers had sent my manuscript to the last surviving Inkling, Owen Barfield, for review.

I need not have worried. He responded with the opinion "...*because of the combination of understanding and insight on which it is founded,* The Magical World of the Inklings *is more than outstanding. It is not in the same league with anything else I have come across.*" This was praise indeed from a man whom even C. S. Lewis rated as the "wisest and best" of his unofficial teachers.

The Magical World of the Inklings was published by Element Books towards the end of 1990 and was well received by academic as well as esoteric sources.

Not all esoteric activity at this time was workshop or lecture based. The main Hawkwood series had been in some respects an initiation and empowerment for me, insofar that I found myself particularly open to archetypal figures and forces. It was as if I had been contacted on to a certain level of the national subconsciousness or group soul where certain long standing complexes seethed away. My function seemed to be, in personal realisation, ritual work (either with my own group or other experienced operatives beyond it), or public articles and lectures, to give vent to these issues. A form of national psychotherapy perhaps, although not being directed by me. Other intelligences upon the inner called the shots. I merely followed them up. This worked in various ways and at various levels, sometimes crossing national boundaries, as in my trips to France and America.

The immediate period of 1987 through 1988 was particularly volatile in this respect, being tercentenary years of a time of particular national crisis, the execution of Mary Queen of Scots and the menace of the Spanish Armada which followed upon it. However, this was but a particularly obvious node, for the archetypal powers stretched over much of the Tudor and Stuart period, when it might be said that the consciousness and self awareness of a modern nation state was being formed.

I did not have to go in search of archetypal powers, rather they seemed to come in search of me! It would be tedious and indeed impossible to go into the detail of all the inner activity going on at this time but a few instances that come to mind may indicate some of the issues at hand.

One memorable focus of attention was High Cross. High Cross lies at the very centre of England, where the old Roman road, called Watling Street (now the A5) runs diagonally across country from south east to north west, and crosses the ancient Fosse Way that runs from south west to north east. Only a dilapidated monument marks the spot but it has a modern icon close by in the form of a radio tower, thus with a dual functional and symbolic role that Dr Dee would have found of absorbing interest.

A visit to Norwich brought awareness of the underground caverns below the city, so great that on one occasion a double-decker bus fell into one after some road subsidence. Here there was the remarkably powerful imagery of singing canaries coming from the depths, birds closely associated with the city, and flying skyward. The experience of such a vision beggars all attempts to explain it after the event.

East Anglia indeed revealed many spiritual power points. Not only in the site of the cell of Lady Julian of Norwich but the great "Milky Way" or star road to Walsingham with powerful dynamics in the replica of the Holy Sepulchre.

Another was at Sutton Hoo, the great Saxon ship burial site, and relics of Redwald, the local king who hedged his bets by embracing Christianity whilst hanging on to his pagan god affiliations too. Although not excavated until the late 1930s Dr Dee had got there first, and remains were found of his attempt to dig for buried treasure there – which indeed existed, although he was, for better or worse, a few yards off target.

Then attention focused on Westminster Abbey and its mysterious Cosmati Pavement, laid in 1268, upon which all coronations are enacted, and which claims to contain the mysteries of the creation of the universe. At the Vernal Equinox of 1989 when I first approached the abbey in search of this symbolic paving, Big Ben chimed noon, which seemed to have some kind of synchronous significance. The work developed over the year to culminate in a remarkably powerful series of visualisations where ancient royal personages sat at the quarters, including the throne that covers the Coronation Stone, to enact some rite of Sovereignty. In events such as this, one is not so much conducting a rite of one's own devising but being called to witness one that is conceived and played out by inner plane powers.

A similar occasion required the visualisation and tracing out of a great triangle that conjoined the abbeys of Winchester, Canterbury and Ely. Canterbury was a particularly powerful magnet, that on two or three occasions put in such an urgent call to me that I took an unexpected day off work to drive down and walk the interior of the abbey, and the site of the martyrdom of Thomas á Becket. While the great windows that commemorated the Battle of Britain also seemed to hold a great significance.

In 1991 a series of workshops I had given at Bath culminated in a powerful contact with a Roman Temple of Unitas. Looking for some reading material at my lodgings for the night, R. J. Stewart's latest book *The Way of Merlin* almost fell off the shelf into my hands and drew my attention to the importance of tree and well spring. So in the current workshop I suggested a lunch time visit to a massive chestnut tree that grew in a nearby square, where somewhat to my embarrassment my students spontaneously formed a ring round it, clasping its trunk, to the combined amazement and amusement of the assembled tourists. Our attention was then drawn to a strange circular structure built around a well, watched over by a volunteer lady guardian who used to swim there as a child and was trying to prevent its demolition. Its inscription also rang a few bells for me as being dedicated to Mary of Modena, wife of James II and direct ancestor of the Stuart claimants to the throne. This was not the end of it however, for the configuration later figured prominently in an inner image of a Temple of Unitas – a circular temple of seven pillars with a god allocated to each, and open at the top where doves could sit. The site being one where once all had been boggy beech forest where Bladud, an early Merlin figure, had traditionally been a swine herd.

This was followed in June by a London conference which also served as a promotional event for the publication of *The Aquarian Guide to Legendary London* where I had written about *Towers of Sound and Light*, combining many of the issues that were homing in on me at this time.

The principle of the city came to me as the expression of a cosmic pattern, rather after the fashion of Dion Fortune's *The Cosmic Doctrine*. First a crossways of two elements, a road and a river, causing a centre that is then ring fenced by a city wall or Ring-Pass-Not and then the pointing upward to the heavens of all the spires and towers of the little parish churches, of which there were very many in London.

Along with this came the significance of towers and of bells, and the esoteric powers of sound – which can be of considerable practical interest in the technicalities of bell manufacture – the dimensions of which affect the type of sound that goes out – and also the principle of change ringing – in which a mathematical combination is pursued throughout its entire course of possibilities. This is a phenomenon unique to Britain, as on the continent the practice is for carillons of bells that play tunes. All this seemed to have some connection with the mathematical researches and angelic tablets of Dr John Dee.

In pursuit of all this I found myself much concerned with St Mary le Bow, and other churches constructed by Wren after the Great Fire of London. And as part of the conference I was able to lay on a guided tour to a selection of his churches around St Paul's cathedral – St Martin's on Ludgate Hill, St Sepulchre opposite the Old Bailey, St Vedast's Foster Lane, St Mary Le Bow, St Mary Aldermary, St Nicholas Cole Abbey, St Benet Paul's Wharf, St Andrew by the Wardrobe, St Brides Fleet Street, in a clockwise circumambulation that ended in St Paul's cathedral itself at a power point marked by a brass grating directly under the midpoint of the dome and over the crypt.

There was some talk of Sir Christopher Wren being associated with a secret society of his time called the Fedeli. I do not know. It would not surprise me, for at about this time amongst the other archetypal contacts that seemed to be wanting to make their presence felt, was a contact that seemed like Wren himself. Not giving any messages but just as some kind of power in the background. Although one remarkable coincidence occurred when driving through Wiltshire, when I had the sudden urge to pull up at a little village and visit the church. The village was East Knoyle and turned out to be the birth place of Christopher Wren, where his father had been rector and he had lived the first four years of his life.

Another positive indication that came from this source was to attend the inaugural meeting of Kathleen Raine's Temenos Academy in September. I had enjoyed the occasional meeting with Kathleen since she first came down to attend my little house group in Tewkesbury back in the 1960s and visited her house where she astounded me with the depth of her scholarship – having not only read all the works of William Blake but all the books known to have been read by him, in their original editions, before presenting me with copies of her great two volume work on William Blake produced for the Mellon Foundation in America.

I considered her Temenos Academy to be somewhat above my head, albeit an important flag waver for the esoteric tradition in high academic circles. Nonetheless we had an intuitive level of understanding of each other, and she knew exactly what I meant when I told her that "Wren had sent me". I was in later years able to help out her Academy by putting some money her way via the Society of the Inner Light and even to give a couple of talks there.

Just prior to this, however, in August 1991 I had a remarkable experience at the celebrations marking the 1000th anniversary of the Battle of Maldon which is not far from where I live. In common with many such occasions a mock battle was staged between the Anglo-Saxons under the command of the local ealdorman Brythnoth and the invading Vikings. After due process of belabouring each other with makeshift weapons the field was left with a number of the fallen, at which, apparently in accustomed formula the commentator announced "Let the dead arise!" whereupon they did so and all trooped off. However, the land over which they had been fighting was the actual site of the original battle, and the announcer was a Welsh lady with a very evocative voice. Thus I found the hair on the back of my neck standing up as there were actual dead arising – as from the original battle.

I have no favoured theory by which to explain this. All I can record are my own impressions at the time, and if the conclusion is that I simply have a very suggestible and credulous imagination then so be it. However, I have been around long enough and undergone considerable training of myself and others in sorting the wheat from the chaff of subjective impressions to think that my inner perceptions were ringing true. So much so that I had little sleep that night, seemingly enwrapped in the regrets and feelings of guilt of Brythnoth himself for having lost the battle. However, the next morning when I attended a service at the local church to commemorate a memorial window, at which part of the service was conducted according to an ancient liturgy in Old English, I felt the passing on of Brythnoth and many others in relative peace. I was later to become involved with much work of a similar nature in connection with the battlefields of the 1st World War, but to have this kind of clearing up to do after a space of a thousand years of earthly time was hardly to be expected by any conventional theories of post mortem conditions.

By the mid 1990s I more or less called a halt to my workshop activities. Although there was a growing demand for elementary instruction I felt there were plenty of teachers who could meet this demand as well as me, and were probably more suitable for this kind of work. However I was willing to take part in the occasional conference that occurred in my own back yard, and two important ones laid on by American organisations came up in 1998 and 1999.

The first was under the auspices of the New York Open Center and took place at the University of Wales at Lampeter, on *The Grail, Arthurian Mysteries and the Grail Quest*. At an afternoon workshop I stirred up quite a powerful vortex with a thinly disguised ritual called *The Chess Game of Queenly Sovereignty*. In medieval times Jerusalem was regarded as the centre of the world, thus its sovereignty took on cosmic importance. Using the basis of the symbolic chess game that appears in Celtic legend, I applied some of the inner dynamics that might be applied to Queen Isabella of Jerusalem (1172-1205) and the four dynastic husbands of her short life. This represented a stage I had reached in my esoteric French studies that culminated twenty years later in my books *The Faery Gates of Avalon* and *Melusine of Lusignan and the Cult of the Faery Woman*.

A remarkable coincidence accompanied my talk to the whole company on the last day, 13th August, on the subject of *Faery Tradition, the Crusader Kingdoms & the Holy Grail*. A fair bit of my talk had covered Eleanor of Aquitaine and Rosamund Clifford, the wife and mistress respectively of Henry II, both historical characters about whom romantic legend had grown. There was considerable astonishment when pictures of these two ladies appeared on the front page of the *Guardian* newspaper that morning. It was a story connected with some artwork depicting them but it was certainly something of a rarity for 12th century characters to appear so prominently in the national press, and on this particular day. Again, one of those seemingly pointless synchronicities!

The following year, in May 1999, I spoke at a Conference on *Kabbalah and the English Esoteric Traditions* at the Ashmolean Museum, Oxford, sponsored by The Kabbalah Society of New York. I took as my subject *Kabbalah and the Occult Tradition*, and bearing in mind the predominantly Jewish audience took the opportunity to make some kind of apology for the way that we Gentile occultists had more or less moved in and taken over a Jewish mystical tradition and bent it to our own purposes. Each Sphere on the Tree of Life was originally a sacred space for the Emanation of the Most High God into which we had deposited a great deal of symbolic furniture for our own convenience. Nonetheless, the system worked, at least according to our own understanding and esoteric purposes. And this was really no more than Anthony Duncan had demonstrated at Hawkwood some twenty-six years before.

My presentation was very well received, for the audience covered a broad spectrum, although I inadvertently disillusioned some eager young Americans when asked about the origins of some native Craft traditions. Regrettably what I had to say was taken as a hint of cynicism in some quarters although it was nothing other than the unvarnished truth!

This had all come about when an American gentleman had written to me seeking information on the origins of an organisation to which he belonged that promulgated faery traditions. Their leader claimed that in a tour of England in the early 1960s he had met a woman called Margaret Lumley Brown at Glastonbury, who had initiated him into the witchcraft tradition. My enquirer sought to know the details of her "coven" and if Dion Fortune had been one of its members. In support of his enquiry he sent me some of the instruction papers issued to members of the group. As I read them I experienced a strong feeling of *déja vu* and realised I was reading articles from the first two issues of *New Dimensions* magazine!

As I have mentioned earlier, what had happened was that an American back packer of the time had happened to meet Margaret Lumley Brown and been given a couple of copies of the newly published magazine. That was the extent of the training and initiation. The knowledge papers consisted of an article written by her for the first issue, and a couple of articles on faery tales by my old colleague David Williams, a former Helios associate and later Warden of the Society of the Inner Light.

However, over the years a thriving group had apparently developed in America on the strength of it. I simply told the assembled company that there was nothing much wrong with this, and that a great deal of material had been composed by the likes of Gerald Gardner, Doreen Valiente and other revivalists of the time, but was none the worse for not being of ancient origin. Professor Ronald Hutton of Bristol University has since amply demonstrated exactly this in *The Triumph of the Moon – a History of Modern Pagan Witchcraft* (1999), an important contribution to the study of neo-pagan religious thought and belief, even if, in my view, he has not got his assessment of Dion Fortune's significance and development quite right.

Anyhow, with regard to the slightly disillusioned young Americans, when all the chips are down there is greater merit in accepting things as they are than investing them with glamour.

Glamour may be a useful veneer at a certain stage of the game but not when case hardened into self-deception.

22

Voyaging West
1988-89

Since the Hawkwood "Drake" event of 1985 national archetypes involving "voyages west" came very much to the fore, particularly relating to the colonisation of the eastern seaboard of north America. This extended from Dr John Dee's efforts to find a northwest passage to the Orient via Canada, to Sir Walter Raleigh's foundation of the Virginia Company and later search for Eldorado. Then the Tolkien based event of 1986 emphasised a more mythopoeic element in the history of the Far Havens of the Elves and the tradition of Númenor, in many respects a version of the Atlantis tradition, roots of which had been touched as far back as 1983.

Something of this pressure, felt by a number of us, was back of a December 1986 Hawkwood weekend run by R. J. Stewart, Caitlín and John Matthews and myself on the subject of voyaging. It was in keeping with all of this that I chose to talk about John Dee at the second Merlin conference of June 1987, seeing him as an Elizabethan Merlin.

Although John Dee has tended to be regarded in latter days as a somewhat foolish and superstitious old man in view of his esoteric experiments with Edward Kelley, and the much abused Angelic Tablets, he was, on the contrary a man of great brilliance and dedication, and from my inner experience seemed to maintain a powerful presence when he had a mind to. Not that I ever received any detailed verbal communications in this respect but it was felt as a steady intuitive pressure to research certain topics, go to certain places, or to draw attention to his importance, as in the Merlin conference. And at one or two workshops I provided an empty chair for him.

Oddly enough, although I did not realise it at the time, in the early days of my association with W. E. Butler, Ernest had remarked that psychically he was aware of a Tudor gentleman associated with me, who in an effort to communicate his identity put forward the symbol of a green triangle. This meant nothing to me at the time, nor apparently to Ernest. Any inner plane Tudor figure I tended to regard as one of the Inner Light's putative contacts, Thomas More. However, it did not seem to be that. Only much later did I come to realise that the green triangle was in fact the Greek letter delta – or D. That is to say, code for Dee.

Dee was in fact one of the first scholars of Greek (along with mathematics) when at Cambridge university, at a time when these were very advanced and modern subjects. Classical studies hitherto concentrated on Latin, whilst mathematics was considered by Puritans to be a form of Roman Catholic black magic. Above all, Dee put his theoretical knowledge into physical practice as when he invented a flying scarab for a production of Aristophanes' *The Clouds* that was so realistic that he came close to being accused of sorcery.

He also became a mathematical geographer and while a lecturer at the University of Louvain in his early twenties became a close friend of Mercator, with whose name we are still familiar in Mercator's projection, which is a convention used in map making to depict a spherical world on a flat sheet of paper. Indeed Dee brought back with him two objects of great wonder and curiosity – a pair of Mercator's globes. They may be familiar to every school child now but they were not so then. What we are seeing is the first attempt of modern mankind to conceptualise the world as a physical celestial object. To do this, man had to stand out from the world, so to speak, and view it as if an observer in space, from the background of the stars, almost indeed as if he were himself a star being. So these mathematical geographers of the time were the first modern "planetary men". This marked a great step forward in human self-consciousness, and John Dee was at the forefront.

But with Dee this was no mere theoretical knowledge; he invented and instituted the manufacture of navigational instruments that were of supreme importance in making England a powerful maritime nation. So we find men like Drake, Raleigh, Frobisher, Gilbert, Hawkins, making their way to Dee's house on the Thames at Mortlake to learn how to navigate and where to sail.

Dee himself financed a voyage by Adrian Gilbert to try to discover a north-west passage to China, via Canada, and had it been successful he might well have owned most of Canada north of the 50th parallel. Unfortunately Gilbert died in the attempt, but Dee himself accompanied Frobisher on another voyage to Labrador.

The Pope had granted exclusive rights to the Spanish and Portuguese to exploit the newly discovered West Indies and Middle and South America, which John Dee challenged by recourse to legendary history. He justified the right of England to settle colonies and trading posts on the North Atlantic seaboard of America, (or Atlantis, as he chose to call it), by citing the legend of Madoc, a 12th century Welsh prince, who had not only discovered America but settled there.

An early development of this claim came with the founding of the

Virginia Company when under the initiative of Sir Walter Raleigh, the colony of Virginia was founded, named after Elizabeth, the Virgin Queen. Accordingly I also found myself being bombarded with imperatives to follow up on this archetypal figure too. Particularly his old house at Sherborne, where, somewhat to my astonishment I found Dion Fortune's magical name plastered up all over the place: *Deo non Fortuna*. It turned out to be the motto of the family who took over the house after Raleigh's fall from grace. The head of which was much addicted to alchemy, as indeed was Lord Northumberland "the wizard earl" who was a close companion of Raleigh when both were confined in the Tower of London. Northumberland for suspected involvement in the great gunpowder plot to blow up king and parliament, Raleigh for falling foul of the new Stuart king James I.

Raleigh ended his incarceration by seeking permission to go in pursuit of a myth, the Land of Eldorado, the failure to find which provided his enemies with the chance to end his life on the scaffold. There was in Raleigh's, as in Dee's life, so much of hinted mysteries that I had my hands full in following some of them up. There seemed no end to them. There was the mystery of Raleigh's head. There was the mystery of his School of Night that was suspected of witchcraft. There was the fate of John Smith, a captain of the Virginia Company, whose life had been saved by the Indian princess Pocahontas – in what looked suspiciously like an initiation ceremony rather than a tale of romantic love. So many things connected up in a veritable web of coincidences and resonances, some of which became the pabulum for various articles and talks and workshops or for ritual work with my group, which was beginning to cohere as a small but powerful unit on a par with what I had seen in the Greater Mystery levels of the Society of the Inner Light, back in the 1950s.

There is not a lot that can be said of the detail of this kind of work. What survives of it in miscellaneous documentation may prove pabulum for academic theses in the future for those who find profit in sifting over the cold ashes of the past rather than juggling with the hot coals of the present.

However, these things also have an outer side, one of which was the foundation of what I called the Keepers of the Planetary Flame, a world wide vigil by a body of volunteers meditating on the sacredness of the Earth. This began shortly after the 1985 Drake event with a letter out of the blue from a young man in Argentina. He had just come upon the western esoteric tradition through *A Practical Guide to Qabalistic Symbolism* and books by W. E. Butler, Dion Fortune and Israel Regardie and wanted to know more. This came upon the back of a number of my books, including the *PGQS* being translated into Spanish although my contacts had a good enough command of English to study the originals. I do not usually take on personal correspondence with readers but in this case it seemed worthwhile for, as I said to him, my recent occult researches had led me to an interest in the traditions of South America; and secondly in the interests of peace on Earth I thought it important that some bond of friendship might heal the breach between Britain and Argentina over the conflict on the Falkland Islands, or Malvenas as they preferred to call them.

Another Argentine connection came quite unexpectedly when an unusual madonna statuette caught my eye in the shop attached to the Roman Catholic Westminster Cathedral. I was so taken with it that I bought it, and then discovered that it to be Argentinian. *La Virgen de Lujan* was indeed the patron saint of Argentina. Its original is a two foot high terracotta figure of the Immaculate Conception, crowned, with stars about her head, robed in blue with red and white flowers, standing in the sun, a crescent moon at her feet.

However, the time was coming when it seemed I needed to take a voyage west myself and visit the United States of America. This came about at the beginning of 1988 with an invitation to give a weekend workshop at the Open Center in New York.

Roma and I decided to make a holiday of it by signing up to a week long package tour. This included staying at a hotel on the West Side, at news of which a couple of American students were horrified. They had apparently spent their childhood and teenage years there in more violent times and greatly feared for our safety. Whilst not finding this possible reception very welcome, nonetheless I felt we stood a reasonable chance of not being mugged, raped, kidnapped or exterminated – so we pressed on with the great adventure. At this our well wishers consoled themselves with the thought that one so esoterically advanced as me would probably be impervious to any foul play on the streets. It is quite amazing what qualities are sometimes expected of an esoteric teacher!

In fact we found little to worry us, although the tour company's transfer arrangements having broken down, making our way through the New York Port Authority bus terminus was a bit of a trial, fending off a young black man aggressively eager to carry our bags.

It turned out we were located in the heart of theatre land, which if it did seem a bit seedy in the light of morning, was no worse than some areas of London we knew, and all seemed as bright and beautiful and tawdry as London's West End when the lights went up in the evening. Apparently theatre owners had recently insisted that the reputation of the district should be improved in order to protect their trade and what cops we saw seemed to congregate in threes.

In fact we loved New York, and did all the sights, including the Empire State Building, which was iconic to anyone who grew up in the 1930s, when we all thought New York to be the capital of the world. The energy of the place was amazing, whether due to the city being an island situated between two great rivers, the Hudson and the East, I do not know. And all the natives very friendly.

We were much aware however of the psychogeography of the place. As R. J. Stewart had remarked, in places like this there is a kind of layered structure on the inner. You plunge down into the past – which in any major city can be pretty murky – and in cities like London or Paris, or indeed almost any place in Europe, you find yourself going back through centuries before coming to bed rock – but in America you hit that level not very far from the surface.

Shortly before going I had felt strongly impelled to do a lot of walking the streets of the City of London. I could not fathom any reason for this but it seemed to be an important issue with those upon the inner planes with whom I have worked over the years so I happily went along with it.

I then discovered, when I got to America, much the same compulsion to tread the streets of New York. Somehow it seemed that I was subliminally linking up the ambience of the two cities – and particularly those parts most associated with financial power. That is to say the environs of Wall Street in New York and of Threadneedle Street and the Bank area in the city of London. This included a subtle connection between London Wall, that marks the Roman boundary of Londinium Augusta, and Wall Street, which derives its name from the stockade that bounded the original settlement of Dutch traders in New Amsterdam – and beneath the razzle dazzle of Broadway I was conscious of its origins as an old Indian trail.

I had no theoretical blueprint for undertaking any of this but it just felt an important thing to do. However it did lead me to discover other links between the two cities. A notable esoteric one was a pair of basalt obelisks that once stood before the Temple of the Sun in Heliopolis in ancient Egypt at the time of the Pharoah Thotmes III. One stands in Central Park and the other on the Thames Embankment, where it is commonly known as Cleopatra's Needle.

There was also an odd temporal synchronicity in that my own crossing the Atlantic coincided with that of a strange and impressive artefact that is normally kept in the crypt St Paul's cathedral. Destined for a public exhibition in New York it was the "Great Model" of the cathedral constructed by Sir Christopher Wren. I had recently been doing a great deal of research on Wren and had been much impressed by the design of this great model which seemed to incorporate a number of magical features.

When one talks of it as a model, it should be said that it is a fantastic example of 17th century joinery, 15 feet long and large enough for a man to get inside. It was Wren's original conception for the new cathedral but the design was rejected by the ecclesiastical authorities as not conforming to what they thought a cathedral should look like. Or perhaps they suspected that something was being swung upon them. At any rate they condemned it for "not being traditional enough" although in fact it is based on very ancient traditions indeed. That is to say the magical principle of an equal armed cross, in the centre of which is a great circular dome surmounted by a steeple. The magical secret behind this lies in the mirror image of this dome and spire immediately below them, in the form of a hemispherical crypt with a deep well corresponding to the spire sunk down towards the centre of the earth just as the spire points to the heavens. A further esoteric touch is provided in the design for a library and office facilities at the western end, where a figure of the patron saint stands on a cubic stone at the summit of a seven stepped pyramid.

Another link that accompanied us across the Atlantic was William Blake, an exhibition of whose artwork was also on show, although we were also keen to see what the New World had to offer by way of exhibition of its spiritual heritage.

If the extension of Broadway had originally been an Indian trading track, beyond Central Park it seemed to be as much frontier territory as ever it was in the remote past. That is to say we were told we could not possibly visit the Museum of the American Indian because it was situated in a no go area called Harlem. Despite such scary tales however, having survived the worst that the West Side could throw at us, I figured that if we went fairly early in the morning any prowling desperadoes would probably still be in bed. So off we went for an enjoyable and instructive day.

An unexpected pleasure in getting there was riding on what remained of the El (or elevated part of the New York subway) which we had seen before only in comic books. Most people we met seemed to be Hispanic, as might be expected from many of the advertisements being in Spanish. Whilst the nice young Caucasian lad behind the counter in the museum shop assured us that he had never experienced any bother while going to or from his place of work – nonetheless there were moves to relocate the museum to where tourists might feel safer.

As to the main purpose of our visit, this was to start with a Friday evening talk on the Western Mystery Tradition, have Saturday devoted to the Tarot, and Sunday to *The Secret Tradition in Arthurian Legend*.

The Friday evening lecture was a sell out, in fact people were being turned away at the doors. One distressed lady buttonholed me to ask if I could possibly find a place for her as she had flown up from Cleveland specially. I did my best for her but was told that there was no way any extra person could be admitted because of the city Fire Department regulations.

The Saturday and Sunday lectures, in morning and afternoon, were also well attended but in a downstairs studio, albeit with the opposition of a fairly noisy air conditioning system. I based the Saturday Tarot sessions on the new system I had developed to teach it by magical visualisation (later published as *The Magical World of the Tarot*). This meant an initial detailed description of the image of the Fool and then of the Magician, who acted as introductors to the magical locations to be described and experienced.

I was somewhat disconcerted when half way through this opening a gentleman politely raised his hand for permission to ask a question. Having been invited to do so he equally politely went on to say that he found what I had said so far was an insult to his and everybody else's intelligence. That they knew all about what I had said so far, and expected more than just a description of the cards!

Lesson one in the difference between a British and an American (or at any rate New York) audience! If not satisfied they do not sit there in silence and quietly go away afterwards – they put their dissatisfaction right up front! However, I had got to the point when it was a question of throwing themselves into a visualisation of what I had just described and so, with that explanation, all passed off well and a successful day was had by all. One exception was a weird little old lady, festooned with pocket watches, who towards the end of the afternoon began to protest volubly that I had not said anything about telling the future. One of the brighter students later apologised to me for the old lady's presence, as she had charitably paid for her admission on finding her standing at the door that morning without any money to get in. Nonetheless, despite getting a free ride, the old lady obviously felt she had been robbed!

On the second day I based my talks on *The Secret Tradition in Arthurian Legend*. This time, toward the end of the afternoon I uncharacteristically ran out of material despite having developed the technique of speaking without notes. There was a significant culture gap between a Hawkwood audience and a New York one and I found that the depth of the book did not easily adapt to the knowledge and expectations of my current audience. But Roma came to the rescue. She had in her handbag a number of slide transparencies of Arthurian related sites we had visited over the past few years, and this travelogue approach worked wonders.

Anyhow things went well enough for me to be invited back next year although this time I went on my own, and stayed as a guest of Paul and Lois Sugar in New Jersey. Paul had in his salad days been an early student of the SOL and had known and worked with Ernest Butler at his cottage near Southampton. Roma and I had met Paul and Lois the year before, when they had taken us out to dinner at a swanky restaurant on Fifth Avenue where Paul showed his disregard of protocol by asking for a superior kind of brandy that he had had there once before, but could not remember the name. He tried to be helpful by suggesting to the waiter that it had tasted rather like gasoline.

Closer to home he took me for a joy ride in an open Model T Ford, whether a restored original or modern replica was not entirely clear. It seemed in immaculate condition and had been modified to the extent of having a three and a half litre Chevrolet engine and automatic gearbox installed. At any rate it certainly was a head turner among the citizens of New Jersey.

I also had the chance to meet up with Bernie and Mark, two members of my group, one American and the other Canadian, who had been initiated at Hawkwood meetings.

Bernie hired a car for the purpose of taking me up country into New York state to investigate with me some stone constructions thought by some to be of a similar age and type to many found in Europe, but in a better state of preservation, not having been raided for building stone or been psychically messed about with.

This did not begin too propitiously. Leaving the car to trek some little way off road to look at one of these sites, we returned to find a police car waiting for us. The cop checked Bernie's credentials and warned us of the dangers of wandering into other people's private property. Bernie had apparently been seen visiting the place previously and the owners did not like it. The cop was mainly concerned that no one got shot on his patch. To the local land owners these structures were known to be old, but not considered that old, and generally regarded as root crop stores built by the Dutch in the 18th century. Bernie produced the book that contained the theory that they were indeed much older, which the policeman took all in good part but advised us to go look at a more accessible site further down the road that was not located on some sharp shooter's land.

However this was but a preliminary to the main object of the trip which was to a more isolated location up an old Indian trail that led to where more megaliths were said to be found. It was also marked by notices pinned on trees warning off trespassers but Bernie seemed quite unconcerned, whilst I reflected on the irony of having survived Harlem and the West-side of New York City if I were now to fall in the country riddled with bullets from the guns of red neck vigilantes.

But my attention was diverted from these musings by excited equine cries from across the fields, where a white horse started wildly galloping around its paddock at the sight of us. Perhaps it always did this at the sight of strangers. Or was there more significance in all this excitement from a totem animal? The Uffington white horse was a major ancient site back home for the focus of our group work, whilst at the other end of the spectrum another Canadian member of our group spent a lot of time investigating Indian lore up in the Yukon in the far northwest, based at a place called White Horse!

Be this as it may, we progressed further up the trail without incident to an ancient structure similar to the ones we had already seen, and which seemed to have a considerable power about it. Whatever its origins, to stand within it with psychic centres opened was to become aware of an inner sunlit radiance with a pathway leading to what can only be described in the familiar Indian term of "happy hunting grounds", a kind of primeval paradisal world.

Bernie was also much taken with a tree and spring close by that might have something to do with this inner gateway. At any rate a remarkable synchronicity to do with spring and tree occurred back at the Open Center. As the climax of one of my workshops I had chosen a reading from an Arthurian romance by Chrétien de Troyes, the story of *Yvain, Knight of the Lion,* sometimes called *The Lady of the Fountain.*

The story tells how the questing knight is directed to sprinkle water from the fountain spring over a mysterious stone nearby, which brings about a most furious thunderstorm of such severity that the knight feels threatened for his life. In the run up to this point a certain degree of amusement was caused by the sound of light rain on the roof and windows, as we imagined the waters from the fountain being sprinkled upon the emerald tablet. When it came to the description of the storm however, I looked up from my script and to see my audience gazing wide eyed with astonishment and even terror at the plate glass window behind me. I turned to look, and saw that the sky had turned black! A sudden storm was unleashed on the city, short lived but so severe that it stopped the traffic.

I should say that I have used this sequence since without any like disturbance, otherwise I could perhaps hire myself out as a rain maker. However I had experienced similar atmospheric effects before, as in the celebrated storm when I was visiting the bluestones of Merlin, and again when a snow shower fell in April as we visited the Merlin stone on the Wrekin. Also in a minor way at Hawkwood, when as I made a contact with the priestess at the first of the rituals, a sudden gust of wind rattled against the window, whilst some saw significance at the conclusion of the Drake weekend when five naval helicopters flew over as I was making my final peroration.

These two visits concluded my travels to America, although in years to come Americans I had met turned up in increasing numbers at various events such as the Open Centre Grail week at Lampeter in 1998, the New York Kabbalah Society at Oxford in 1999, and a week long Grail event that John Matthews and I put on at Hawkwood in 1994.

The three transatlantic members of my Group, Bernie, Mark and Rab, continued to act over the years as outriders, so to speak, of the main group, following their own vision of renewing links with the native Indian traditions. These were becoming increasingly to the fore in those years, and it was interesting to recall that back in the 1930s Dion Fortune had drawn attention to this ground base for American esoteric work but nobody took much notice, and I recall even in the 1960s being asked by puzzled Americans what she might have meant by it. In keeping with the "lands to the west" dynamic evoked by Tolkien it was also notable that our three members resident also did some work in connection with the Fellowship of the Valar that came out of the 1986 Hawkwood event. Mark, in later years, was responsible for publishing some of my works, including first editions of *Pythoness* on the life and work of Margaret Lumley Brown, and Dion Fortune's lost manuscript *Principles of Esoteric Healing*. And later still, the reconstitution of the Keepers of the Planetary Flame.

There is one final element in this tangled skein of coincidence concerned with my American trips. On the second one I was taken by Paul, my host, to the top of one of the great Trade Towers where we had lunch. As we looked out over the vista of Manhattan Island with all its densely packed streets and skyscrapers, Paul remarked how inspired he felt at such a sight, as representing the achievements of man over the natural environment. I did not fully concur with his sentiments but they obviously sincerely moved him. This was in 1989. Track forward a dozen years to a ritual in which I was taking part in London. Part of this consisted of a ritual officer taking up a stack of Tarot Trumps and placing them upon the altar, announcing the name of each one as he went.

When he came to the 18th – the Lightning Struck Tower – it turned out to be missing. Where could it have gone? We had no alternative but to leave it out, and carry on reading out the rest. In fact the explanation was simple, it had stuck to the back of the card in front of it.

But on my way home I was surprised to find the trains packed with office workers. They said they had been sent home early because something terrible had happened in New York. The date was September 11th. The tower at whose summit I had been standing with my friend Paul had been struck down.

Coincidence? No doubt. But why do such coincidences as the missing card occur? For some reason it seems that on occasion strings are being pulled upon an inner level for purposes we cannot comprehend. Maybe just to remind us that strings and string pullers are there?

cfRench Connections
1987-99

From an early age things French held a great fascination for me. This manifested itself in a number of childish ways. Attendance at a performance of Franz Lehar's tuneful and dramatic travesty of medieval French history *The Vagabond King* combined with early cinematic experience of the French comedian Maurice Chevalier at the height of his popularity, and in particular his hit song of the time, *Louise,* the words of which remain in my memory to this day – although I should perhaps say that they hold no esoteric significance. In my seven or eight year old mind I fantasised about some kind of ideal world where men walked about with rapiers at their sides, and wearing straw boaters – which eventually led to a fascination with Alexandre Dumas' romantic novel of *The Three Musketeers.*

I did quite well at French at school, although not all that well, being in the words of the French master "un garçon intelligent mais très très paresseux." Eventually I did get my act together, on retirement from full time employment, to enrol in 1992 as an external student at Royal Holloway College of the University of London to take an honours degree in French – which took me eight years to accomplish, eventually graduating at the age of 70. I was not quite sure of the reason for doing all this, but it came in very handy later.

In the meantime Daniel and Marie-Noelle Lhernould, an enterprising French couple, had set up their own spare time publishing company, Ediru, and published a translation of *A Practical Guide to Qabalistic Symbolism* back in 1983, and later went on to produce French versions of *A History of White Magic, The Rose Cross and the Goddess,* and *The Secret Tradition in Arthurian Legend.*

My first trip to France was when they asked me to help promote my books by a lecture tour in 1987. My French was by no means fluent at this time, not having practised it since leaving school, but I was able to pronounce it reasonably well if provided with a script. So I wrote out my talks in English, the Lhernoulds translated them, and I read out the result in my best schoolboy French. This worked well enough and seemed better than the Greek experience of speaking in English with interpolations of a translator.

However, Daniel and Marie-Noelle did not believe in doing things the easy way, and for each lecture they asked for a different script, even though I did not address the same audience twice.

The venues and circumstances varied widely. The largest audience was an annual meeting of the *Philosophes de la Nature*, at the prestigious Pompidou Centre in Paris. I was quite amazed at what I saw there. The *Philosophes* were devoted to alchemy, and when the French go for something they go for it in a big way. There was an impressive display of actual stills used for recent experiments in alchemy, with a strong contingent from the south of France, where the sun shone brightly and reliably enough to be used as a source of gentle heat in the search for gentle transmutation of base materials into gold.

At the other end of the scale was a hotel in Auxerre, where my talk on *The Return of the Goddess* attracted only five people. The reason, it was thought, was because of a lecture on Buddhism going on elsewhere in the town.

Another date at Dijon, the capital of Burgundy, was something of a test of nerve after a local supporter hinted that there might be some kind of student demonstration at this conservative old university town in protest at a talk about magic. In fact my subject was *The Holy Graal* and was well received by a small discerning audience at a branch of FNAC, the large retail bookselling chain.

Back in Paris I gave a talk on *The Quest of a Knight of King Arthur* (that is to say, Sir Gareth) to a small group at the *Centre d'Etude des Therapies de Demain* in what seemed like a garret in a warehouse. And another on *Images of the Tarot and the Tree of Life* to a Martinist group in a remote courtyard in the 18th arrondissement – not the most salubrious part of Paris. Nonetheless this was a venue I came to know well over the years.

It was the headquarters of an old branch of the Martinist Order that had been founded in 1887 by Dr Gérard Encausse (better known as "Papus" – author of *The Tarot of the Bohemians)*. I was a little wary about my possible reception here, given the subject of my talk, as the Golden Dawn Tarot attributions that I used were at complete variance to the system generally accepted by the French who followed the system favoured by the 19th century occultist Eliphas Levi. All depended upon the position of The Fool in the sequence of Trumps. MacGregor Mathers and his colleagues had placed it at the very beginning of the series, whereas Eliphas Levi, followed by subsequent French writers such as Dr Encausse, had placed it toward the end of the series, between Trumps XX and XXI. Consequently the whole allocation of Trumps to Paths and Hebrew letters differed by one.

I need not have worried however; neither then, nor since, did I have the slightest question or challenge over the matter. Qabalists on each side of the Channel seemed happy to work in blissful ignorance of each other. In any case I did not press the point in any of my lectures. It was only after long meditation on this anomaly, and practical work of my own, that I came to realise that there is no "one and only true" system of correspondences. Any magical system derives its validity from the understanding of the individual, and paradoxical as it may seem, is none the less valid for that.

A severe test of my rudimentary linguistic skills was being interviewed on radio. The radio station, though small and specialist, was in the highly impressive Paris headquarters of the American Rosicrucian organisation AMORC. They had naturally been attracted to the title of *Le Rose Croix et la Déesse*. My French was hardly up to being interviewed in the language, although I did eventually manage to fudge through, albeit with a heartfelt protest to Daniel Lhernould about dropping me into the deep end so unexpectedly.

One slightly amusing incident concerned our alarmist colleague from Dijon, who wrote and performed esoteric music. Daniel had produced a cassette of this for sale which he proposed should be played as an introduction to my interview. However, as the cassette began, the expression on the faces of the interviewer and technicians was a picture to behold – of great puzzlement and even *"quelle horreur!"* They had to be assured that there was not any technical fault on the tape, and that it was meant to sound like that. Fortunately it did not come through my ear phones.

Beyond this, I did find the language problem a burden at times, combined with over-hospitality of my hosts. The worst experience was a visit to the abbey at Vezelay, starting point of the 2nd Crusade, where a very keen amateur guide had been specially laid on for us. Although his full itinerary could take five hours to present, we were accorded a shortened version, over an hour in the fast excited French of a great enthusiast. Most of it was lost upon me but I did my best to show appreciation by faking acceptable signs of comprehension. My cover was almost blown at one point however when Roma asked me for translation of what had just been said.

A similar problem came at a reception held by the Lhernoulds at their home. Whilst preparations were being made to receive the guests we were sent out for a walk in the surrounding country accompanied by a highly voluble occult student from Paris. Although he claimed a knowledge of English, when excited – which was frequently – he broke into long streams of French, or a mixture of both languages. After about an hour of trying to keep up this kind of conversation I was in a state of nervous exhaustion. Only to be introduced to a poor depleted looking soul who looked like I felt. It was said this man had suffered from an occult attack of some kind and it was obviously hoped that I might be able to do something about it. One of the problems of being an alleged guru is that people expect you to live up to their fantasies of what a guru can do! At least they did not start bringing out their dead!

On the other hand, the French have a high regard for writers, and it does not seem to matter very much what you have written. Thus I was surprised to find that a good proportion of those who were introduced to me had no interest in the esoteric at all, but were simply happy to meet an *écrivain* of whatever kind. However, these minor gripes aside, it is not given to everyone to be invited into the home of a French family and I must say we were treated very generously and sympathetically by Daniel and Marie-Noelle and all we met.

Not least among these were Emilio and Maria Lorenzo who were a Spanish (or perhaps I should say Catalan) couple who headed up the Martinist group at which I spoke earlier. Emilio spoke no English and it became something of a standing joke that although the French sometimes found his French difficult to comprehend I could understand him perfectly well. An example of the old observation that it is easier to understand a fellow foreigner speaking French than one of the French themselves, who do seem to go at quite a rate!

Despite my initial reservations, my first talk to the Martinists had been deemed so successful that I was regularly invited back to take part in the annual reunion of all their branches spread throughout France. This invariably took the same form of a meeting on the Friday evening where I would give a talk, then Saturday was devoted to business meetings in the morning followed by an esoteric meeting behind closed doors in the afternoon, a private dinner of the leading lights on the Saturday evening at a local bistro, and Sunday devoted to a meeting at the vast and famous Père Lachaise cemetery in the morning around the grave of "Papus" – Dr Encausse – and then a great banquet in the afternoon.

This pattern gradually developed throughout the 1990s, a period during which my French improved somewhat through my university studies. It was also a period which saw my renewal of membership of the Society of the Inner Light, and there did as a result seem to be an important link being forged upon the inner between the esoteric traditions of England and France. I was generally accorded a table at the banquet occupied by English speakers, which included Professor Antoine

Faivre, who to my astonishment at the time, occupied a chair devoted to the history of esoteric movements at the Sorbonne in addition to visiting professorships in the United States. It seemed that occultism was becoming respectable after a fashion in academic circles.

I was also gradually able to increase the esoteric content of my talks, introducing some guided visualisations, which at first they seemed rather nervous about, due it seems to possible abuses of the technique in less than experienced or ethical hands. And eventually I was also admitted to their secret esoteric meetings, ritually robed, somewhat to the disquiet of some of their more conservative members it has to be said. I can say no more about the detail of these, save to say that the emphasis was not so much on ritual as upon waiting upon the spirit of individuals to speak what came into their heads at the time. Not unlike, indeed, a Quaker meeting but biased toward the thoughts and teachings of Louis-Claude de Saint-Martin. Here I was expected to contribute my share, and thanks to my academic French studies I was able to account for myself in reasonable fashion. It has to be said that I was aware of a considerable spiritual force at the time, that seemed to welcome my presence as forging an inner link between French and English esoteric traditions.

The public Sunday morning meetings at Père Lachaise cemetery were not devoid of their peak moments. On one occasion the place being evacuated by the gendarmerie because of an approaching wind storm, or "tempête", that was thought likely to blow down some of the old trees upon anyone unfortunate enough to be beneath. It looked as if the meeting would need to be conducted in the street outside. However, at the last minute, the storm alert passed, and we were able to file in for the accustomed graveside ceremony.

It was here I began to pick up on some of the deeper esoteric links that concern the unconscious minds of nations. The wall against which many of the communards of 1870 had been shot was particularly moving, and even more so the sequence of memorials to the thousands deported and murdered by the fascist forces in the 2nd world war. It was here one sensed a link between the French and British group souls as a result of 20th century alliance in times of conflict against dark forces, when Churchill had even at one point offered unification of the two nations. If one is deeply contacted to the inner side of things this level of work can be something of an ordeal as well as opportunity for service. During my first visits to France I tended to be challenged as something of an alien on the inner levels, no doubt a consequence of earlier conflicts between the two nations, from Joan of Arc onwards, although I felt I could have done without some later ostensibly friendly contacts from old

French Resistance fighter sources intent on justifying the use of torture in extreme circumstances. All is definitely not sweetness and light in the service of the Mysteries.

A deeper concern with the darker side of things was to come later in work among the war graves and battle grounds of the 1st World War, and on the brighter side with the opening up early Arthurian contacts via Chrétien de Troyes, and of faery contacts via Melusine of Lusignan. But of all this – more later.

24

The Tarot
1984-91

My first close engagement with the Tarot came about through my individual research in writing the second volume of *A Practical Guide to Qabalistic Symbolism* in which I described them in terms of the Spheres and Paths of the Tree of Life to the best of my ability, along with notes on the major esoteric packs that had been published up until then. This study was supplemented by being asked to design a set of my own, intended originally to go along with the book, with the artwork done by Sander Littel. Owing to various financial problems this work did not see light of day for some time.

Then, thanks to Stuart Kaplan of US Games Systems Inc., the *Gareth Knight Tarot* was eventually published in 1984. Stuart, perhaps the world's leading collector of Tarot cards, offered to get Sander Littel's artwork out of hock, where it had been in limbo for the past twenty two years. So what would have been leaders in the field of esoteric packs back in 1962 now came trailing along at the back of the massive explosion of published esoteric packs in the late sixties and seventies. Not that I think this long delay was any great loss to the world.

However, designing my own set of cards had been a very educative experience, so I gave every budding member of the Gareth Knight group the task of producing their own original set of designs based on their meditations on the Tree of Life, which led in turn to my conducting a Hawkwood workshop in December 1984 on the Tarot as a basis for magical work rather than personal divination, which in turn led to another book, originally called *The Treasure House of Images* but, less obscurely, *Tarot and Magic* in a later American edition.

Here I took the opportunity to introduce a modicum of informed academic research into the origin, naming and numbering of the cards. This thanks to a book on *The Game of Tarot* by Sir Michael Dummett, a distinguished philosopher and Professor of Logic at the University of Oxford. This massive tome, published in 1980, was devoted to the history and evolution of Tarot as a card game and had little sympathy for occult interpretations of the subject.

According to Professor Dummett's research Tarot had appeared in northern Italy in the early 1400s by the addition of a set of more or less arbitrary Trump cards to the standard pack of four suits. The resulting game gradually spread to the rest of Italy and then France and central Europe, and its association with occult tradition could be dated back no earlier than the late 18th century. So much for occultists who liked to regard the Trumps as a compendium of secret wisdom originating in Ancient Egypt and even further back in the mists of time!

I already knew most of this from my own more modest research for *A Practical Guide to Qabalistic Symbolism* and found no problem with it. As far as I was concerned the Tarot worked as an occult system, and so the history of its origins was largely an irrelevance – and the truth never hurt anybody. However, to any occult enthusiasts who embraced the legendary history of Tarot as part of their belief system these revelations could be upsetting. If their historical assumptions were called into question they felt it to be the destruction of their cherished spiritual beliefs – rather like fundamentalist Christians faced with textual Biblical criticism.

For myself, I very much welcomed some professional scholarship being applied to the esoteric field. As far as I could see, there was no problem in reconciling the two apparently conflicting standpoints. It seemed to me that whoever conceived the original Trump designs was simply drawing upon a common stock of archetypal images from the inner planes or collective unconscious. Whether they were the random choice of an imaginative wood block artist using the first pictures that came into his head, or the directions of a lordly patron with hermetic philosophical ideas we shall never know. From a practical point of view the images worked, whatever their date or source of origin. Although from my study of Frances Yates' historical works on magical philosophy it seemed quite likely that whoever designed the Trumps was quite well versed in Hermetic tradition, which was then popular within the courts of Renaissance Italy.

In support of my views I had the good fortune to be in Paris when the Bibliothèque Nationale laid on a comprehensive exhibition of Tarot cards. From what I saw it seemed unlikely to me that they originated as only a card game. I could not conceive that such sumptuous hand painted and gilded sets as the Visconti-Sforza cards and others could ever have been put to practical use over a card table even by the most opulent of princes. They were more like iconic images. And if they were *objets d'art* for display (and it seems that they may have been popular as wedding gifts) they could equally have been subjects for meditation as magical images by those who were in the know.

It should be said however that Professor Dummett, who had indeed had a hand in mounting the exhibition, had not been similarly impressed. As far as he was concerned it originated solely as a game, and occult interpreters of the system were as superstitious and ignorant as those whom they fleeced into believing them. However, I think I did persuade him to take a more charitable view when I had the opportunity to meet him.

This came about when he approached me some time later, after publication in 1996 of *A Wicked Pack of Cards* – a book devoted to the origins of the occult Tarot and its development up to the end of the 19th century, which he had written in collaboration with two art historians Ronald Decker and Thierry Depaulis (who indeed had been responsible for setting up the Bibliothèque Nationale Tarot exhibition back in 1984.) He was now intending to follow this up with *A History of Occult Tarot 1870-1970* for the purpose of which he was interviewing contemporary practitioners.

I have to say I was somewhat surprised by his approach and not a little daunted at meeting a distinguished and rigorous scholar who evidently did not suffer fools gladly. Nonetheless I accepted his invitation to lunch at the Charing Cross Hotel and, perhaps to our mutual surprise, we got along with each other famously. Far from being an intimidating fire breathing dragon he came over as a chain smoking old charmer with the most alarming of bronchial coughs that put me more in fear of his health than his invective. And when I came to read his book I was impressed with the incisiveness and retention of his mind. He had taken in accurately all that I told him despite making very few notes.

He also seemed to have come a long way since his initial negative impressions about the occult fraternity, and willing to accept that at least some of us were far from being a conspiracy of frauds. Indeed later on I was pleased to respond to his plea for me to wangle admission for him to attend Warren Kenton's conference on *Kabballah and the English Esoteric Traditions* in 1999 at Oxford after all seats had been booked.

However, having given a Hawkwood course and a resulting book on the magical aspects of the Tarot it began to occur to me that something radical ought to be done to bridge the great divide between the Tarot as a fortune telling device and its use as an initiatory system of magical wisdom.

Most instruction books on the Tarot seem little more than recipe books with the outlines of a simple spread and then a list of meanings to look up. It seemed to me that the public deserved better, and it would be in their interest to introduce the practical magical principles behind the system. Rather than rely on blind adherence to printed meanings in a book why not encourage the student to start back at first principles?

It also occurred to me that there was more than one way of looking at the Tarot, and that it could be a valid system in its own right without relying upon correspondence to other symbol systems such as the Hebrew alphabet, the Tree of Life, or astrology. So in 1988 I started work on a course with a view to launching *The Gareth Knight School of Tarot*.

The principle upon which I worked was aptly summed up in my descriptive brochure for the course: *The Tarot: Four-fold Mirror of the Universe*. For I realised that in addition to the obvious four fold system of the suits of Wands, Swords, Cups and Coins, the Trumps would also divide up into a four-fold system if you knew what to look for. And the hint for this I found from the design of one of the earliest Tarot packs that I had seen at the Bibliothèque Nationale exhibition – the Gringonneur Tarot.

In this pack four of the Trumps are distinguished by a female figure who has a halo or aureole about her head. These cards are **Temperance**, **Strength**, **Justice** and **the World**. Temperance holds two cups, Strength restores a broken pillar, Justice holds sword and balance, and the World stands upon a disc. It occurred to me that they had a certain resonance with each of the suits, over which they rule as Cardinal Virtues, of Temperance, Strength, Justice and Prudence. Not only that, these cardinal virtues each rule over four of the other Trumps.

Under **Strength** come the Hierophant and the High Priestess (spiritual power in male and female aspect respectively), and the Emperor and Empress (outer executive male or female power).

Under **Justice** come the apparently malefic images of the Devil, Death, the Lightning-struck Tower (once also called Hell's Gate or Mouth), and the Hanged Man (formerly known as the traitor, for all such, or their images, were hung upside down).

Under the wings of **Temperance** come conditions of human life, the Hermit (as Father Time) along with the three goddesses of Victory, Love and Fortune. These cards have slightly changed their imagery over the years. The Hermit's lantern was once an hour glass, and like time, went slowly on crutches when one was having a bad time, and yet also had wings when it seemed to go quickly as when one was having a good time. The figure in the chariot was once female, the ubiquitous classical figure of Winged Victory. The Lovers shows a procession of lovers, overshadowed by Cupid, the son of Venus, goddess of love. And the Wheel of Fortune once had the figure of the goddess Fortuna who turned it.

Under **the World** are shown different states of the universe – the heavenly world represented by the angel who summons all to the Last

Judgement (on the card which was once called the Angel), the celestial world represented by the Star, our own solar system represented by the Sun, and the lowest world, anciently called the sub-lunary sphere, encompassed by the orbit of the Moon.

This accounts for all of the Trumps save two, the Fool and the Magician, which oversee and act as introductors to the rest. **The Fool** is the direct representation of the Spirit of the Tarot itself, the creative fount of the whole system, and **the Magician** is another aspect of the same character, this time not wandering free, dancing among the other images as he danced before they existed, but the executive or controlling focus of them all.

As I had acknowledged in my book on the magical Tarot, between them these two represent whom I was referring to when I wrote: *And finally my thanks to the spirit of the Tarot itself. Despite all the abuse it may have had from less than spotless hands and intentions in the past, it revealed itself to me as a very wise and gentle source of wisdom and encouragement, deserving much respect.* And it was a direct approach to this **Spirit of the Tarot** that I tried to induce in each student.

For the key to success in working with the Tarot is a very simple one, but so simple that most people overlook it. It may sound unlikely but the proof is there for anyone who will try it. It is to approach the Tarot as if it were a real person. If you treat the Tarot like a person it will respond like a person – a very wise and friendly person to whom you can turn for advice. It is no good trying to take a kind of superior, "scientific" attitude and subject the Tarot to psychical or statistical experiments. The Tarot will not be put to the test in this way. It opens up, like a friend, only to human warmth and trust.

But this means that we must still be careful as to how we approach it, for it will deal with us exactly as we deal with it. If we go to it just for a laugh or a lark we will receive only misleading answers, for it will be having a laugh or a lark of its own at our expense. We have said it is a very wise person. This means it is not easily fooled. And what is more, it will deal with us for our own good if we approach it in the wrong kind of way. It will not be abused for evil or selfish reasons and is likely to teach us a sharp lesson if we try to make it do so. Similarly, if we become too addicted to it or over reliant on it, pestering it for advice on every minor decision in life, it is likely to respond by giving misleading answers so that we are led in a circular dance until we realise the necessity and wisdom of learning how to make up our own mind. However, if we approach the Tarot as we would a wise and trusted friend, for advice and discussion, we may rest assured that it will respond in similar good faith, and prove a friend and wise counsellor indeed. And, it has to be said, not necessarily an infallible one!

From these simple beginnings, which apply to most if not all avenues of practical occultism, having made initial contact with the Fool and the Magician we can then enter in imagination each of Four Halls where one of the Cardinal Virtues rules over the principles of the remaining Trumps along with their extension into the appropriate numbered suit and court cards.

Not content with just relying on the theory, I tested out the method and principles as well as I could in a series of one or two day workshops throughout 1988 and 1989, mostly at Bath under the aegis of Arcania, a local esoteric bookshop.

Then I produced a six lesson course, including cassette tapes, and launched it with a series of full page advertisements in *Prediction* – the one remaining commercial psychically-oriented journal of the day. I found the experience of teaching students in this way a very rewarding one, but after a time not something to devote the rest of my life to. Over the first couple of years I had expended about £10,000 on this venture, £7000 of it on advertising, and had just about broken even. I could probably have gone on covering my costs and even making a modest profit over the years but the prospect of devoting myself to this kind of commitment did not appeal to me. Ever the typical Aries native I needed to keep breaking new ground.

Fortunately Aquarian Press and later Weisers in the USA were willing to take on a book based upon the course, entitled *The Magical World of the Tarot,* which in addition to the original course text had a great deal devoted to actual questions and answers between myself and the students who had successfully passed through the course.

This was not however the last book I published on the Tarot. Many years before, inspired to some extent by C. S. Lewis and his *Chronicles of Narnia,* I had written a children's fantasy, called *Granny's Magic Cards.* In effect it was a thinly disguised extended pathworking through all twenty-two paths of the Tree of Life when a couple of children experiment with their grandmother's Tarot cards, encounter the Fool, and with his dog go on a harum scarum adventure all the way up from Malkuth to Kether. Although, having said that, the book more or less wrote itself, and in retrospect it was in some respects an early experiment halfway between creative fantasy and channelled material.

I was aware however that there was very little prospect of it being published as it stood, and so consigned it to a bottom drawer. Then having written *The Treasure House of Images/Tarot and Magic* and finding myself a little light on material I decided to strip it of the children and present it as a more conventional series of pathworkings at the end of that book.

However, I think it lost a great deal by this slaughter of the innocents and I was very happy to find a small publisher to take it on in 2004, embellished with a series of charming and evocative illustrations by Libby Travassos Valdez. Unfortunately, as commercial winds blew bleaker in the publishing world, only a few copies were printed before the publisher ceased trading. The consolation for the relatively few people who have copies of the very limited Sun Chalice edition is that they are likely to be sitting on a good long standing investment on account of its rarity!

But things took an unexpected turn in 2010 with the launching of Skylight Press, one of the first of whose publications was a re-issue of the story under the title *To the Heart of the Rainbow* – and drawing attention to the fact that it was not simply a book for children, but for those who approached it in the right way, a way of approaching the Paths of the Tree of Life in a direct and personal way. In other words, it was my version of the standard Rosicrucian device of a *ludibrium* – an amusing tale that has an inner meaning approached by means of the imagination rather than the intellect.

25

The Group
1973-98

As already recorded, the Gareth Knight Group saw light of day on Sunday 15th April 1973 at tea time in the dining room of Hawkwood College. My co-founders were a young couple whom I met during the weekend of lectures by the Rev. Anthony Duncan entitled *The Two Qabalahs*. The hostile reception he received from a group of supervisors convinced me that the *Helios Course on the Practical Qabalah* was not likely to be a suitable vehicle for developing my own ideas. It was very much Ernest Butler's baby and of course none the worse for that. So when Helios Book Service divested itself of course work to concentrate on selling books, we assigned management of the old course to Michael and Dolores Ashcroft-Nowicki under the title chosen by Ernest as the Servants of the Light. At the same time I branched off on my own with the *Gareth Knight Course on Christian Qabalah*.

It took me two years to find possible students and write a series of lessons for them, which I backed up with a textbook, published in 1975 as *Experience of the Inner Worlds,* and launched a small magazine to attract new students – using the old title of *New Dimensions* as already described. As a group of serious students gradually enrolled upon my course I issued a humbly produced handwritten newsletter for them – a photocopied single sheet, but at least it provided a personal touch. However, in 1977 I launched a 24 page quarterly magazine specifically for them under the name of *Quadriga,* and abandoned *New Dimensions* as having now served its purpose.

And so things quietly proceeded, entirely by correspondence. Following the traditional pattern of the old Society of the Inner Light the student membership was divided into three Lesser Mystery degrees and the beginnings of a Greater Mystery group. Some statistical reports survive from 1981 and show I then had 21 students in the 1st Degree, 18 students in the 2nd Degree, 7 students in the 3rd Degree, and 4 members in the Greater Mysteries. Greater Mystery initiations were performed in the early days at my house, with me speaking the necessary parts until such time as we had enough members for a ritual team.

A more practical element of work developed as, from 1979 on, senior members began to assist me with guided visualisations and thinly disguised rituals at the Hawkwood workshops. The prominent role they played led some of them to want to write rituals of their own and find occasions for working them, and so we endeavoured to begin to meet regularly as a private group.

We had no regular place of working but made informal visits to various sites, including the London Planetarium where an astronomical programme on Stonehenge was on offer, and undertook one or two evocative excursions on the Thames from Westminster to Greenwich and the Tower of London – later extended westward to the site of Dr Dee's old house at Mortlake.

One early meeting was at a public house in Warwick, the location chosen because it was more or less in the centre of England. It turned out to be a fairly low key affair in a beer-smelling upstairs room that was not exactly congenial to higher things. However things sparked up quite well when we adjourned to Warwick castle, with its significant historical associations. Already historical archetypal dynamics were beginning to make their presence felt, and I began to realise why there had been a large section on history and historical biography in the old Inner Light library. Tewkesbury and its abbey became a focal point for us although one meeting we held in the town, at the Royal Hop Pole (favoured watering hole of Charles Dickens' Mr Pickwick), maintained a Dickensian flavour when our booked table for eight was mistakenly given to another party, and our afternoon deliberations accompanied by a child banging away on a piano in the next room. Then a meeting at Street, near Glastonbury, owing to a mix up of keys, found us banished to the stage of a hall where a bring and buy sale was going on in full swing behind the curtains in the main hall below. Things markedly improved when we later climbed together up Wearyall Hill to visit the holy thorn as the sun went down over the western sea.

Perhaps the first of our "proper" meetings was in September 1984 at Caerdeon in west Wales. Paradoxically, it was in an old house that had associations with the evolutionist Charles Darwin but it also seemed somewhat obscurely haunted. There was a sense of being observed discreetly in the corridors and rooms – as if by a psychic system of closed circuit television.

Be this as it may, the strangest experience we had was the result of a path working I conducted. It was largely along stellar lines, which is all that can be said of it, because immediately and ever afterward, none of us – not even I who had conducted it – could remember what had been said. However, all agreed it had been a deep and beneficial experience, although, at any rate in detail, it could hardly be regarded as "memorable"!

Here we were also able to conduct a formal initiation ceremony of a new member. The beginning was however slightly delayed by news that my mother had suffered a heart attack. Nonetheless the show had to go on. Roma and I left early the next day for the long drive back across England and Wales – to find my mother quite recovered and demanding to know what the fuss was all about! But such are the nature of "lions in the path" that often beset us at key points in esoteric ventures.

The meeting was not without its spectacular signs following however, as a water spout afterwards careered around a nearby bay – whatever that may have signified!

An outdoor group meeting at Brean Down, Somerset, mid 1980s.

However, despite these early teething problems, things went from strength to strength, and we had some powerful meetings together with R. J. Stewart and various invited friends in his attic just across the road from the hot springs in Bath. These shared meetings were helpful in their way, as well as performing an important magical purpose in reconciling Christian and pagan dynamics, but we still felt the need for a regular meeting place of our own.

We tried Runnings Park in the Malverns in March 1985 where we staged two initiations but found its facilities and ambience not entirely to our liking. Apart from being overlooked by other residents if one could not book the whole establishment, an indoor swimming pool seemed to add to a cloying and uncongenial psychic atmosphere. Then we discovered the stable block at Hawkwood.

Here, in January 1986, we had the first of our regular ritual weekends, operating at Greater Mystery level, which became a staple part of the group from then on. The location met with general approval as a place that was relatively calm and quiet, and indeed almost "waiting" for us. Whether my role in helping to find funds for the repair of the roof had anything to do with this, remains subject to speculation. Thanks to the generosity of Carr Collins, I had been able to help renovate the roof of the stables. Anyway, the stable block became the virtual home of the Gareth Knight Group for many years to come.

During that first year we had five Hawkwood meetings and one at Bath and carried out no less than five initiations. The initiations came comparatively thick and fast as we began to realise that our major purpose was not to be a general occult school but to be a close knit magical group working at an intensive level and experimenting with new techniques.

Therefore the Lesser Mysteries were closed down and those within striking distance of completing the 3rd Degree given the opportunity for Greater Mystery initiation. From now on new members for the group were recruited and trained by individual members until fit to attend meetings in their own right. This was along the traditional apprenticeship lines of magical training.

The GK Group, as it later came to be called, continued to meet five or six times a year in the stable block at Hawkwood, over a 24 hour period, from lunchtime Saturday to lunchtime Sunday, during which time we contrived to fit in three ritual workings. These were usually robed, with all the trimmings, and we had furnished ourselves with some highly effective mobile three foot high candlesticks and pillars, fabricated from plastic drainpipes, which are light in weight and easily portable. In later years we were able to scrounge a cupboard on the premises in which to keep such basic materials.

The general pattern was for me to delegate three people, each to be responsible for one rite each. They had a free choice on what they did, along with responsibility for choosing their own officers from those attending. Each rite magus had a period of an hour or so for any necessary rehearsal of officers, and then the performance was done. One on Saturday afternoon, one Saturday evening, and one Sunday morning. One of these might, when occasion demanded, be an initiation, when a member felt ready to offer the Unreserved Dedication.

It was interesting how, with no prior collusion, rites would correlate so that in effect we had a meeting that consisted virtually of one ritual in three acts, so to speak. This, to my mind, clearly showed that the group was genuinely "contacted" and inner plane adepti were working effectively behind group members.

In 1986 and early 1987 we also initiated the first of our overseas members who later became active in trans-Atlantic activities of their own as "out riders" to the main group. Demonstrating healthy signs of independent growth, members of the home group were also active in promoting their own local groups. 1987 saw the foundation of a western sub-group in Wales, initially called the Rose and Unicorn, and another called the Crystal Gate, and in 1989 an eastern sub-group performed rituals in a well appointed converted loft at Leigh-on-Sea.

However this did not detract from participation in the main meetings where the opportunity was opened to all to experience leadership of a full working group when in 1988 we introduced a revolving headship system, with a new Group Magus appointed each year. This meant we had a functioning training group for adepti in which the curriculum was in effect: (1) attendance at ritual meetings, (2) opportunity to take office, (3) to write and act as Magus of one's own rituals, and (4) if desired, to offer the Unreserved Dedication to the Mysteries by ritual initiation. This could pass on to (5) experience of running the entire group, first as Magus Elect, then as Magus, leading on to Immediate Past Magus. After this however there often came (6) a Daath-like crisis when the individual concerned went on "walkabout" for a year or so before (7) returning to the group or taking up some kind of group leadership elsewhere.

The Gareth Knight Group at Hawkwood, 1998.

So things continued over the years with the development of a highly creative group which in course of time built a vast library of original rituals. Some of the better ones might be repeated from time to time but by and large the emphasis was not on repetition but creativity, and acting in response to changing inner plane needs and requirements. We were certainly not the type of group that devoted itself to an ancient formula or set of rituals of which no jot or tittle could be changed.

1995 was a crucial year, ratifying a phase change and testing our abilities at a new level. In February of its 21st year the group formally "came of age" when I presented it with the Founder's sword, which meant that the group was no longer an appendage of myself but a self-governing entity in its own right. It had for some time been this in practice, but now this was formally and ceremonially recognised. The group was fully responsible for its own survival and direction from now on, under the current Magus of the day. This ceremony was thus very much in the nature of a group initiation.

Two challenging events very soon followed. The first was a relatively simple test of magical technique wherein at a July meeting the group was put to the task of corporately making up a ritual from scratch and then immediately performing it. A more rigorous testing was experienced in October in the circumstances surrounding an experimental public Open Day which developed a difficult wobble. The immediate problem seemed to have been a consequence of Hawkwood having naïvely played host a little time before to a group of dubious reputation who had, by accident or design, left behind some distinctly negative elemental entity.

The first indication of this was one of our members apparently being led astray in a spontaneous directed visualisation, which uncharacteristically went deeper and darker and more convoluted, ending up with a feeling among the more sensitive members of our having been deliberately attacked. In my own case it was like a stinging welt across the heart centre. Although not overly serious in itself, being more like getting in the way of a cat suddenly let out of a bag than a deliberately malicious assault, discussion of it induced some fear in a few of the guests. Maybe we should have said nothing about it in order not to frighten the horses – for in certain circumstances ignorance can be bliss – but I have ever favoured transparency as much as possible.

Members of the group who followed on with their own workings had to cope with this as best they might. Nor was the general ambience helped by one or two of our number having a row as to who might have been to blame, thus leading some visitors overhearing to feel that the group might be in deep crisis. Hardly an entirely successful public relations exercise altogether, but all's well that ends well, and we emerged from the event intact and the wiser for the experience.

A follow up event the following year went completely smoothly. One sage piece of advice from one of the inner plane adepti whom I have learned to respect and trust is "Learn to fail well." We all fall short from time to time, sometimes grievously. But the important thing is to learn from the experience, dust yourself down, and start in over again.

As a leader of groups I have never been grieved by people making mistakes. It is one way by which we can learn, even if it can be a hard way. It is only when people make the same mistake twice that I begin to get tetchy. Should they make the same one three times then probably the time has come to wave farewell.

The time was coming however, during 1998, when I went off to answer a call to service back at the Society of the Inner Light. Coincidentally all current members had had their turn at being head of the group, so it seemed we were due to start another round, yet things did not continue in a simple circle but went off into a new spiral of progress. With my moving on it was no longer appropriate to call the group after me, so at the beginning of 1999 it became the Avalon Group, initially under the joint headship of Mike Harris and Wendy Berg – which is the beginning of another story – although we had not seen the last of each other by any manner of means.

26

Merlin and the Stuart Line
1986-88

In a sense the May 1986 Tolkien Hawkwood marked the end of a series of powerful workings that had grown from strength to strength over the past seven years. It was not the end of Hawkwood events altogether, but the series to date seemed to have acted as a kind of springboard for individual and small group work with powerful inner archetypes.

I also began to be asked to take part in other functions, the first of which was a conference devoted to Merlin, organised by R. J. Stewart at the Conway Hall in London. Speakers were the Arthurian scholars Geoffrey Ashe and Count Nikolai Tolstoy, John and Caitlín Matthews, R. J. Stewart and myself. Somewhat to our surprise it was packed to capacity, with many people being turned away.

My contribution, on *The Archetype of Merlin*, led on from my recent work on Tolkien. I followed the story of Merlin as told in Layamon's *Brut*, a Middle English version of the 12th century Latin *History of the Kings of Britain* by Geoffrey of Monmouth. Although the Celts rightly get most of the credit for the magical material in Arthurian legend, the Anglo-Saxon Layamon was the first to introduce elves to the story and the account of Arthur being carried away in a boat to Avalon. How much Tolkien's history of the elves has in common with events in Arthurian legend is a matter of conjecture but it seemed worthwhile to look at the magician Gandalf as a Merlin figure.

The talks were later reproduced in a hardcover book – *The Book of Merlin* – in which I was able to add a couple of Merlin adventures of my own, the drenching at the bluestone outcrop at the time of the Fastnet yacht race, and my contact with aspects of Merlin and Nimué at a local meeting point of oak and ash and thorn.

The following year, 1987, at the second of R. J. Stewart's series of Merlin conferences, entitled *Merlin and Woman*, I talked about *John Dee, the Elizabethan Merlin*. This was closer to the feminine theme than might appear, for Dr Dee had close connections, off and on, with Queen Elizabeth I, focus of the Tudor cult of Gloriana, or Astraea, the Virgin of the Stars.

I must confess that in my earlier Arthurian studies I had never paid much attention to the Scottish traditions of the great mage. These however were brought very much to my attention when, following our successful celebration of the Celtic mysteries at the 1984 Hawkwood, Roma and I intended to take a simple family holiday on the Scottish borders. Something of a busman's holiday it turned out to be, for it developed into a highly charged few days involving Merlin traditions along with Stuart connections.

We might have known what to expect when Bob Stewart telephoned us on the eve of our departure, in high excitement over an ancient local guidebook he had come across, that mentioned an altar stone connected with Merlin. He suggested we try to find it and also spoke of some mysterious Bear Gates connected with the Stuart cause. The Bear reference, to our minds, also carried with it a strong resonance to King Arthur, associated with the Great Bear, or Arthur's Wain, and, like the deposed Stuarts, another "king over the water" whose possible return was the stuff of legend.

We followed the trail of Merlin in the border country, climbing the Eildon Hills above Melrose where legend has it that King Arthur and his knights are sleeping, and explored the valley of the Tweed. At the little village of Drumelzier, the traditional site of Merlin's grave under a thorn tree, we found the Powsail brook associated with his "three-fold death". Versions vary – in flight from being stoned, falling into the stream, his foot caught on a branch, where he became like the Hanged Man of the Tarot, suspended with his head beneath the surface of the waters.

The Powsail brook runs into the River Tweed close by and there is also a Stuart connection here in view of an ancient prophecy, perhaps by Thomas the Rhymer, that:

> *When Tweed and Powsail meet at Merlin's grave*
> *Scotland and England one monarch shall have.*

This was fulfilled in 1603 when the Powsail and the Tweed overflowed their banks at this site, the year that the crowns of England and Scotland were united under King James VI of Scotland and I of England.

King James' mother had of course been the tragic Mary Queen of Scots and on the journey up we stopped at Jedburgh abbey, near which is a house in which she stayed, and in which her strikingly beautiful death mask is displayed along with a copy of her letter on the eve of her death. Here I experienced a feeling of intense claustrophobia – not so much afflicting me personally, but in the general atmosphere of the place. This was particularly strong in an upper room, and temporarily finding I had the place to myself, I felt impelled to fling open all the windows, which cleared the atmosphere at a stroke.

Later, in Holyrood palace in Edinburgh, we experienced a similar claustrophobic sensation in the room where she had been with her favourite Rizzio when her husband Darnley stormed in and with his confederates inflicted fifty or more stab wounds upon the unfortunate Italian by the time his corpse landed at the bottom of the staircase. Did we but know it, this was a foretaste of further encounters with the egregore of Mary Queen of Scots.

The main thrust of our interest on this occasion was however concerned with the Scottish Merlin and a search for the mysterious altar stone. This seemed destined to failure as we drove up and down a minor road that runs parallel to the River Tweed. Then almost on the point of giving up the hunt, we realised we had stopped outside a place called Altarstone Farm. The stone surely could not be far off, and realising this we now discovered a large flat topped stone set in the roadside wall opposite the entrance to the farm.

Some say that the marks resembling the imprints of claws on the top of the stone were those of a witch turned into a hare when being hunted by Merlin. We felt the stone more likely to be associated with St Kentigern, the saint whose hermitage chapel is about a mile away at Stobo, and who is supposed to have converted Merlin to Christianity, which led to him being stoned by irate pagans, perhaps leading to his legendary three-fold death.

Stained glass window in Stobo Kirk depicting Kentigern and Merlin.

Another theory is that the altar stone is simply left over detritus from a nearby quarry, and takes its name from the farm, which was originally Arthur's Stane rather than Altar Stone. It is odd how even in this attempted rationalisation of the story the name of Arthur crops up, as with the association with the Bear Gates at Traquair House.

Traquair House is an old Stuart stronghold, with priest holes and the walls six foot thick in places. The gates, with the statue of a bear on each pediment, stand at the end of a long drive, now entirely grassed over, and have never been opened since Bonny Prince Charlie passed through them in 1745. Nor is it intended they ever will open until a Stuart is returned to the throne.

Whether or not this will ever come to pass, the power behind this ancient tale was palpable; we even seemed accompanied by an inner group of mounted cavaliers. We were also intrigued to note a Rosicrucian resonance with the archery butts that had been set up at the near end of the drive.

There was also a great surprise for Roma, who hails from Somerset, to find at the eastern end of the Tweed valley the house of Bowhill was the seat of the Duke of Monmouth and Bucleuch, who was leader of the Protestant rising against the Catholic James II. This led to the carnage of the Battle of Wedmore which was followed by the merciless "bloody assizes" held by the notorious Judge Jeffries – events which still stir passions of resentment in the locality. The Duke of Monmouth paid with his life, and there was a poignant childhood relic of his cradle on display.

All this points up symbolic elements in national history that act as foci for unresolved inner conflicts – what might be called neuroses of the racial unconscious – and that in some fashion were being evoked and confronted at the Hawkwood sessions and elsewhere. The importance of symbolic artefacts as a stimulus to the imagination also came to mind on a visit to Abbotsford, the home of the pioneer historical novelist, Sir Walter Scott, where a long room is absolutely jam packed with ancient arms and souvenirs that he must have used as a spur to his imagination. The techniques of magic are where you find them.

We later became closely embroiled in some unfinished business in relation to Stuart archetypes at a group meeting on February 8th 1987 which, although we had not realised it, was the 400th anniversary of the execution (or martyrdom, as some would have it) of Mary Queen of Scots.

There was also a certain synchronicity with our current ambiance of looking westward, as the candidate we had due for initiation was an American, and who also happened to be, like Mary Stuart, a Roman

Catholic. Indeed the weekend was full of other portents, in retrospect, not least as also being the anniversary of the most powerful earthquake in Britain, in 1750, when the shocks were so great that the church bells rang of their own accord.

The atmosphere for the initiation was notable for a deep mystical atmosphere of religious dedication, and it turned out that the name given to the candidate coincided with his confirmation name in the Roman Catholic church. At a point in the ritual when a sword is placed on the candidate's neck, I experienced, as initiating magus, a powerful emotional kickback associated with the execution of Mary Queen of Scots, and her figure, clad in black, seemed to circumambulate the lodge, so palpable as to be almost visible to physical sight. Whilst to the vision of one of us, who was much moved by this experience, she seemed almost to dance, proclaiming joyously that she was free, before standing beside him, saying that he was so affected because he had Stuart blood in his veins.

The final working of the weekend was also very significant in this respect. Although intended to be mainly a rite of Spring it picked up coincidentally on many facets of the Stuart queen – indeed the central altar bore a vase of daisies (the first time flowers had ever been so used in any of our workings) which, unknown to the individual concerned, were her special emblem.

The ritual also incorporated the pattern of visualisation described in the last chapter of my book *The Rose Cross and the Goddess* wherein a bright goddess above and a dark goddess below are harmoniously counterchanged in a polarity of heavenly and earthly powers. On this occasion it became apparent that this could also represent an element in the healing of ancient wounds afflicting the soul of the nation, in that Mary Queen of Scots (identified, at least in part, with the dark goddess) was being lifted up in an exchange of polarity and forces with the bright goddess, Astraea (represented in the body politic by Elizabeth I of England). Both queens, together and equal, were recognised as vehicles of high spiritual, racial and national significance.

These resonances were all the more remarkable insofar that the individual who wrote the ritual had no idea of any associations with the tragic queen – and indeed felt slightly miffed as well as bemused that he had been unconsciously used in this way.

All this seemed to bring to a head much that had been experienced by various members of the group in the immediate past, of strong and often uncomfortable contacts with Mary Queen of Scots. Her presence could be quite turbulent and disquieting, particularly to women in the group. One even felt she might be losing her mind through an intense and irrational impulse of hatred towards a much loved ginger cat. The explanation for this became apparent on a subsequent visit to an exhibition of Mary's tapestries at Oxburgh Hall in Norfolk. Designed and made by her when she was imprisoned, one of them showed herself in the role of a mouse, with her feared and hated rival Elizabeth as a ginger cat.

So much for practical experience of these matters, but I find myself somewhat challenged to find a theory to fit much of these archetypal contacts. I have reason to believe they are not confined to me or my own group. In the context of ritual it seems that in the deeper strata of occult work we are involved with what might be described as unfinished business in the group soul of the nation, or at worst some festering psychic sores that need attention. Not that this implies a politicisation of the Mysteries, but rather forms a safety valve for unresolved conflicts that might otherwise result in political fanaticism or even terrorism. In ritual that has an inherent self balancing tendency I suspect that we produce an inner pattern or mandala that can be used by the forces of light to take some of the heat out of the hot spots than can be so readily exploited by the agents of "spiritual wickedness in high places".

This, at any rate, is my main justification for a belief in the importance and efficacy of magic, despite its frequent trivialisation or misunderstanding on the part of those outside it. "Dabbling in the occult" is a much bruited trite phrase used by those who do not understand it. I would fully agree with their reservations, bearing in mind the famous couplet by Alexander Pope:

> "A little learning is a dangerous thing,
> Drink deep or taste not the Pierian spring."

27

Sherwood and Alfred Noyes
1990

Alfred Noyes (1880-1958) was an immensely popular poet in his day, who wrote verse with strong rhythms and vivid images which struck a responsive chord in a huge readership. Since his heyday in the Edwardian and Georgian era he and his work have suffered an eclipse. Indeed it is not uncommon when one speaks his name to meet the response "Alfred who?" Yet with those of a certain age one has only to quote the opening lines from his narrative poem *The Highwayman* to meet with instant recognition and positive response.

> *The wind was a torrent of darkness among the gusty trees,*
> *The moon was a ghostly galleon tossed upon cloudy seas,*
> *The road was a ribbon of moonlight over the purple moor,*
> *And the highwayman came riding –*
> > *Riding – riding*
> *The highwayman came riding, up to the old inn door.*

Indeed it has claims to being the most anthologised poem in English literature.

He has fallen out of fashion now but I became increasingly fascinated by parallels between subject matter that attracted Alfred Noyes and archetypal themes that kept cropping up in my magical work. It seemed he had an intuitive and emotional link to the group soul of the nation, and beyond that even to the English speaking peoples, for he was highly popular in North America too.

He had no intentional "magical" aims or interests, and would probably have been horrified at the suggestion. Yet in his work magical resonances do arise, of which he seemed to have been for the most part unconscious. In his autobiography *Two Worlds for Memory* he admits to some kind of elfin guide called "Shadow-of-a-Leaf" that had accompanied him since childhood, but nevertheless is inclined to pass it off as some kind of psychological quirk.

My attention was first drawn to Noyes after the remarkable Drake weekend at Hawkwood in 1985, when I learned that early in his career he had written a twelve part epic poem *Drake* (1906-08). Then I discovered further archetypal themes in his *Tales of the Mermaid Tavern* (1913), in a long faery inspired narrative poem *The Forest of Wild Thyme* (1905); and in a play, *Sherwood* or *Robin Hood and the Three Kings* (1908). Whilst in later work, *Watchers of the Sky* (1922), his treatment of the astronomer Tycho Brahe fell into a typical fourfold magical pattern, with the Odin-like Brahe, complete with golden mask, his peasant wife Christina, and his helpers the Pythagorian mathematician Johannes Kepler and the prophetic dwarf Jeppe; all ensconced in the Venusburg, a castle on an island dedicated to the study of the stars. All this was based on historical fact – if given a romantic and at the same time unconscious magical twist.

Noyes' play *Sherwood* led me to perform a quite unexpectedly powerful magical working with my group. In Noyes' vision Sherwood forest is an overtly magical place, with the gates of the faery world or "the Shining Glen" as part of the scenery, and the King and Queen of the Forest Sprites as characters. As their intermediary we find Maid Marian's Fool is the half human, half elven Shadow-of-a-Leaf. And it is by his sacrificial efforts that Robin and Marian are able to pass through the Shining Glen into legendary immortality – all this with the underlying theme of "the return to the King" – in this case Richard the Lionheart.

There is a good deal of Edwardian poetic whimsy and romantic folk history in all of this it has to be said. And despite his charisma Richard the Lionheart was far from being an ideal king of the realm, which he taxed up to the hilt! But this is of small consequence alongside the magical relevance of the powerful archetype his memory carries – of the once and future king, of the absent king, or the returned but unrecognised king. The archetypes and legends are bigger than the historical characters and events, which are merely convenient hooks upon which to hang them. There is a power of magic, with high mystical dynamics, bursting to come through.

Prompted by Alfred Noyes' play, I wandered through Sherwood forest myself, and found it, like all ancient deciduous forests, a magical kind of place. This led to my attempting a relevant working with my group at the Summer Solstice of 1990, and it may bear description here as an example of the kind of work that the Gareth Knight Group did.

Although based on the Robin Hood characters and legend, the emphasis of the rite was upon "the Return of the King". This was an old Hawkwood theme dating from 1981 that was also infused with a mystical Christian dynamic – of the Second Coming. The Robin Hood legends, with their firm base in the greenwood, and their tradition of Anglo-Saxon and medieval yeoman practicality, seemed to offer a grounded balance for a rite which aimed to touch the mystical heights without becoming attenuated in neo-platonic abstraction.

A cosmic framework was provided by means of a ground plan of the Tree of Life, by which the very episodic and anecdotal fragments of the Robin Hood tradition could be sorted into a meaningful pattern. Accordingly **Kether** was located in the East as the position of the King beyond the water, with **Malkuth** in the West presided over by Maid Marian in her wider context as Planetary Being, giving a fundamental East/West polarity between Spirit and Matter, Heaven and Earth.

Between these fundamental polar points a series of images was built representing spheres and power points on the Middle Pillar of the Tree of Life. In the very centre, at **Tiphareth**, the great oak which was the traditional rallying point of the outlaw band. At the point corresponding to **Yesod** a cauldron upon a camp fire, the "foundation" of the outlaws' existence in the forest. At the position of **Daath** and the Abyss a stream with a narrow bridge across it that figures prominently in many of the Robin Hood stories.

Between cauldron and oak tree (in traditional Qabalistic symbolism the 25th Path or "Path of the Arrow" of aspiration), a weapon store full of arrows was visualised. And between oak tree and narrow bridge a great stag with curving antlers, physically represented in the lodge by a large menorah, or 7 branched candlestick, that recalled the branching tines of a stag.

So much for the Middle Pillar. The spheres on the side Pillars of the Tree of Life were each represented by a single candlestick manned by an officer representing one of the characters of the Robin Hood legend. Will Scarlet at **Hod**, Robin Hood at **Netzach**, Little John at **Geburah**, Friar Tuck at **Chesed**, Alan o' Dale at **Binah**, and Much the Miller's son at **Chokmah**. At first sight these may seem bizarre and arbitrary attributions, however there is magical reasoning behind the selection of each – and in the event they worked!

Will Scarlet and Robin Hood at the base of the Pillars of Manifestation represent the lower "Dragon powers". It is Robin whose horn summons the outlaws and Will who issues their weapons. In magico-mystical terms this is a summoning of the lodge (and the individual) to focused attention and aspiration towards the heights, marked by "the path of the arrow".

Little John and Friar Tuck at the midpoint of the side Pillars beyond the central oak represent guardians of the bridge over the Abyss. In magical terms they are polar aspects of the Dweller on the Threshold in any attempted rising on the planes. Little John as tester of resolution by challenging the right to approach the bridge; Friar Tuck in a more positive test of carrying across the waters, as in the legends, with his traditional pack of red-eared other-world hounds to assist in the chase once the quarry has broken cover.

Alan o' Dale and Much the Miller's Son have comparatively minor roles in the legends but in this magical scenario their supernal positions are of considerable importance as suggested by their legendary attributions. As a minstrel Alan's harping is that of the harmony of the spheres, overseen by the angelic realms; whilst Much, being a miller's son, provides a connection to the Cosmic Axis around which the heavenly spheres turn. Additionally the side Pillars, at whose head they are situated, are associated with two mythical trees, one of green and one of gold, a gateway to the inner realms at whatever level one may be operating. (They also feature in Tolkien's mythology.)

The operation of the rite was relatively simple. A roll call of the outlaw band was made and their identity and position affirmed. Then the hunt of the mystic stag was commenced, consisting of a journey in consciousness after the stag, past the oak and over the bridge, to pursue it to the sea shore. Here it plunged into the water, swimming to a far destination, to return in the form of a ship (with resonances to the earth encompassing Golden Hind!) bringing the Return of the King.

Empowered by and identified with the King, the Magus of the Lodge in the East then lit the menorah, and moving in the path of the Lightning Flash upon the Tree of Life, lit each of the Sephirothic candles on the way, and presented the illumined menorah to Maid Marian, who then passed up the Middle Pillar to sit in the place of the King in the East, in a species of cosmic interchange. Finally the officer representing the King spontaneously danced out of the Lodge.

To anyone who has not experienced ceremonial magic this may well sound like no more than primitive amateur dramatics or a crude and somewhat arbitrary symbolic charade, but the recorded response of some of those present bears witness that something took place that was rather more than that.

1. *"What can one say? It was a privilege to be there. The part which took me by surprise and filled me with wonder was at the end when the Magus wove between the Pillars leaving a trail of light and then strode round in circumambulation leaving footsteps of light. Christ most assuredly came through. After sitting in the atmosphere for some while when it was over, I found myself stumbling up between the Pillars as though walking through soup to arrive at the East and mumble 'Thank you' but I'm not sure who to."*

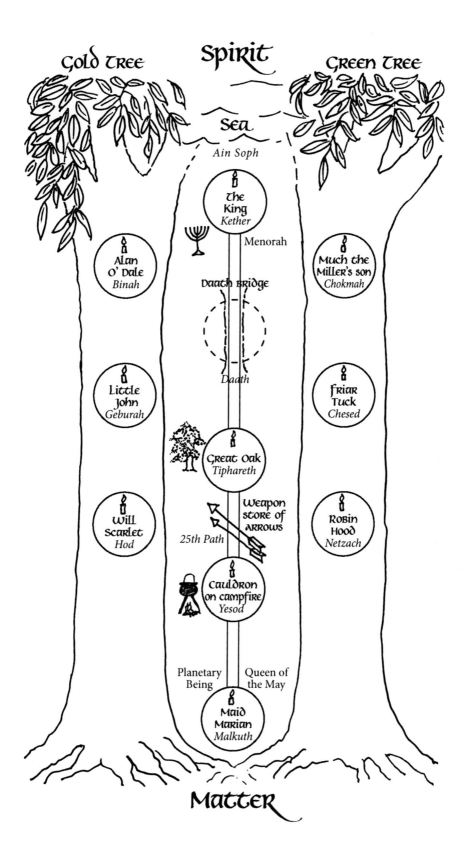

2. "Its construction as a piece of ritual magic was stunning and words fail me to adequately describe my reaction. The back of my neck felt as though all the hairs were standing up through much of the working. I feel that it was a great privilege to be a small part of such a working..."

3. "The giant oak reared up within the circle and the officers were the respective participants, the pillars of green and gold stimulated thoughts of Tir nan Og ... The aroma of the cauldron filled the greenwood (and if the sheriff had been around he would have only to follow his nose!) Trees played a role at the stations also, the lyre being hung upon an ash tree, whilst a yew stood at the bridge, aspen at the ford and holly grew round the weapons cache. Robin's horn hung from a beech tree. The significance of some is plain but others obscure at the moment. The Tree of Life superimposed over all and the path of the Lightning Flash formed as the lights were lit. Although certain passages are difficult to recall the final circumambulation of the King set up a vortex which continued after his departure, and the impulse to draw arms and, bearing the light, follow after, was irresistible."

4. "As suspected, this 'merrie romp' turned out to be the inevitable tour de force associated with a Hawkwood Sunday morning! The rite tied all the facets of the weekend's workings together, from the mystical high spiritual to the ecological, and set the stamp on the earth/heaven interchange with what can best be described as a 'rite of the second coming'. The Magus played the Fool. I mean this of course in the profoundest sense. The Kabbalistic setting was a superb innovation with the Lightning Flash coming down to contact the officers – the Word, as it were, echoing down the planes in the names of the officers as servants of the King over the sea... The most moving moment, however, was when Richard came to the clearing and I saw the King from over the sea with pierced hands and feet. What started out as the flicker of light between the green tree and the golden tree became an interchange between the powers of Chokmah and Binah – working through and in the world. The Merrie Romp then became the Dance of the Fool, with the skipping between the Pillars, and finally after those affirmations from 'The Lord of the Dance', a demonstration of the Chokmah 'whirling force'... Perhaps the best thing to say is that it was a privilege to be part of this. Yet again our magic (or whatever it is) opened the gates of heaven."

5. "I don't think I have been so powerfully moved by any ritual before: the Officers of the East and West were no longer people we knew, but pure archetype, radiating with inner light. This Sherwood was the eternal Garden of Eden, the return of the temenos. I found myself at the end holding a lit candle on which the flame was literally jumping in time to the pounding of my heart-beats! This was the true celebration of the Second Coming – Christ the King who will enter our own lives and minds and hearts – in accordance with the promises of the continual revelation. It was quite wonderful, and the scripts should be ceremonially burnt because we are NEVER going to be able to repeat it in just that way again."

In fact there were only vestigial scripts in this largely improvised working, and no repetition has been attempted, in line with the traditions of the group, which has always been to break new ground. The above reports are given, not in the spirit of a collection of favourable theatrical notices, but as evidence of the power of the dynamics that were evident to tuned consciousness.

This was not the only instance of working with subjects that also fascinated Alfred Noyes. I found much common ground in a work of his called *The Torch Bearers*. This was devoted to cultural heroes of human progress and written in three parts: *Watchers of the Sky* (1922), *The Book of Earth* (1925), and *The Last Voyage* (1930). The first celebrated great astronomers, including Tycho Brahe as already mentioned; the second, great scientific discoverers from Pythagoras through to Goethe and Darwin; and the third, the development of radio communication, a semi-occult wonder which we nowadays take so much for granted.

All this had led me to undertake writing a book to be called *Stars, Crystals and Heroes,* so-called from the fact that most of the chemical elements have their origin in the **stars**, the remarkable qualities of their combination into **crystals**, and a projection of these general principles into human life which brings one to the consideration of **heroes** in the broadest sense, leaders in all fields of human endeavour. Back of this was a statement made in Dion Fortune's *The Cosmic Doctrine* about the first creative hierarchies that laid down the physical world we know: with Lords of Flame laying down the laws of physics, Lords of Form laying down the laws of chemistry, and Lords of Mind laying down the laws of biology, and Lords of Humanity faced with laying down the laws of sociology or civilisation.

So I spent a fair amount of time following in Pythagoras' footsteps studying the laws of harmonics, with the help of a monochord generously given me by an American student and which I wielded at one or two lectures, to demonstrate the phenomenon of whole numbers in divisions of a vibrating string to form a musical scale. From this I passed to Mendeleev's Periodic Table, which shows how all the chemical elements fall into families of similar reactivity according to the number of electrons or gaps in their outer shell. There is a fascinating field of speculative research into the function of each element in the formation and maintenance of organic life upon the planet, and later in the history of the discovery of each chemical element, and its subsequent uses, whether as coinage metals or silicon chips.

It is arguable that I was attempting to bite off far more than I could chew. Certainly I was overtaken by events when new management at Aquarian Press came to a similar view and the project was cancelled. Some of the material ended up as journal articles or papers for dedicated students and also for the presentation of a 1992 workshop on *The Angelic Hierarchies*, whilst my group also performed some interesting rituals based upon eightfold atomic structure which might be regarded as an approach to a new kind of alchemy. (Without any "get rich quick" associations it has to be said!)

In the end it seemed that fascinating although much of this might be, there was not a great deal of scope for it in a published book short of encyclopaedic proportions embracing everything from ritual magic and angelic mysticism to particle physics and radio astronomy. Something for some future genius to bear in mind perhaps. But all a bit beyond me.

28

Renewing Ancient Springs
1990-2000

I chose to celebrate 1990 as the centenary of the birth of Dion Fortune; an event which was taken up by a wider concourse of people than my own group, and also, did I but know it, within the portals of the Society of the Inner Light.

I had begun to suspect some changes were being made there from my contact with Simon Buxton of the Arcania bookshop in Bath for whom I had done a number of workshops. He had become a member of the Society but his demeanour and attitude to the esoteric world seemed so much at variance with the enclosed and reserved atmosphere of the organisation that I remembered that I had some difficulty in believing my ears.

This came into closer focus when, in July 1991, I was invited to meet the new Warden. The occasion was to see if I was willing to edit a volume of Dion Fortune's war letters. I felt this might be a somewhat delicate interview as I had already been issuing a cassette tape of extracts from these letters for some time. A former member from the old days had given me a complete set, and much in the spirit of Israel Regardie when he published the papers of the Golden Dawn, I determined that such valuable material was not going to remain hidden under a bushel. Anyhow, I trusted I was not likely to be hanged for piracy – as Dion Fortune thought she had been in a previous incarnation.

It turned out that the new Warden of the Society of the Inner Light was an old acquaintance from Helios days. David Williams (not to be confused with the earlier David of the corporal's club) was, like me, an aspiring small publisher back in 1963. Indeed we shared some of the Helios distribution and production facilities, and he also wrote some articles for me on the esoteric lore in fairy tales, which I published in *New Dimensions*.

I was invited to meet him for lunch at his London club, the Oxford and Cambridge University in Pall Mall, although plans misfired at the last minute because Simon Buxton was not allowed through the door of the august establishment because he was not wearing suit and collar and tie. Nonetheless David and I carried on successfully without him and I came away with the commission to produce a volume of edited letters, to be called, somewhat sensationally I thought, *Dion Fortune's Magical Battle of Britain.*

I completed the assignment quite quickly for I was already familiar with most of the material. But as I worked on the letters I began to be subject to the impression that I should follow Dion Fortune's example in writing some kind of esoteric novel. I resisted this thought. Despite my limited success in the theatre I was convinced I had little talent for fiction. However, so persistent was this feeling that in the end I gave way, if only to prove that I was quite incapable of such a task! Thus began a visualisation sequence which rose before my inner eyes and ears as I wrote – which led to most unexpected consequences.

I started getting a scenario persistently pushed into my head of being in what seemed to be the saloon bar in the Queen's Hotel at Burnham-on-Sea. I was present in a crowd of people who were about to set off to a vicars and tarts fancy dress party. I kept getting this coming through with the impulse to imagine I was there and if I wrote down what happened I would learn something to my advantage. Eventually I did, only to find that the party goers then went off, leaving one chap who seemed dressed up in somewhat old fashioned army officer's uniform. He was feeding money into a slot machine, or trying to, and asked for my assistance. When I went over I saw that he was trying to use old money – big pre-decimal pennies. I accidentally knocked against him, I think, and he appeared to be suffering from some old war wound or something, as he was obviously pained. I realised then it was David Carstairs, who contrived to persuade me to rush up to room number 7, which I had thought to be mine, but when we got there and opened the door, who should be sitting there but a couple of the Masters associated with the Society of the Inner Light – one sitting in the armchair and the other looking out of the window. It was then I realised that I was expected to start writing down what they told me by way of instruction.

I was too flabbergasted to do anything about this immediately but the power of this imaginative sequence was sufficient for me to try to follow it up systematically a while later, when over the course of ninety days, from 24th July to the 21st October 1993, I took dictation from all three of them.

The technique I used was simply to visualise them talking to me and to write down what they said. This could be quite tiring, doing it regularly night after night, but if I failed to sit down to it, the chances were that I would be roused out of bed, fully awake, in the small hours of the morning, to get on with it then. I was therefore quite glad when the job seemed finished to their satisfaction.

I have no desire to make specific claims as to the ultimate source of all this, whether it be contact with superior intelligences or my own subconscious or even superconscious mind. Although I had a clear idea of the personalities with whom I conversed, I simply referred to them in the script as the Chancellor, whom I visualised as Thomas More (who had subsequently taken the place of Dion Fortune's original contact of Thomas Erskine – another Lord Chancellor), the Philosopher, whom I visualised as Socrates, and the Soldier, whom I visualised as David Carstairs.

The worth of any of this kind of material must rest on its internal validity rather than any claims as to its source. Certainly the process seemed similar to literary composition, except that it came through a lot easier, just writing down the words, or sometimes phrasing blocks of ideas, that came into my head. The main difference being that it came through at about two or three times my usual speed of conscious composition. On average about 1200 words per hour as opposed to 500.

Having written down all this material I was not at all sure what to do with it.

The material fell into three parts. *The Approach to Magical Images*, a direct teaching on the inner mechanics of forming a magical group. *A Guide to the Inner Abbey*, a sequence of directed visualisations based upon the structure of an abbey church much like Tewkesbury, via crypt and various chapels and tower and environs, to form a complete curriculum of training in making contacts. Whilst *The Magical Vortex* gave instruction based on principles first enunciated in *The Cosmic Doctrine* on the dynamics of inner contact.

Some years later, somewhat to my surprise, the Society of the Inner Light published it as *The Abbey Papers*, and it remains a guide for any who wish to form their own groups, or to follow an individual curriculum of training. It was later augmented by material my daughter Rebecca developed while working with it, and issued as an expanded edition.

One thing led on to another, however, and in a certain sense these old contacts began to externalise – in the form of publishing opportunities. This despite things beginning to look quite dire on the esoteric publishing scene.

For various commercial reasons, it was becoming increasingly difficult for medium sized publishers to survive. Element Books, a promising esoteric publishing enterprise that had commissioned *The Magical World of the Inklings,* went out of business, fortunately not before selling out the complete edition of my work. Whilst Aquarian Press, the one time eager home for most of my other books, was acquired by a large multinational. Following this there came a ruthless purging of the books.

As a former executive in a large publishing company I could see just what was happening. In a large company with large overheads the accountants are pretty ruthless about how much warehouse space (costed at so much per cubic metre) is taken up by stock (or "product" as they like to call it) that does not move fast enough to generate sufficient "return on assets used". I was never allowed to print stock that would not sell within 18 months and was expected to make a return of 65% profit (of which 50% was gobbled up by overheads – including of course my salary, the office block, the car park, the pension fund, etc., etc.)

A hard fact of life is that few esoteric books of any quality will meet with these criteria. Consequently, at this time in common with a number of fellow authors I found my books being put out of print. On the brighter side of this, in dumping large quantities of stock, as an alternative to sending the books off to be pulped as waste paper, the new owners were quite willing to sell them off at bargain prices. This seemed to me a great opportunity for some small bookseller/publisher of the type that Helios had once been. Indeed had I been some decades younger I might perhaps have grabbed the opportunity. However, I came across a similar kind of concern in the form of Magis Books, an occult mail order bookshop, with ambitions to publish in a small way as Thoth Publications. Having made the acquaintance of its principal, Tom Clarke, I put to him the opportunities that were becoming available, most of which he took up, to equip himself with an enviable list. And a perfectly viable one if you can keep your overheads low.

At the same time, Tom was also eager, and apparently had the means, to do a certain amount of original publishing on his own. This happened to coincide very helpfully with my recent role as an outrider to the Society of the Inner Light, as I realised there was a great deal of interesting stuff by Dion Fortune that had not yet been published. Thus the launching of a series of books, "co-authored" to greater or less degree by myself, and the late Dion Fortune.

An obvious first choice was the collection of her articles on ritual magic that I had published in *New Dimensions* magazine back in the 1960s. I now produced these in volume form. Each article of hers I accompanied with one of my own on the same subject, bringing some of her insights up to date, and giving practical examples of modern magical practice in areas where she had, in the climate of her times, felt obliged to be more reticent. Hence the publication of *An Introduction to Ritual Magic* by Dion Fortune and Gareth Knight.

I followed up with *The Circuit of Force,* an important series of articles that she had written for her magazine in 1939/40 and which I had heard

Dick Mallock describe as "rather dangerous"! I did not think so. They were the result of her colloquies with Bernard Bromage in 1938 on some of the practicalities of yoga and the etheric vehicle. Here I was able to provide a useful accompanying commentary by a lucky find on a bouquinist's stall in Paris. It was an 1893 guide to etheric magnetism – *Théories et procédés du Magnétisme – Cours professé á l'Ecole Pratique de Magnétisme* by Hector Durville, a mine of useful practical and historical information on a lost art.

I continued with *Principles of Hermetic Philosophy* along with *The Esoteric Philosophy of Astrology* which were Dion Fortune's last works in her Monthly Letters to students a short time before she died. Like me, she was no great astrologer, but she provided some interesting insights into magical applications of an astrological birth chart.

After that it was natural to produce a collection of her writings on mediumship, of which she had considerable personal experience. Indeed it had been her firm belief that it formed the power house of any esoteric group, and she certainly bolstered theory with practice right up until the time of her death. Taking the opportunity to reprint her early work *Spiritualism in the Light of Occult Science*, I enhanced it with her descriptions of how she undertook trance, and her personal experience of doing so, to provide a rare and useful book on the subject in *Spiritualism and Occultism*.

Finally, using as a core a reprint of her little book *Practical Occultism in Daily Life* I added a pot pourri of interesting bits and pieces from her pen, including early work with David Carstairs, in *Practical Occultism*.

This was not the end of the game however, as I was able to follow through with an esoteric biography *Dion Fortune and the Inner Light* with the advantage of full access to the Society of the Inner Light's records. This satisfactorily summed up the old millennium with its publication in 2000.

Not that the bottom of the barrel had yet been reached! One day David Williams asked me to cast an eye over some papers left by Dr Edward Gellately to see if they might be worth publication. I remembered him from being a guinea pig in his researches into the Alexander technique back in the 1950s, and later unsuccessfully urging him to write a book about his unique knowledge. The file marked with his name appeared to contain – in considerable disorder – voluminous notes for a book, but which to my amazement turned out to be largely by Dion Fortune. They included details of her ambitions, with her husband Dr Penry Evans, to form a healing arm to their esoteric school back in 1927, under direction of an inner contact they called the Master of Medicine.

For one reason and another this had never come to fruition but Dion Fortune was still at work on it in 1942. In company with her old Golden Dawn mentor, Maiya Tranchell-Hayes she had conducted an experimental series of contacts with the Master of Medicine in the presence of other medical men, now that her husband was no longer with her. They resulted in a series of monographs with a very limited circulation entitled *Esoteric Therapeutics*. And after 1946 it appeared that the material had later been further worked on by Dr Gellately and Margaret Lumley Brown.

It was no easy matter to sort through this conglomeration of assorted material but I eventually hacked out a reasonably coherent *Principles of Esoteric Healing* by Dion Fortune. One interesting fact was to discover that the method used by Margaret Lumley Brown in my esoteric review back in 1959, of scrying the Sephiroth of the Tree of Life in my aura, was originally formulated as a psychic diagnostic technique in esoteric medicine.

The last element of Dion Fortune's writing I was able to lay before the public was *The Arthurian Formula*, the evocation of which had formed the basis for the memorable Hawkwood of 1981 in the re-calling of Arthur and which inspired my writing of *The Secret Tradition in Arthurian Legend*. The eventual coming to light of this old material, competently augmented by Margaret Lumley Brown, I felt deserved another useful expansion in the form of a paper by Wendy Berg, whose research into the possible faery origins of Queen Guenevere were to spark another line of investigation and experiment for me, much encouraged by R. J. Stewart.

29

This Wretched Splendour
1996-98

When Dion Fortune began to open up her psychic faculties back in 1922 one of the first to make contact was a young man who went by the name of David Carstairs. He had a very breezy likeable personality with comments far from the weighty teachings of those whom he shortly introduced who worked with Dion Fortune for the rest of her life.

> Do I know the name Carstairs? Ought to. Signed cheques with it. My father was a cycle manufacturer in Coventry. I couldn't get on with office work. I was in the Cycle Corps. Of course I am pretty close to the Earth. Haven't been over very long. That is why I was put on this job. Makes it easier. The others have been dead a long time. Lucky to get this job, wasn't I?

Carstairs seems to have had the function of what in spiritualist circles would be called a "control". That is to say, one upon the inner side who organises those who wish to communicate with the medium. Although the bulk of the teachings relayed by Dion Fortune came from two or three of these other "Masters", or Inner Plane Adepti as they came to be called, contacts with Carstairs, at a lighter level, continued to be made for many years to come.

He had apparently been killed in the 1st World War and although some doubt has been placed upon his identity, for no army records confirm his existence, he was certainly capable of making his presence felt over the years. This became evident in 1979 to Brenda, one of the co-founders of my group, after looking through some old war papers, military instructions, trench maps and diaries kept in the family. This induced next day a vision of young boy soldiers marching and singing. Then there flashed into her mind an old time music hall with an audience of soldiers, and a man on stage tap dancing with a walking stick and singing in a mock cockney voice "She's my lady love…etc" (part of a popular 1st World War song *Lily of Laguna*). Then came a feeling of heat and a voice saying "Carstairs, it's Carstairs!"

Apparently he had homed in on the old maps and papers of the previous evening and said that physical objects could be effectively used to make and sustain contacts. This initial contact was short but he was pleased that such contact had been made, and it developed over time.

Announcing his presence by means of an old 1st World War song seemed to be his trade mark and became something of a joke with members of my group, three of whom experienced in their heads the call sign of a scratchy old-fashioned gramophone record playing another popular hit of the times, *Roses of Picardy*, as a preliminary to his making contact.

However, apart from his input to me in the course of receiving *The Abbey Papers* in 1993, his major involvement in the work of the group did not occur until the advent of my daughter Rebecca a couple of years later. Shortly after joining my group, when doing a simple meditation, she suddenly became aware of a young man in military uniform sitting in front of her on a wooden chair, smoking a cigarette (much to her annoyance). He immediately smiled and said "Aha, so you made it then!" That was the last she heard from him for a year and a half. Then in February 1996, after a Hawkwood meeting, she began to hear his voice in her head, and since it came through rather sporadically (and often inconveniently) she decided to formalise it by writing it down.

The first sessions were little more than jovial banter on personal mundane topics, for Carstairs was keen right from the start to avoid excessive formality or reverence, as it could stifle the communicative faculty. Thus there developed an informal style of dialogue, including numerous asides, puns, facetious wise-cracks, slang expressions, insults and even the occasional swear word. This jovial attitude was a very positive thing, as if proving that it is possible to approach the Mysteries in an easy-going, human sort of way, without undermining the validity of the work itself.

I quote Rebecca's description of how these contacts were made, for they were exactly the way I experienced them myself, not only in *The Abbey Papers*, but later in my contacts with Margaret Lumley Brown. All was a far cry from Dion Fortune's technique of falling into a complete trance, being unconscious of what is going on, and in need of an independent scribe.

Although my early contacts with Carstairs had strong visual imagery and no words, as soon as the verbal communication began the visual aspect disappeared; it seems that since the images are only there to focus the mind they can be dispensed with as soon as a decisive contact is made. So when I take down the communication I don't 'see' him at all, I am merely aware of his presence. Sometimes it feels as though he is standing behind me, looking over my right shoulder (he rarely appears at my left, for some reason). The voice is in my head but unobtrusive, so it is difficult to distinguish it from the voice of my own thoughts – it has the same articulation that you might find if you were reciting poetry silently to yourself. There is no strong sensation of having somebody else inside my head, it feels more like having my own mind split into two parts, a 'me-brain' and a 'David-brain' both sharing the same channel of consciousness. The only way I can tell that the communication is coming from him and not from my own subconscious is by its consistency of character, the sort of things that are said, and the rate at which it comes through – considerably faster than I could write if I were making it up myself. And with experience I have developed a 'feel' for when he is there, in much the same way that you can be in a room with somebody you know well and sense their presence without actually seeing them. One interesting aspect of his communicative technique (so subtle that it took me a while to notice that he was doing it, and it seems to reflect his experience and skill as a communicator) is that each piece of information comes through twice. First he drops it into my consciousness all in one go as a complete block of intuitive understanding, and then he immediately feeds it through line by line in actual words. Thus there is never any necessity for me to blindly write down words without understanding the concept behind them, or to struggle to express a concept which I understand on an abstract level but have to put into my own words.

In all such 'mind to mind' contacts there are of course difficulties in guaranteeing accuracy, for the communicator can only use words and concepts that are in the subconscious mind of the mediator. Thus all communication of this kind has to be judged according to its inherent quality at all stages, not on the assumed or claimed esoteric rank of any of the parties involved. And, like long-distance radio communication, quality can vary.

As far as the mediator is concerned the experience is very much like that of a novelist or playwright who finds that a character within his or her mind seems to be taking on a life of its own. This is a common occurrence in creative thought processes, whether or not inner plane contacts are involved. It also occurs of course in common day-dreaming, and indeed in forms of neurosis and psychosis. However, the magical applications should be familiar to all, at least in theory. We build a magical image of the contact within the mind and then see if it does or says anything.

With regard to our experience of Carstairs from 1996 to 1998 he certainly said plenty – and also did plenty.

Among the initial written communications taken by Rebecca was a ritual based upon Chapels of Remembrance, first performed in the GK Group and on a number of occasions since. A rite conducted for the relief of the victims of conscience in war, innocent victims of warfare, the physically and psychologically shattered in warfare, and the dissipation of the shadows of war from locations. In many respects, this type of ritual might be seen as a type of intercessory prayer, for many souls, living or dead, still in torment or in conflict. It differs from intercessory prayer however by being a detailed and deliberate construct.

A further development of the Carstairs contact came in a GK Group meeting in April 1997, when Rebecca produced a ritual aimed at opening up the Carstairs contact to others, and which led me to remark in my summary report: "I do not think ritual magic is ever going to be quite the same after this working!"

Although based upon very traditional methods of evocation – processing round a picture while evocatively singing – what was new was the use of humour, even light hearted sarcasm, in ritual. Far from destroying the ritual atmosphere as might have been expected, it served to point up the deeper points of contact in the working. A kaleidoscopic sequence of visions started with the poet Wilfred Owen acting as a guide in Tewkesbury Abbey at an adorned altar of remembrance, leading on to the sacraments being administered to those about to go to the Western Front. All then left through the great west doors to meet Carstairs which was followed by a visit to Coventry Cathedral, bombed to obliteration in the 2nd World War and dedicated as a site of international reconciliation. Thence embarking on a troop train, seeing the ruins of Ypres, a weeping Madonna in a dug-out, and then the ultimate sacrifice of troops going over the top in trench warfare.

This was an inner "magic lantern" show of a very powerful sequence of imagery in which a very wide range of emotional stops were played upon, from the opening *Roses of Picardy* – in which it was difficult to keep a dry eye – to the concluding light hearted panache of a reverse circumambulation with the community singing of *Goodbye-ee! Goodbye-ee! Wipe the tear, baby dear, from your eye-ee…*

Who said that ritual magic had to be portentously solemn and self-important? The fact was demonstrated that there can be dedication and spirituality in the midst of innocence, joy and laughter. It is extraordinary how the apparent near-doggerel of some of the songs of the time could be vehicles for great depths of emotion – including a brief snatch of *The Bells of Hell go Ting-a-Ling-a-Ling* as David Carstairs, an officer in the Cycle Corps, appeared to fall off his bike!

Coincidentally there was a television programme later in the day, *The Roses of No Man's Land*, with the fascinating and at times harrowing reminiscences of some former nurses and hospital assistants of the 1st World War, by now aged between 96 and 108. The multifaceted and enduring expression of the human spirit coming across very strongly and poignantly in the faces of these very old ladies alongside photographs of the bright and glamorous young things they once had been at the time they were facing these horrors.

Between this event and the next meeting in June my book *An Introduction to Ritual Magic* was published which included examples of Rebecca's initial contacts with David Carstairs, describing not only modes of contact, but how "synchronicities" could be produced from an inner plane initiative. That is to say, actions as well as words.

Things moved on further at the GK Group meeting in June in which I was moved to perform a working based upon the war-related poetry of Rudyard Kipling. I had been attracted on more than one occasion to visit his old home at Batemans (administered by the National Trust) which I found extraordinarily evocative. He seemed another Edwardian poet, like Alfred Noyes, who had direct links into the national group soul.

There was in his work and in the house occasional hints of his affiliation to Freemasonry, but if he had any more esoteric contacts he was always very reserved about them. His sister had been a spiritualist medium and he went on record to say that he hoped no-one would attempt to contact him by such means in the afterlife. A similar reservation against the practice as had been voiced by Alfred Noyes. However, his collection of stories for children *Puck of Pook's Hill* (followed by *Rewards and Fairies*) was directly inspired by his friend and contemporary Edith Nesbit, author of a series of esoteric children's books and, whether he knew it or not, a member of the Hermetic Order of the Golden Dawn.

My feeling is that his esoteric connections were largely intuitive. They show up in the children inadvertently evoking the friendly nature spirit Puck to visible appearance by a little bit of unconscious ritual magic in their acting out a part of *A Midsummer Night's Dream*. Then Puck provides them with means to contact him in the future with leaves of oak and ash and thorn. I had lately become much aware of a special place near my home where an oak and an ash tree grow like two pillars by the side of a meadow, with a thorn bush between them, and where I had picked up quite a strong Merlin and Nimué contact.

For my Hawkwood working I had strewn leaves from this place on the floor of the lodge, which as the rite went on seemed to act almost like a magic carpet. The rite was of a very simple nature, virtually little more than reading of a sequence of relevant poems in a dedicated environment, which indeed was much the same technique as had had such remarkable effects in the legendary Arthurian workshop at Hawkwood back in 1981. The poems I selected were, however, poems that had come to Kipling by his experience of the 1st World War, which included the loss of his son John at the Battle of Loos, and whose body or grave was never found during Kipling's lifetime, although he went to immense lengths to try to discover it. It was this that led Kipling to play a major part in the War Graves Commission, and the words placed on the gravestone of any unidentified soldier, "Known Unto God", were Kipling's own.

This kind of magical work makes for pretty hard going at the time, as emotions sweep through you, and *The Children* was the most difficult poem to get through in this respect, particularly with its imagery of the long term desecration of the dead, tossed in the mud and on the barbed wire by continued shelling, victims of an uncontrollable machinery of war – a monster created and let loose by 20th century man. I felt pretty close to Kipling in this one and could feel a tickling sensation as if my face were changing to a replica of Kipling's and others remarked that my voice changed markedly at the same time. One member of the group had a big surprise on finding that a pebble he had been holding during the ritual had shattered into four pieces in his hand!

The Charm at the end seemed to have a very healing resolution to the rite, which concluded with the placing of earth upon the altar to fashion a model grave from it. The earth in question, from my garden, contained a fair sprinkling of mud gathered from the Somme the previous year, since when they had been growing cornflowers (*bleuets de France*) and

Rebecca Wilby

poppies, some of the latter from seed taken from the dug-out that once sheltered Wilfred Owen on the battlefield. The wild flowers too, evoked in this poem, also brought in the faery element again and thus helped to round off the rite to a conclusion. Although in a sense it was not a conclusion, but a staging post for much that was to follow.

The working had a marked effect upon Rebecca. The energy did not seem to be building up for her in the way it usually does, and then she realised that, for her at least, this was only the opening up of what was meant to be an on-going ritual, and one which would have to continue outside the lodge. Feeling a bit lost and helpless immediately afterwards she climbed the fence and went across the fields that face on to Hawkwood college, and in the soggy bit by a pond at the bottom picked up two handfuls of English soil and sang the song version of Kipling's poem *Have You News of My Boy Jack?* which though not of spectacular literary merit is really harrowing. As she was bellowing this out to the rather suspicious sheep gathered round, it became clear to her what she had to do next. With a tremendous surge of energy and peace and well being, she was prompted to pick up a couple of large bits of log and run back up the hill with them.

She realised that one of them was destined for John Kipling's recently discovered grave at Lone Tree, Loos – a site also strongly linked with Gloucestershire, the 10th Glosters being almost totally wiped out there in the same battle as John Kipling.

And so on our return visit to the Western Front immediately after this meeting, she engraved a memorial in poker work upon one of the logs, which she placed on John Kipling's grave. This second visit to the Western Front included the Ypres salient, the site of David Carstairs' war, where as I lit a candle for him in the cathedral it fizzed like a firework. "Ah yes, typical Carstairs!" I thought.

One of the most moving moments for me was at the village of Messines. It had been completely wiped out during the war, but the rebuilt church had been dedicated as an international focus for peace with the flags of all nations in it, along with an evocative Black Madonna. Here the custodian asked if I would like to play the carillon of bells. As a result I was able to ring out *Amazing Grace* over the surrounding battlefields, still littered with the fragmented bones of the dead and unexploded shells and bombs of the type that had shattered them.

By some kind of synchronicity, just before our trip David Williams, the Warden of the Society of the Inner Light, presented me with an old war map, in the centre of which was the town of Albert. On visiting there we discovered it had once been known as "the Lourdes of the North", on account of miracles following the discovery of a golden statuette of the

Virgin and Child in medieval times. A large figure of the golden virgin holding out the Christ child high above her head was placed on the topmost point of the basilica. This had been toppled early on by shell fire during the war but remained leaning at an acute angle over the town, as if holding out the Christ child in blessing.

WORLD PREMIERE

THIS WRETCHED SPLENDOUR

by Rebecca Wilby
a new First World War drama by a Cheltenham playwright

7.45pm
Directed by   6th—13th
David Wheeler   September 1997

THE PLAYHOUSE THEATRE
Bath Road, Cheltenham

Box office open daily 10am–4pm. Telephone (01242) 552852

This line of work initiated by Carstairs was not to be restricted to the confines of an esoteric lodge. He went on to inspire Rebecca with the need to write a play based upon his life at the Western Front. Of course it is one thing to write a play, and another thing to have it performed. But amazingly, this occurred in two separate theatres in the course of the next six months.

This Wretched Splendour was first performed in an amateur production at the Playhouse Theatre, Cheltenham from 6th to 13th September 1997 and then snapped up for professional production at a London fringe theatre, the Grace Theatre, Battersea, from 10th to 28th February 1998, evoking an enthusiastic review from Michael Billington, dramatic critic of the *Guardian* newspaper:

> The standard first world war play is still R. C. Sherriff's *Journey's End*. But Rebecca Wilby, a 29-year-old from Cheltenham, knocks it into a cocked hat with *This Wretched Splendour*. Where Sherriff's play is steeped in the public-school ethos, this one conveys the eccentric humanity and the tragedy of life at the front line. ... A more than promising debut.

How much Carstairs himself or Rebecca was owed this accolade is a moot point. I rather fancy that the honours should be shared. The script has subsequently been published by Skylight Press.

Whether as a result of Carstairs' efforts, or whether they were simply part of a new wave of consciousness in the soul of the nation, Remembrance Day celebrations had seemed in danger of petering out as survivors of the 1st World War conflict died – but since then it has come to be celebrated with increasing enthusiasm and recognition of its significance.

30

Che Return of the Native
1998-2010

Nothing ever happened quickly at the Society of the Inner Light. From my initial contact with the Warden in 1991 seven years elapsed before I was invited to their headquarters in Steele's Road. But although it was 38 years since I had last crossed the threshold, and many changes had been made in that time, I must say it did feel like going home – not quite as the prodigal son – but once an Inner Lighter always an Inner Lighter I suppose. Certainly there was no mistaking the genuineness of the welcome I received, complete with the presentation of a rose from the garden – most unusual for the time of year!

Inside the house, all was much as I remembered it. The Lesser Mystery Lodge was just as I recalled. Indeed it was a replica of its prototype in Queensborough Terrace where I had first been initiated back in 1954. Even the Greater Mystery Temple appeared much the same, although it had operated as such only for about a year after the move to the new house. When the old degree structure had been abandoned there was no use for it apart from a general meeting room as an alternative to the library. Now, however, it had been fitted up again, with the addition of some impressive pillars at the entrance.

I was invited to sit in there and was formally welcomed by the Warden on behalf of the Chancellor, at which point I felt moved to say that I still regarded myself, as I always had, as server of the Masters behind the Fraternity and was willing to help out in any way I could. I had already done something of course by way of publishing, but now the requirement seemed to be on a more esoteric level.

To my inner senses, seated in the old Greater Mystery lodge, it seemed as if there was a great layer of power hovering at about ceiling level, but with a gap between it and the temple below. An immediate task seemed to be to facilitate a conjunction, to form a powerful circuit when all would be in effective magical action once more. And I recalled some of Margaret Lumley Brown's remarkable work in this very place in the latter days of the old regime.

So began another phase of my membership of the Society of the Inner Light. I was formally re-admitted with the title of Tutelary Magus – a non-executive position rather after the style of a management consultant in the business world – with a remit to suggest ways of introducing procedures and levels of working that I had known in former days. An advisory capacity was all I sought – I had no wish to take over the place.

In recent years, from the outside, I had felt the Fraternity to be somewhat like a hearth fire banked up behind a thick level of ash, that needed only a good kick and a poke for it to burst into flame again. But in fact the actual kicking and poking were not quite so easy. A whole generation had gone by since the old days, and although there was a general desire to get back to being a graded esoteric fraternity, the years between had instilled a deeply conservative and cautious streak, a desire to make an omelette but fear of breaking any eggs.

To be frank I wondered if I was really the best person to undertake this refurbishment of the Fraternity. My experience with public workshops and the GK Group over the years had given me quite a radical attitude to custom and practice. It seemed to me that my more conservative old Inner Light chum Alan Adams, who like me had left in the 1960s and founded his own organisation – the London Group – might have been a better choice for the task. Indeed I thought about trying to set up a meeting with him to discuss best ways forward and his possible cooperation. However, this came to nothing when after a brief correspondence he fell sick and died. Thus my hoped for meeting with him turned out to be attendance at his funeral. So for better or for worse, as fate or whatever powers would have it, the work of renewal lay squarely at my door.

Four levels of action demanded attention – the House of the Order, the Study Course, the Lesser Mysteries, and the Greater Mysteries – the latter but recently opened and still in somewhat embryonic form.

The house had indeed been refurbished as a first requirement when the current team had taken over in 1990, but the extensive garden had become something of a jungle. I recalled the great plans when we had moved in back in 1960 – to make it a carefully tended plot of symbolic holy ground. Indeed I had put in a fair bit of digging and planting in it myself at the time. The problem was that although the ideal remained to have it tended by initiates, as membership had dropped there was just not enough of them to do so. Arthur Chichester, a stickler for perfection, would have turned in his grave to see the state of the garden now – particularly as his ashes are reportedly scattered there!

Once more I turned out, this time with motor mower and heavy duty secateurs, and with a small band of volunteers gradually things were turned round – but not without a struggle. Real estate can no doubt be a stabilising element for an esoteric group but can also be a heavy burden to maintain.

The Study Course had also badly gone to seed and needed heavy pruning. Over the years different Directors of Studies had added their own bits and pieces and it could now take years for a student to work through. It was therefore not surprising if no initiations had taken place for some time. The main need was to cut out dead wood, such as great gobbets of advanced *Cosmic Doctrine* material, along with unnecessary administrative delays. In short to prepare a keen student for admission within a year.

The Lesser Mysteries appeared to be in reasonable shape, although with some accretions I found difficult to live with, mostly in the form of long drawn out preliminaries before the action started. I had trained my own initiates to be ready for inner action almost at the turn of a switch, but the tradition within the Fraternity (largely it would seem to suit the personal preferences of one or two senior members) was to build things up painfully slowly, rather like bringing a kettle to the boil by putting a penny candle under it.

There was also, in the eyes of some, great emphasis on minutiae of words and procedures even if the reason for them was not understood. My own experience was that imaginative creativity and attuned intuition were the essence of magic, not repetition of ill-understood formulae. Indeed, in my opinion, the latter is not magic but superstition. And when it came to the occasional "path working" in the newly opened Greater Mystery level, I was at pains to demonstrate that effectiveness was dependent on creative storytelling at a pace congenial to building evocative images – and not wordy vehicles for moralising sermons or intellectual speculation.

When it came to old Greater Mystery rituals, which to my surprise were still preserved despite a holocaust of old material during the 1980s, I was rather touched to find my old Isis ritual still there – albeit with a ban on its use because it mixed Christian and pagan symbolism. Not that I felt any need to resuscitate it. To my eyes it now appeared no more than a fairly routine example of apprentice work; and the fact that it had been so lauded at the time of its original performance back in 1959 was a useful marker to see how my own work at any rate had progressed since then. It had indeed been largely refurbished for work with my own group under the title of the Assumption Ritual in the mid 1980s.

Over the succeeding months and years I wrote a series of rituals of various kinds for performance at Greater Mystery level – and encouraged others to write their own – a prospect greeted with considerable trepidation at first. What did encourage me was that with the working of these rituals the power and effectiveness of the Lesser Mystery workings increased considerably as if by osmosis. Also the initiation of Study Course students increased markedly – balancing and then surpassing the death rate of elderly members – which had been a worrying statistic in the past.

On a more informal level I was asked to help develop a couple of senior members in techniques of receiving inner plane communications. I was not too sure how to go about this, but conducted a series of sessions wherein we sat in lodge and built up the images and tried to discern if they did or said anything.

Whatever it did for my students it blossomed forth in a remarkable way with me. I started to get a series of contacts with Margaret Lumley Brown every evening back at home, much after the fashion in which I had received the Abbey Papers. This went on for a whole year and I duly wrote it up each week and sent a copy to the Fraternity. This met with some excitement when it appeared that MLB in her discourse had coincidentally answered one or two questions that one of the members had had in mind to put to her.

That was about as far as it went though. We were obviously not going back to the old regime where all inner communications, received by a team of mediums (and later one lone "mediator") were routinely duplicated and circulated to members. This was all one to me, but I felt that being filed away in a cabinet was not quite all that was called for, so under the title of *The Temple Papers* I passed them round to various individuals in and outside the Fraternity who I thought might benefit from them, and with a view to possible publication, in whole or in part, at some future time.

Meanwhile, as previously described, Rebecca and Carstairs had been hard at work. What came across loud and clear was that the Chapels of Remembrance work deserved to be put on some kind of permanent basis. David Williams in particular greatly supported this and they were incorporated into the regular programme for celebration in November each year. To get this initiative off the ground I thought it appropriate to have Rebecca in attendance, who was plainly at this time acting as David Carstairs' amanuensis in a very remarkable manner.

The suggestion met with severe reaction – almost of shock and horror. No stranger had been admitted into the Lodge for at least fifty years. In fact I think it was the so-called Irish mage, Art O'Murnaghan, a little before my time, and before that Maiya Tranchell-Hayes in 1941/2 under conditions of the utmost secrecy.

Despite the "democratising" efforts of Arthur Chichester in the 1960s there ever remained an underlying sense of "them and us", probably a hangover from as far back as the twenties and thirties. One problem of a long standing esoteric group is the weight of past custom and practice that can build up almost like a burden of karma, inhibiting new developments and creativity.

As an example of this attitude, in the early 1970s, when John Hall and I drove up from Gloucestershire for a bulk delivery of copies of *The Cosmic Doctrine* to the house, we wondered if, as old initiates, we might perhaps be invited in for a cup of tea for old time's sake. We were soon disabused of that however. Our reception by John Makin, a senior member and general factotum of the Society for many years (indeed the Magus who had initiated me back in 1954) was polite and cordial enough, but he insisted on taking delivery of the load on the pavement outside. As souls who had chosen to walk in outer darkness we were not even admitted beyond the garden gate.

However, things had now improved, at any rate just a little. After some heart searching, Rebecca was admitted, but only under solemn warning that this was a unique occasion never to be repeated or even divulged to anyone. (Shades of Maiya Tranchell-Hayes' temporary admission in 1940!) However, to my mind, Rebecca's presence was the thin end of an essential wedge. With existing members in short supply and they with little magical experience beyond their own four walls it seemed vital to consider major surgery. If I had looked at my own contribution to the society up to now as somewhat in the nature of a blood transfusion, I began to think that we should now be thinking more in terms of an organ transplant.

I had to introduce the idea with considerable finesse, and was also aware of its dangers. As in the analogy of a physical organ transplant, the primary problem was the matter of rejection, with all kinds of possible consequences, to host or implants alike. Anyhow I went ahead, at first with what was billed as a one off experiment in cooperation with members of my group – after all we all gave allegiance to the same inner plane adepti. The first meeting was a reasonable success, although as expected, attended by some violent reactions in certain quarters on both sides. Indeed it caused a rupture in the Avalon Group, then run by two co-magi, one of whom fled from the place in horror, declaring it to have the atmosphere of a Jesuit seminary and wanting to forbid any of the group to attend the SIL ever again.

Then, as luck would have it, a precedent was discovered in the archives. Occasionally members had been admitted in the past without having to go through the Study Course or Initiation, by means of a short Rite of Obligation. This simple device was reintroduced and so members of my old group who felt so inclined could now be admitted to the Fraternity. This was in no sense a formal merger, but as I saw it, the opportunity for some cross fertilisation to mutual advantage. And so it turned out, with the Avalon Group members being referred to, semi-officially, as the "away team" as opposed to the "home team" of Inner Light initiates.

At the same time there were external forces afoot to change the existing culture. The Society in the distant past had, presumably for tax purposes, sought and obtained the status of an educational and religious charity. In the new climate of the times the Charity Commissioners had begun to take a more active interest in what established charities were doing to justify their existence as charities. With the past parsimonious aloofness that had characterised the 1980s the Society had accumulated a large bank balance that the Commissioners required be put to some demonstrable good works.

In response to this the Society founded a lectureship at an Oxford college and also undertook a little private publishing – from which I benefited from the publication of *The Abbey Papers* and a couple of volumes of collected articles I had been writing for the *Inner Light Journal*. Another welcome and significant initiative was, at my suggestion, to fund a series of lectures at Kathleen Raine's Temenos Academy at which I gave the opening and the closing talk.

I felt all this to be a welcome change of focus from a very much inturned and defensive attitude to the outer world which had, in the past, resulted in the somewhat bizarre action of making the name Dion Fortune into a registered trade mark. This had been because it was felt that certain outsiders were making claims to be the true representatives of her tradition. My own reaction to this was that if they felt they were being upstaged by outsiders they had only themselves to blame for virtually disowning her in the first place back in the sixties – and that if they had created a cultural vacuum then it was obviously going to be filled by others. The important thing was to take the Dion Fortune banner and wave it themselves, not try to stop others from doing so.

I never managed to organise any external activity by way of lectures or workshops but at least the way was paved by the initiative of my old GK Group colleague, Mike Harris, who on his own initiative began a series of annual Dion Fortune seminar/conferences at Glastonbury. I spoke at the first two of these in 2006 and 2007, the first in the town hall, which to our surprise was filled to capacity, and the second in the evocative precincts of the Assembly Rooms, in which Dion Fortune in times past had recorded her enchantment at witnessing the first performances of Rutland Boughton's faery musical drama *The Immortal Hour*.

So things developed for the rest of the decade, although with a gradual falling away of members of the "away team", who had been trained in a more informal and freely creative way of going about things, and who at times felt that their best efforts were not entirely appreciated. Whilst one might sympathise with the feelings of old stagers to the introduction of shamanic drumming on occasion, there were those who felt threatened by the slightest deviation from established opening or closing procedures. More significantly, senior members of the "home team" could not bring themselves to undertake the more intensive training and reporting procedures that, as far as the "away team" was concerned, were essential for Greater Mystery development.

Eventually at the beginning of 2010 all old Gareth Knight Group members had finally departed, leaving just myself as a kind of Elder, now into my 80s and finding travelling up to meetings something of a physical burden. It came to me that my work there was in any case done as well as it was likely to be, and that I did best to stand aside and let the Fraternity continue to develop under its own steam, finding its own way with a combination of the old and the new, as a new generation came in with some quite bright sparks among them.

Having served my apprenticeship at the Inner Light in a twelve year period from 1953 to 1965, I felt I had returned something to them in my second twelve year stint from 1998 to the present, to the best of my ability, and the rest was now up to them. I really think they have the potential to attain great things but Rome was not built in a day.

As to my own future, far from being pensioned off, fresh woods and pastures new now beckoned.

31

The Gates of Faery
2004-2010

In December 2004 I had been invited to be a guest at the annual meeting of "The Company of Hawkwood" which John and Caitlín Matthews had continued to celebrate over the years since I first coined the phrase back in the early 1980s to describe the kind of work we were doing at that time. A more positive cognomen than the early, slightly shell shocked "Hawkwood Survivors Club".

The occasion was a jolly romp, with the place filled to capacity, and a rich variety of activity. Power was not ramped up to the degree that it had been in the old Hawkwood days, which is probably no bad thing in a large gathering with individuals at various stages of progress and levels of experience.

It concluded with a celebration by the whole company of an enactment of "The Joy of the Court" culled from Chrétien de Troyes' Arthurian romance of *Erec and Enide* or the Mabinogion *Geraint and Enid*. It was probably more group theatre than heavy magical working but at the same time it may well have been the spur that pushed me into a greater study of Chrétien de Troyes that led to my book *The Faery Gates of Avalon* four years later. It also gave me the opportunity to present to John and Caitlín the actual horn I had blown on that memorable Arthurian weekend of 1981.

Of course I already thought I knew quite enough about Chrétien de Troyes from my French studies but with one of those irrational but persistent urges that in the end brook no denying, I took upon myself the task of going through each of Chrétien's romances as if both he and I were present, travelling through the whole scenario from start to finish as a kind of directed visualisation, and writing it all down.

Having done this there did not seem very much I could do with it as a piece of literature, but then there filtered into my head the realisation that much that I had "witnessed" in this way was not chivalrous knights going to the aid of damsels in distress but accounts of their initiation into faeryland – for there was a strong case for seeing the principal female characters as faery rather than human. This meant that in earlier Arthurian literature the ladies might be more important than the knights.

Other elements contributed to my coming toward this conclusion.

- In visits to Lusignan in France where the faery Melusine was said to have founded the town, the church, a castle and a dynasty.
- A fascinating book called *Red Tree, White Tree* by Wendy Berg, who put forward a case for considering even Queen Guenevere to have been a faery.
- The books of R. J. Stewart describing some of his workshops on the faery tradition, and in particular the doctrine of a Three-fold Alliance between human, animal and faery kingdoms, which rang many bells for me.

This eventually led to my writing three books. *The Faery Gates of Avalon* and *Melusine of Lusignan and the Cult of the Faery Woman* were published by R. J. Stewart Books in 2008 and 2010. The first a detailed analysis of the faery elements in the works of Chrétien de Troyes, and the second making Melusine of Lusignan more widely known in the English speaking world. The third was a translation of André Lebey's novel *The Romance of the Faery Melusine*, published by Skylight Press in 2011. In all three books I gave a brief account of what a faery contact may feel like, at any rate in my experience, and how best to go about it.

I found they could come in at various levels. After visiting Lusignan I began to find a contact coming in at an intuitive level. It dealt in imagery

The church crypt at Lusignan, said to have been built by the Faery Melusine.

but with a philosophical intent, yet a wisdom expressed more through the medium of story than by intellectual definitions. To make the contact it was necessary to build a scenario something like a questing knight discovering a castle in a particular symbolic shape, and then entering into it. This was perhaps not dissimilar to entry into an Abbey complex in *The Abbey Papers,* but in this case with a more direct feeling of relationship with the fabric of the building itself. As if it embodied the faery in its very structure.

A typical verbal contact illustrating something of this, ran as follows:

This is the magic castle of Melusine. It is I Melusine who have built it, and you will know that I am one who is and was famous for building castles or churches or many another kind of building for those who chose to work with me, and who are in turn, my chosen consorts.

All the beings, the characters in my castle, work to do my bidding. For they are expressions of myself. I can manifest in many ways, for am I not one of the race, the daughters of Proteus, the great Sea Father, who can change shape and form like the waves on the sea, from tumultuous billows that can wreck and destroy ships and the fortifications of men, or weave rainbows and visions within the spray, of sea horses and sea maidens?

The whole castle, the towers and the walls and all that is expressed between, from the upflowing waters of the hidden fount below it all, to the high towers and the contacts that may be discerned from them, and all the characters and their actions within, are an expression of myself in my completeness, or as complete a way as you are able to discover.

This is the type of the fabled tower of Merlin and of other enchanted castles or edifices, whether in the hollow hills or hawthorn towers that have ever entered the traditions of men. This is also the pattern of the so-called mating between elementals and men, although this is a far higher and elevated thing than is realised by the common speculation of ordinary men and women in the world. This is an aspect, a meaning, of the title of the Tower, given to the Virgin, the Queen of Heaven – Tower of David, Tower of Ivory. These are the gates of wisdom and dream.

This wisdom of my castle is not one of theory and speculation of the intellect, although wisdom of that kind may later come, by personal realisation with the male and concrete mind, but my wisdom is given in another way, by story, and by being, and experience and by human contact. This is ever the woman's, the feminine way. And so to enter my castle of wonders you have to bow the theorizing intellect to the burden of experience. Simply to walk in faith into the corridors of my being, and experience and record what you find. This is in itself an act of faith, but it is the steps of faith that open up further the way. Without those steps of faith you will ever stand outside the walls and wonder – building your theories in the air, thin air.

This kind of thing was at a different level from local countryside experiences where contact was virtually devoid of intellect but impacted more on the emotional and etheric levels. With the latter if felt as if one's aura lit up like a Christmas tree often accompanied by a sense of euphoria. On one particular occasion I noticed I was standing on quite soggy ground, although it was a hillside, and that I was standing over a spring – with a rowan tree just beside. This opened up a whole range of contacts including the rowan tree faery to whom I dedicated *The Faery Gates of Avalon*.

Along with contacts such as these came a greater sense of presence and communion with the world of nature, and particularly trees. I know that it is with a sense of derision that people are said to be fond of talking to plants and trees, or communing with animals or birds. As with any level of higher or inner perception including the mystically religious, we can only leave the blind to mock on until the scales fall from their eyes.

It may well be that experience and wisdom of this nature comes with age, which is another aspect of the Merlin and Nimué story. As the chemistry of the body alters away from the physically reproductive to the psychically perceptive new visions may open up that are not all geriatric folly. Age was once equated with wisdom. But there is no real need to await one's dotage for a realisation of these things.

There is of course the old and much misunderstood tradition of adepts forming relationships with elemental beings. And so I find it odd that this latter day faery work should echo in a sense that very first magical text tentatively revealed by that most unlikely guide – mystagoguic Dave of the corporals' club. An edition by "The Brothers" of *Le Comte de Gabalis* by the Abbé Montfaucon de Villars, which I did not understand at the time – and whose relevance I should realise only much later, from personal experience.

But as Dion Fortune was ever fond of saying – an ounce of experience is worth a pound of theory!

And whether I shall be carried off or disappear into the ground one day, like Merlin or Robert Kirk, Tam Lin or Thomas the Rhymer remains to be seen. In the meantime it seems I have various jobs to be done, given the time, part of which is to try to elicit just how much evidence there is for faery activity in the history of the middle ages. All of which, if any, is probably best passed off as fiction rather than fact to a secular and cynical generation!

32

Through the Skylight...
2010...

My old RAF companion and fellow initiate Alan Adams once remarked that he saw in me, not so much the Arthurian Sir Gareth as the Greek hero Ganymede – the cup bearer to the gods (although he hastened to add this implied no comment on my sexual orientation). And although I have also been likened to a fire raiser (lighting fires for others to tend), or sower of seeds (for others to cultivate), neither flames nor seeds have been my own, I have simply been their distributor.

For this reason publishing has been a principle activity of my life – even beyond the esoteric scene. Apart from my scrabbling on the periphery of the publishing trade to spread the light and seeds of wisdom of the likes of Dion Fortune, Israel Regardie, Margaret Lumley Brown, William G. Gray, Anthony Duncan, and umpteen others whose brains I have picked, I have made a living by publishing other peoples' knowledge and wisdom in the disciplines of engineering (electrical and mechanical), building, business studies and other vocational areas. Which when push comes to shove are areas as important to our welfare and happiness as expertise in the nuts and bolts, circuit diagrams, bricks and mortar, flow charts and balance sheets of the inner worlds.

Nonetheless much seems to have happened by accident, which leads me to believe that there is a certain background pattern to our lives (whether ministered by our own higher selves or by ministering spirits or even directly by God) that serves to make necessary connections even when we are blundering dimly around uncertain of what direction to take.

What was it that caused me to light upon Dion Fortune's *Esoteric Orders and their Work* at a particular time when it would have meant most to me – for in earlier or later years it would not have had such an effect upon me as to change my life. What chance brought Carl Weschcke to commission me, an unknown, to write *The Practical Guide to Qabalistic Symbolism* and edit *New Dimensions*? How was it that Anthony Duncan and I met up at Tewkesbury when each of us were ready to make such an impact upon each others' life and thought? What brought about my meeting with William Gray, by no means an easy relationship, which had significant results upon the esoteric world? What orchestrated the odd interchange of meetings between myself and David Williams, Warden of the Society of the Inner Light, over half a century? The bizarre coincidence of Margaret Lumley Brown collapsing at my wife and daughter's feet? One could go on...

From such interconnections, unforeseen and in some instances against all the odds, even of conscious intentions, came the commissioning of *A Practical Guide to Qabalistic Symbolism*, the rescuing of neglected little works by Israel Regardie such as *The Art of True Healing*, crusading on behalf of the mystical insights of Anthony Duncan in *The Christ, Psychotherapy and Magic* and *The Lord of the Dance*, the magical innovations of W. G. Gray in *The Ladder of Lights* and *Magical Ritual Methods*, plus the magazine work of *New Dimensions* and *Quadriga*, courses on *Practical Qabalah* and *Christian Qabalistic Magic*.

Then the Hawkwood workshops, when publishers such as Aquarian Press and Element Books came to me, followed by American publishers such as Weiser and Inner Traditions International during the 1980s for a series including *The Secret Tradition in Arthurian Legend, A History of White Magic, The Magical World of the Inklings, Magic and the Power of the Goddess, The Magical World of the Tarot*, until boom turned to bust with the advent of multinational publishers. The return to niche publishing via Thoth Publications in the United Kingdom and Sun Chalice in the United States to produce a series of previously unpublished works by Dion Fortune, from *Introduction to Ritual Magic* and *The Circuit of Force*, to *Principles of Esoteric Healing*, including my biography of her, *Dion Fortune and the Inner Light* and an appreciation of her much neglected follower *Pythoness, the life and work of Margaret Lumley Brown* and Dion Fortune's lost manuscript on *Principles of Esoteric Healing*.

Finally, out of the blue, came the Skylight Press, brain child of my daughter Rebecca and a kindred spirit Daniel Staniforth. A trail blazer to retain in print old titles of mine, other occult classics, and to help me indulge in what I regard as the heart and soul of publishing, the encouraging of literary talent and specialist lines of interest. Works that would otherwise be neglected by the worldly wise and financial bean counters to the mighty. With the coming of the world wide web has come methods of printing technology that make life a lot easier from the time when Morris Kahn and I first started up, our books set up in hot metal on Linotype machines, to be stored in bulky slabs in printers' warehouses, with the need to print (and sell) in thousands to make the figures turn out right.

So, with this last turn of the spiral, and to sum things up, let me repeat what I wrote at the beginning of this book concerning the guiding light of my life.

I called it magic – Kathleen Raine called it poetry – J. R. R. Tolkien called it enchantment – others have called it a variety of things – from mysticism to mumbo jumbo. All I know is, that it works – and that for better or worse I have lived most of my life by it. Now seems the time to take stock of it – not so much in self justification – but in order to dust it off, look it up and down, and make some kind of appraisal of what it was all about. Was it all worth it? What did it serve? Was it a public service for the greater good or a fanciful diversion – a flight from the real in pursuit of the ideal?

I don't know that I am any closer to answering these questions than I was at the beginning. Although I look upon them on the optimistic side. And you, as reader, are entitled to your own conclusions on the strength of what you have read. I like to think that you too will come down on the favourable side – insofar that if you did not you would probably not have even picked up this book in the first place!

If however you have picked it up and read it despite being at odds with all it contains then perhaps you had better beware – for something may be pushing you from within that you have not come to recognise yet. You may run a distinct chance of being converted. Not necessarily by me – but by your own inner self – call it inspiration or delusion according to fashion or fancy. Just recall the fate that befell Saul of Tarsus upon the road to Damascus, who ended up espousing what he thought he hated!

Each of us can but follow our own lights. Which is what I have endeavoured to do. And although much of the time it may have seemed like groping in the dark, a certain pattern seems to have been traced out by my steps. Odd chances and coincidences have caused me to meet the right people at the right time – including my nearest and dearest. And if the course of life has seemed like treading a dimly lit labyrinth, the way has not been without significance, has formed some kind of pattern, led to a series of goals. Even if each goal turns out to be a gateway – to be passed through to find something new. Whilst the final gate in this life I suppose one might liken to a skylight!

I seem to have relied a lot on largely unseen folk who apparently live on the roof of the world, whispering down through the skylight to give a little encouragement and advice. Even to catch a glimpse of them against a background of stars, or a sunlit sky that encompasses wider horizons than we are familiar with, shut within our familiar dimensions of floor, ceiling and walls.

And perhaps in time (or out of it) I may be accorded the chance of looking back through the skylight at folks down here – reading these words – and perhaps even whispering a little guidance too. So keep looking to the skylight as I leave you with the greeting – *Au Revoir* – till we meet again, either in this world or another.

For myself, in faith and hope and charity, I look forward to the possibility of becoming a fiddler on the roof! That can be made of shingle too! Will you come and join the dance?

Gareth Knight Bibliography

A Practical Guide to Qabalistic Symbolism (Helios Book Service, 1965; reissued by Samuel Weiser, 1986; paperback edition by Red Wheel Weiser, 2001)

Occult Exercises and Practices (Helios Book Service, 1969; reissued by Aquarian Press, 1976; Sun Chalice Books, 1997)

The Practice of Ritual Magic (Helios Book Service, 1969; reissued by Aquarian Press, 1976; Sun Chalice Books, 1997)

Experience of the Inner Worlds (Helios Book Service, 1975; reissued by Samuel Weiser, 1993; Skylight Press, 2010)

The Occult, an Introduction (Kahn & Averill, 1975)

A History of White Magic (Mowbray, 1978; reissued as *Magic and the Western Mind* by Llewellyn Publications, 1991; reissued under its original title by Skylight Press, 2011)

The Secret Tradition in Arthurian Legend (Aquarian Press, 1983; reissued by Samuel Weiser, 1996)

The Gareth Knight Tarot Deck (U.S. Games Systems Inc, 1984)

The Rose Cross and the Goddess (Aquarian Press, 1985; reissued as *Evoking the Goddess* by Destiny Books, 1993; later as *Magic and the Power of the Goddess* also by Destiny Books, 2008)

The Treasure House of Images (Aquarian Press, 1986; reissued as *Tarot and Magic* by Destiny Books, 1991; reissued by Skylight Press, 2012)

The Magical World of the Inklings (Element Books, 1990; reissued by Sun Chalice Books in 2001-2 as four separate books: *The Magical World of C.S. Lewis*; *The Magical World of J.R.R. Tolkien*; *The Magical World of Charles Williams*; *The Magical World of Owen Barfield*; revised and expanded edition published in one volume under the original title by Skylight Press, 2010)

The Magical World of the Tarot (Aquarian Press, 1991; reissued by Samuel Weiser, 1996)

Dion Fortune's Magical Battle of Britain (Golden Gates Press, 1993; reissued by Sun Chalice Books, 2003; Skylight Press, 2012)

An Introduction to Ritual Magic [with Dion Fortune] (Thoth Publications, 1997)

The Circuit of Force [with Dion Fortune] (Thoth Publications, 1998)

Magical Images and the Magical Imagination (Sun Chalice Books, 1998)

Principles of Hermetic Philosophy & The Esoteric Philosophy of Astrology [with Dion Fortune] (Thoth Publications, 1999)

Spiritualism and Occultism [with Dion Fortune] (Thoth Publications, 1999)

Merlin and the Grail Tradition (Sun Chalice Books, 1999; expanded edition issued by Skylight Press, 2011)

Dion Fortune and the Inner Light (Thoth Publications, 2000)

Principles of Esoteric Healing [by Dion Fortune, edited by Gareth Knight] (Sun Chalice Books, 2000; reissued by Thoth Publications, 2006)

Pythoness: the Life and Work of Margaret Lumley Brown (Sun Chalice Books, 2000; reissued by Thoth Publications, 2006)

Esoteric Training in Everyday Life (Sun Chalice Books, 2001; reissued by Skylight Press, 2012)

Practical Occultism [with Dion Fortune] (Thoth Publications, 2002)

The Abbey Papers (Society of the Inner Light, 2002; expanded edition issued by Skylight Press, 2011)

Dion Fortune and the Threefold Way (Society of the Inner Light, 2002)

The Wells of Vision (Society of the Inner Light, 2002)

Granny's Magic Cards (Sun Chalice Books, 2004; reissued as *To the Heart of the Rainbow* by Skylight Press, 2010)

Dion Fortune and the Lost Secrets of the West (e-book published by Ritemagic, www.ritemagic.co.uk, 2006)

The Arthurian Formula [with Dion Fortune, Margaret Lumley Brown and Wendy Berg] (Thoth Publications, 2006)

The Occult Fiction of Dion Fortune (Thoth Publications, 2007)

The Faery Gates of Avalon (R.J. Stewart Books, 2008)

Melusine of Lusignan and the Cult of the Faery Woman (R.J. Stewart Books, 2010)

Yours Very Truly: Selected Letters of Gareth Knight 1969-2010 (Skylight Press, 2010)

The Romance of the Faery Melusine (Skylight Press, 2011)

I Called it Magic (Skylight Press, 2011)

Faery Loves and Faery Lais (Skylight Press, 2012)

Index

Pages with illustrations are shown in **bold type**.

Lightning Source UK Ltd.
Milton Keynes UK
UKOW051614250712

196560UK00001B/297/P